Nation and Migration

Nation and Migration

THE MAKING OF BRITISH ATLANTIC
LITERATURE, 1765–1835

Juliet Shields

OXFORD

UNIVERSITY PRESS

OXFORD
UNIVERSITY PRESS

Oxford University Press is a department of the University of
Oxford. It furthers the University's objective of excellence in research,
scholarship, and education by publishing worldwide.
Oxford is a registered trademark of Oxford University Press
in the UK and certain other countries.

Published in the United States of America by
Oxford University Press
198 Madison Avenue, New York, NY 10016, United States of America

Library of Congress Cataloging-in-Publication Data
Shields, Juliet, 1976–
Nation and migration : the making of British Atlantic literature, 1765–1835 / Juliet Shields.
pages cm
Includes bibliographical references and index.
ISBN 978–0–19–027255–5 (cloth) — ISBN 978–0–19–027256–2 (updf)
1. American literature—1783–1850—History and criticism.   2. National characteristics,
American, in literature.   3. Emigration and immigration in literature.   4. British—
United States.   5. Irish—United States.   6. Scots—United States.   7. Welsh—United
States.   8. American literature—Revolutionary period, 1775–1783—History and
criticism.   I. Title.
PS195.N35S55 2016
810.9'358—dc23
2015015621

1 3 5 7 9 8 6 4 2
Printed in the United States of America
on acid-free paper

For Tom

{ CONTENTS }

{ ACKNOWLEDGMENTS }

While my interest in the emigrant experience goes back many years, I began writing this book in 2009 with the support of a fellowship at the Ohio State University's Center for Historical Research. The opportunity to participate in the CHR's year-long series of seminars on diaspora and migration deepened my appreciation of the enduringness of geographical mobility as part of human experience. My involvement in the Anglo-Scottish Migration network run by Professor Keith Brown at the University of Manchester has also benefited the book. I'm grateful to the other participants in the network for their conviviality, enthusiasm for the subject, and determination to dig deep for evidence. A Scholar's Award from the University of Washington's Royalty Research Fund enabled me to complete the manuscript. An early version of a section of Chapter 4 appeared in *The Wordsworth Circle* and part of Chapter 3 was published in *Nineteenth-Century Literature*. I thank both journals for the permission to reprint that material here. The anonymous readers of the manuscript for Oxford University Press provided thorough and incisive comments that inspired me to rethink some key points of my argument. Brendan O'Neill has consistently gone above and beyond his editorial duties in seeing the project through to publication. For their support of this project in a variety of ways I thank my colleagues and friends Bob Abrams, Marshall Brown, Eva Cherniavsky, Alison Conway, Leith Davis, JoEllen DeLucia, Penny Fielding, Nancy Henry, Jeff Knight, Thomas Lockwood, and Roxann Wheeler. Their generosity and integrity as scholars and human beings continue to inspire me. I'm grateful to my parents, whose emigration from Scotland to the United States with a young family gave me the courage to make my own moves later in life. My deepest thanks go to my dear boys: long-suffering Hamish, who has been by my side through many changes; Archie, who died just before the book's completion but who is always present in my heart; irrepressible Nigel, who came hurtling into my life at an opportune moment; and, most of all, to Tom. Wherever I wander, my home is with you.

Nation and Migration

{ Introduction }

Decentering Transatlantic Literary Studies

The stories that late eighteenth- and early nineteenth-century Britons and Americans told about transatlantic migration and settlement, whether from the position of migrant or observer, reveal the extreme tenuousness and fragility of both Britain and the United States as relatively new national entities at the time. Although Britons had been leaving home for the colonies in increasing numbers since the early seventeenth century, the Declaration of Independence dramatically transformed the implications of transatlantic migration. After the War of Independence, migrants no longer crossed the ocean from one of the King's dominions to another; instead they passed from one nation to another, each with a distinct system for regulating membership in its political community. British migrants to the United States now were legally aliens even though Britons and Americans continued to share cultural, familial, and historical ties. These migrants played an important but ambivalent part in shaping American identity during the late eighteenth and early nineteenth centuries precisely because they were at once foreign and familiar: they offered Americans of British heritage a distorted reflection of themselves.

It is true that, as Kariann Akemi Yokota has argued, "The project of nation building and developing national identity in the young United States was as much about its people's struggles in 'unbecoming' what had made them British subjects before independence as it was about 'becoming' citizens of a new country."[1] Yet Britishness during the late eighteenth and early nineteenth centuries was hardly a stable identity against which Americans could define themselves. Scotland and England had united to become Great Britain as recently as 1707, and it was not until 1801 that the union of Great Britain with Ireland created the United Kingdom.[2] The inhabitants of the newly formed United States did not begin to consider themselves Americans as soon as the Declaration of Independence had been issued or the War of Independence won; and, thanks to deeply entrenched political and cultural divisions in the

British archipelago, the unions of 1707 and 1801 were arguably even less effective in creating Britons out of the English, Welsh, Scots, and Irish. Indeed, the adjective "British" first came into popular use not in the British Isles, but in colonial North America where settlers of mixed English, Welsh, Scottish, and Irish origins needed a common term to describe their heritage, the central symbol of which was their common allegiance to the British Crown.[3] These colonists may have identified themselves more closely with Britishness than did many of the inhabitants of the British Isles.

This book contends that the stories told by and about the British migrants who settled in North America during the late eighteenth and early nineteenth centuries illuminate the instability of British identity as much as the formativeness of American identity. Where do we find these stories? Historians of migration concur that "the anonymity or invisibility of the mass of emigrants is generally intractable."[4] We have journals and letters recording the experiences of some migrants, but the thoughts and feelings of the hundreds of thousands of people who left Britain for the United States during the late eighteenth and early nineteenth centuries remain relatively opaque and inaccessible except through imaginative empathy and the accounts of observers. However, stories about transatlantic migration and settlement are embedded in the political and imaginative writing of the era. Samuel Johnson, Edmund Burke, Benjamin Franklin, Thomas Jefferson, and other political and literary luminaries expressed opinions on the effects of migration on national character and on relations between Britain and the early American republic. Migrants and transatlantic migration also figure in the poetry and fiction of late eighteenth- and early nineteenth-century writers including Hugh Henry Brackenridge, Charles Brockden Brown, James Fenimore Cooper, Oliver Goldsmith, Felicia Hemans, Washington Irving, Maria Regina Roche, Catharine Maria Sedgwick, and Robert Southey, among others.

I describe these stories by and about British migrants to North America as "migrant fictions"—a term I borrow from Eve Tavor Bannet—not only for the obvious reason of their content, but also because they do not fit easily into the "nationalist master-narratives" through which transatlantic literary studies is organized.[5] "Migrant" is a term that connotes mobility, rootlessness, and liminality. In contrast to the terms "immigrant" and "emigrant," which in the context of this book imply respectively an American and a British perspective, "migrant" assumes no particular vantage point or category of belonging. Recent studies of transatlantic literary influence have tended to orient themselves around one or the other of these perspectives. Moreover, they have focused primarily on what Stephen Spender describes as the formative United States' "love-hate relations" with England—the political, economic, and, above all, cultural center of Britain's empire.[6] Whether citizens of the early republic manifested the symbolic attachment to English imperial authority that Elisa Tamarkin describes as "Anglophilia" or whether, as

Robert Weisbuch has claimed, outright "enmity" catalyzed Americans' efforts to distinguish themselves from the English, they could not avoid measuring themselves to some extent against England.[7] In either case, however, Leonard Tennenhouse's argument that British migrants were particularly invested in "feeling English," or in "reproducing certain traits of Englishness in a radically non-European environment," does not follow.[8] Many British migrants had never felt English even while living in the British Isles, simply because they were not English.

The United States was not settled only, or even primarily, by the English; and although England held immense sway over the minds and hearts of Americans, the English were far from the only people to contribute to the development of an American cultural identity. Thomas Paine reminded readers of *Common Sense* (1776) that "Not one third of the inhabitants, even of this province, are of English descent," and that "Europe, and not England, is the parent country of America."[9] Paine may have overestimated the multiculturalism of the colonies, which James Belich has described as "less a melting pot than a British stew with a dash of neighbours."[10] But Paine's polemical disparagement of England's contribution to the peopling of the colonies was, in its gist, fairly accurate. Historians have demonstrated that Ireland, Scotland, and Wales sent proportionally more people to the American colonies and early republic than did England, and that these people played major roles in the settlement, government, and defense of the formative United States.[11] In the seventeenth century, seventy percent of the one million people who left Britain were English; but during the eighteenth century, English emigration sharply declined and Scottish and Irish emigration rose, so that over seventy percent of all British settlers who arrived in America were from Ireland and Scotland.[12] It was the significant presence of Scottish, Irish, and Welsh settlers in the early republic that in 1805 led Hugh Henry Brackenridge to testily describe the United States as a "colluvies of all nations: Mac's, O's, and Ap's; Erse, Irish, and Welsh."[13] Settlers came to the United States from throughout the British archipelago and their contributions to American culture differed according to their origins. The mixed reception that met these migrants upon their arrival also differed according to their origins: "Scottishness," "Irishness," and "Welshness" had different meanings for Americans than did "Englishness," much as each of these identities carried different connotations in Britain.

By allowing England to stand in for the British archipelago, then, recent literary scholarship has not only overlooked the significant contributions of Scotland, Ireland, and Wales to the development of American literature and culture and oversimplified the processes through which the new United States differentiated itself culturally from Britain; it has also underestimated the impact of migration on British literature and culture during the late eighteenth and early nineteenth centuries. It is one of the primary contentions of this book that transatlantic migration created a dialectical relationship between American and British literary nation formation during the late eighteenth and early nineteenth centuries. In *Nation and Migration* I seek to demonstrate the robust impact of Scottish, Irish, and Welsh migration on the literatures and cultures of both the early American republic and Great Britain. In doing so, I extend the premises and insights of J. G. A. Pocock's New British History, and of the critical methods that it has inspired in literary studies, from the British archipelago across the Atlantic to the United States. After Pocock pointed out that so-called British history usually offered little more than "the history of England with excrescences," historians began to attend to the interactions among "the various peoples and nations, ethnic cultures, social structures, and locally defined communities, which have from time to time existed in the area known as 'Great Britain and Ireland.'"[14] Following the New British historians, literary critics have begun to practice what John Kerrigan terms archipelagic criticism, and others have called four-nations or devolutionary criticism.

This method of reading traces genealogic and microgeographic connections among the literatures and cultures of the British archipelago, a formation that includes England, Wales, Scotland, and Ireland.[15] While London's literary culture traditionally has been at the center of the British literary canon, archipelagic critics expose that canon to decentering re-readings. Rather than taking England as a stable core entity against which to read the literatures and cultures of the peripheries, archipelagic criticism reveals that "Englishness was a contested resource . . . open to reconceptualization, defined against and meshed with its neighbours."[16] If, for Claire Lamont, "the achievement of the English is to have created a culture which they regard as simply normal,"[17] then archipelalgic criticism helps us to examine how and why that normalization occurred. It shows us that Englishness is not simply a lack of identity or state of neutrality against which all other cultures of the British archipelago can be measured and defined. Instead, Englishness is a repository of historically constructed meanings.

The New British History has in its turn come under criticism for failing to include "the settlements, provinces and dependencies of Greater Britain" in its efforts to put English history in context, or for confining these efforts at contextualization within the geographical boundaries of the British archipelago.[18] Accordingly, historians have begun to extend the scope of the New British History across the Atlantic, exploring how various regions and populations of Great Britain and Ireland contributed unevenly to the settlement, exploration, defense, and government of the American colonies and early republic. In contrast, Kerrigan explicitly excludes the American colonies from his magisterial study of seventeenth-century literature of the British archipelago because "the evidence that British-Irish issues were influenced by events or literary texts produced in America is slight."[19] While this may be true of the seventeenth century, it certainly cannot be said of the late eighteenth and early nineteenth centuries, when people, books, and ideas circulated almost as freely between the British archipelago and the United States as they did within the British mainland on one side of the Atlantic or among the states on the other.[20]

Accordingly, *Nation and Migration* extends the methods of archipelagic criticism across the Atlantic to bring to light hitherto-neglected connections between British and American literary cultures and to explore a body of writing that belongs neither to the British archipelago nor to the United States, but rather to the Atlantic world. Like literary influence, migration was not unidirectional, and did not flow solely from the Old World to the New. Migrants frequently represented the passage from Britain to America through a triumphalist narrative in which settlers undergo hardship and homesickness but ultimately succeed in achieving stability and prosperity in their new home. In reality, though, migration was much more haphazard and contingent than this narrative implies. Sometimes transatlantic migration was forced, as in the case of evicted tenants or indentured servants. Back-migration, or a return home, was not at all unusual; indeed, some migrants left Britain with the explicit intention of returning after they had accumulated a fortune abroad.[21] And often, transatlantic migration was only one part of a broader trajectory of travel and settlement. Historians have shown that internal migration, whether within Britain or North America, was "as major a movement as that across the Atlantic."[22] Rural Britons often migrated to a busy port city like London, Glasgow, or Liverpool in search of work before they chose to seek a new life overseas. Similarly, some of the Britons who initially settled in the eastern United States established a pattern of serial westward migrations as they sought out cheaper, better land.[23] Whereas British migrants brought narratives of origins with them to the American colonies and early republic, return migrants often brought home with them the American discourses of liberty that influenced the development of cultural nationalism in Scotland, Wales, and particularly Ireland. Archipelagic criticism, which encourages us to attend to these literary and cultural exchanges, perhaps stands to shed as much light on the literature of the early American republic as on that of late eighteenth- and early nineteenth-century Britain and Ireland.

My focus on the impact of transatlantic migration on literature of the British Atlantic world brings to the foreground a different set of works and writers from those featured in the numerous studies of literary influence that have participated in establishing an Anglo-American canon of transatlantic literature.[24] The migrant fictions that I discuss in this book make visible the literary and cultural connections among regions of the British Atlantic world often described as "peripheral" or "provincial" in relation to metropolitan England: namely, Scotland, Ireland, Wales, and the United States. As Tamarkin and Joseph Rezek have shown, metropolitan England remained a powerful center of literary and cultural authority in the British Atlantic world well after Britain's loss of the thirteen colonies;[25] but its influence diminished gradually as writers situated in Scotland, Ireland, Wales, and the United States entered into forms of literary exchange ranging from allusion to adaptation that circumvented England and its literary productions. These exchanges contributed to the making of what I am calling a British Atlantic literature.

Through the term "British Atlantic," I aim not only to distinguish this body of literature from the canon of Anglo-American literature that currently dominates transatlantic literary studies, but also to acknowledge the coexistence of multiple other Atlantics—French, Spanish, Dutch, and African, to name just a few—each with its own literature. Arguably, "British Atlantic" is too broad a designation for a body of literature I discuss in this book. I focus primarily on works from the United States and the British archipelago while largely neglecting those from Canada and the West Indies. Although Canada and the West Indies were popular destinations for Scottish and Irish migrants, I have mostly excluded them from this study for two reasons.

First, Canada and the West Indies each lacked a center of publication, and thus a center of literary culture, that could come anywhere close to Philadelphia, New York, or Boston, let alone London, Edinburgh, or Dublin. While a good deal was written *about* Canada and the West Indies during the eighteenth century very little was written by people who might be called Canadians or West Indians. For instance, Frances Brooke's *History of Emily Montague*, often dubbed the first North American novel, was written during Brooke's four-year sojourn in Quebec, where her was husband was chaplain to a British garrison, but it was not published until 1769, a year after her return to England. *The History of Emily Montague*, as Carole Gerson observes, was "the product of a seasoned London author who cannily exploited the exotic setting she encountered" during her stay in British North America.[26] Although Britain had acquired Canadian territory in the Seven Years War, it became a significant destination for settlers only after 1783, when American independence sent a mass of Loyalists northwards to New Brunswick and Quebec.[27] The literary fruits of this wave of settlement only really began to appear at the tail end of the years covered by this study in works like John Richardson's *Wacousta* (1832), Peter Fisher's *Lay of the Wilderness* (1833), Catharine Parr Traill's *Backwoods of Canada* (1836), and Thomas Chandler Haliburton's *Letterbag of the Great Western* (1840). These works were published in either England or the United States, a condition that was to pertain to most Canadian writing throughout the nineteenth century.[28] Migrants to the West Indies had even fewer opportunities for literary pursuits than Canadian settlers. Many regarded their sojourn in the West Indies as temporary, a means of making money before returning enriched to Britain. Extremely high mortality rates due to illness and harsh living conditions may also have precluded the development of a British West Indian literature.[29]

The second, and more important, reason that Canada and the West Indies feature so minimally here is that during years covered by *Nation and Migration*, both remained British imperial possessions. The United Kingdom and the United States were, at the turn of the nineteenth century, new nation-states, both experiencing the struggles of attempting to consolidate a shared culture out of a disparate variety of peoples. Canada and the West Indies had their own, quite different, problems. They were subject to the authority of competing imperial powers, and had to contend with distinctive forms of religious intolerance and racial oppression. Alison Games reminds us that in 1800, Canada still "had a francophone majority while enslaved Africans and people of African descent vastly outnumbered Creoles and Europeans in the West Indies."[30] The nuances of the Canadian and West Indian situations deserve more attention than I can profitably give them in this book. However, I turn briefly to Canada in the epilogue to compare the British archipelagic Atlantic literature I explore in the ensuing chapters to what we might call a British colonial Atlantic literature that would include Canada and the West Indies.

The Literary and Legislative Regulation of Migration

Transatlantic migration was not only the subject of a great deal of literature in the late eighteenth- and early nineteenth-century Atlantic world. It was also a topic of political debate and was subject to new forms of legislation, particularly during the drawn-out struggles between Britain and its American colonies. Together, literature and legislation helped to shape public opinion about the economic and political implications of migration, and influenced general perceptions of migrants.

Prior to the eighteenth century Britons tended to regard emigration as beneficial to the nation's moral and economic health. One of the justifications for establishing American colonies in the seventeenth century had been "to draw off excess population and put to some productive use the swarms of sturdy vagrants who roamed the countryside and infested city slums."[31] By the end of the long and costly Seven Years War, however, the increasing rate of emigration inspired fears that the loss of population would eat away at Britain's strength, whether that was measured in terms of manpower or money. James Anderson spoke to these fears in his argument against attempting to retain the American colonies, *The Interest of Great Britain, with Regard to her American Colonies, Considered* (1782). Anderson acknowledges that "the real strength of a kingdom, consists in the *number* of its inhabitants, and that its riches will be in proportion to the industry of its people," but warns that extending a population over a large territory, let alone across an ocean, decreases its power.[32] On the other side of the Atlantic, Morgan J. Rhees, in a speech delivered to the Philadelphia Society for the Information and Assistance of persons Emigrating from Foreign Countries, welcomed the continued influx of newcomers to the United States because "the strength of a country consists in the number of its inhabitants, more than in the wealth of its citizens. The industrious labourers and mechanics are the sinews, the bones and the marrow of every community."[33]

In *The Deserted Village* (1770), perhaps the best-known piece of eighteenth-century anti-emigration literature, Oliver Goldsmith suggests that the enclosure of formerly common land and the rise of agrarian capitalism would rid Britain not only of laborers, but also of the simple virtues proper to traditional rural life. For Goldsmith, these virtues were the true source of national strength and prosperity. The poem nostalgically recalls a time

> ere England's griefs began,
> When every rood of ground maintained its man;
> For him light labour spread her wholesome store,
> Just gave what life required, but no more:
> His best companions, innocence and health;
> And his best riches, ignorance of wealth.[34]

Small subsistence farmers who held their "rood" on a large estate and who just maintained a state of self-sufficiency were not tempted by the luxuries that the poem deplores as the cause of national degeneration. *The Deserted Village* holds "the rich man's increase" responsible for "the poor's decay," noting that, thanks to the consolidation of small farms into sweeping parklands, "The man of wealth and pride / Takes up a space that many poor supplied."[35] While Goldsmith's depiction of rural simplicity is undoubtedly sentimentalized, it nonetheless affirms the equation between population and national vitality. A nation of "rich men" cannot be sustained without laborers because the wealthy are consumers rather than producers; thus, "This wealth is but a name / That leaves our useful products still the same."[36] The poem charges its readers, "'Tis yours to judge, how wide the limits stand / Between a splendid and a happy land."[37]

While critics have sometimes assumed that *The Deserted Village* depicts the rural depopulation of Goldsmith's native Ireland, there are no details in the poem that decisively mark the location of the village of Auburn.[38] This indeterminacy was surely purposeful on Goldsmith's part, intended to suggest that depopulation in any region of the British Isles would undermine the nation's moral and economic prosperity. Nonetheless, British anxieties about emigration did tend to focus on Scotland and Ireland.[39] Accounts of emigration from the Celtic peripheries may have been exaggerated by landlords who feared losing their tenants and laborers, but Scotland's and Ireland's distance from the center of British government made it difficult either to ascertain the exactitude of such reports or to exercise control over the passage of migrants. In September of 1775, shortly after George III had declared the American colonies to be in rebellion, Scottish emigration to North America was prohibited for fear that Scots were leaving the country with money and arms to support the rebels. British emigration slowed almost to a halt during the War of Independence, but even before the conflict had ended *The Public Advertiser* declared, "*Emigration*, that alarming evil, which threatens all our devoted country through all its coasts, is already beginning its frightful devastations. . . . [G]reat parts of Scotland and Ireland, nay the north and western parts of England itself, will soon be depopulated."[40] British anxiety surrounding emigration increased after the war because migrants could no longer be considered as simply extending or diffusing Britain's might across the globe; instead, they were diminishing it—perhaps permanently.

If the British came to see migration as a decided loss, a gradual draining away of the nation's strength and wealth, Americans after independence were far from unequivocally delighted by the numbers of newcomers pouring into their country, and the early republic's immigration policies were hardly laissez-faire.[41] British attempts to prevent emigration had previously been a sore point with colonists, and The Declaration of Independence included in its list of grievances against George III his efforts "to prevent the population of these states," charging him with "obstructing the laws for naturalization of foreigners [and] refusing to pass others to encourage their migration hither." Yet by 1787, Thomas Jefferson questioned whether America's government might not be "more homogeneous, more peaceful, more durable" if immigration were severely restricted.[42] Most writers did favor immigration—but only of the right sort of people, namely, English-speaking Protestants who were willing to work hard. James Madison warned that "those who acquire the rights of citizenship, without adding to the wealth and strength of the community are not the people we are in want of."[43] Benjamin Franklin similarly was eager to regulate the passage of Europeans into the newly formed United States. His *Information to Those Who Would Remove to America* (1784) aimed to rectify prospective migrants' "mistaken Ideas and Expectations" about life in the United States and thus to prevent "inconvenient, expensive, and fruitless Removals and Voyages of improper persons." In this pamphlet Franklin describes the United States not as the land of opportunity, but rather as "the Land of Labour." While it offers "good Laws and Liberty" to settlers, they must nonetheless "work and be industrious to live."[44] For Franklin, the right kind of immigrants were not just industrious, they were also British. His earlier essay *On a Proposed Act to Prevent Emigration* (1773), written while he was residing in London, lamented that "Germans are now pouring into [America], to take Possession of it, and fill it with their Posterity; and shall Britons, and Ireland, who have a much better Right to it, be forbidden a Share of it, and instead of enjoying there the Plenty and Happiness that might reward their

Industry, be compelled to remain here in Poverty and Misery?"[45] After independence nullified Britain's "right" to people the United States, Franklin nonetheless urged that migration would offer Britain a means of "repossessing" the United States, and asked why Britons would "leave it to be taken by Foreigners of all Nations and Languages."[46]

Informal efforts to control immigration like Franklin's were superseded by formal legislation after the Constitution was passed. During the 1790s, fears that revolutionary doctrines from France would infect the United States in its vulnerable infancy led Congress to dramatically increase the residency requirement for naturalization from two to fourteen years in hopes of deterring the wrong sort of immigrants. Humphry Marshall's *Aliens: A Patriotic Poem* (1798) warns readers that there are two classes of immigrants. The first seek a land

> where temporal things,
> The fruit, of honest purchase, or toil;
> Are safe from force,

and where "honors reward, the wise, the brave."[47] The second are "a malicious crew," "foes to all law, and right," who have come to the United States to sow "The seeds of discord" and "to villify, our government."[48] For Marshall, the distinction between honorable and devious newcomers was transparent. Perhaps presuming upon his position as a senator, he reassured readers that desirable immigrants

> need not feel the penal laws,
> That are now in agitation;
> For as to those, there'll be a clause,
> That shall save them to the nation.[49]

Although some of the writers discussed in this book might have disagreed with Marshall over the transparency of the distinctions between good and bad migrants, almost all of them would have agreed that such distinctions exist and many of them would have attributed these moral differences to migrants' national origins. For instance, J. Hector St. John de Crèvecoeur's *Letters from an American Farmer* (1782) praises Scottish settlers as "frugal and laborious," but notes that they are somewhat hampered by the deficiencies of their native climate, as "it is not easy for those who seldom saw a tree to conceive how it is to be felled, cut up, and split into rails and posts."[50] By contrast, "The Irish do not prosper so well; they love to drink and to quarrel"; and "they seem beside to labour under a greater degree of ignorance in husbandry" than settlers from other countries.[51] Crèvecoeur traces each nation's moral characteristics, as well as its settlers' chances of succeeding in the United States, to conditions of existence like climate, government, and mode of subsistence. Other writers were less ready to attribute national traits to material conditions, representing them instead as innate and perhaps indelible. Chandler Robbins Gilman, a physician and denizen of New York City who journeyed to the Great Lakes to see the Pictured Rocks in 1835, offers a representative account of some Irish and Scottish migrants he encountered during his travels. The main deck of the steamboat on which he sailed "was occupied by a swarm of emigrants, whose lack of cleanliness not less than their brogue, marked them as from the Emerald Isle. There they stood, sat, and lay about the deck—men, women, and children—all huddled together, with an utter disregard of the commonest decencies of life, which was sickening."[52] The upper deck of the boat, in comparison, was occupied by "a band 'of brother Scots'" from Aberdeen. Their "appearance was so respectable, their demeanour so quiet, that no cabin passenger could possibly object to their presence."[53] Gilman's unsubtle contrast between the repulsive indecency of the Irish migrants and the upstanding respectability of the Scots demonstrates that Humphry Marshall's division of immigrants into two categories—desirable and degenerate—persisted well into the nineteenth century, and arguably through our own time.

Writing by and about British migrants to the United States by no means disappeared in 1835, the somewhat arbitrary year with which this study ends. However, in the United States, debates over migration were overshadowed in the following decades by the northern and southern states' profound disagreements over slavery. These disagreements, along with the consolidation of belief in Americans' manifest destiny, turned nation-building efforts increasingly inwards and westwards, away from Britain. Moreover, by the 1830s, far more British migrants were heading to Australia or Canada than to the United States, and mid-nineteenth-century British writers were beginning to regard Americans less as their distant brethren than as bizarre ethnographic curiosities.[54]

Aims and Organization

By bringing Ireland, Scotland, and Wales into my study of the United States' immigrant origins, I aim to provide an account of the development of a British Atlantic literature that is missing from current discussions of transatlantic literary relations. I argue that late eighteenth- and early nineteenth-century migration between Britain and the early republic made three significant contributions to a British Atlantic literature. First, and most obviously, Scottish, Irish, and Welsh migrants brought with them to the United States stories and traditions very different from those shared by English settlers. Americans looked to these countries for narratives of origins—whether cultural, racial, or geographic—through which to legitimate their new nation. Adapting these narratives helped American writers to explore the United States' position as at once a former British possession and, in regard to Native Americans in particular, a formative colonial power. Indeed, Scottish, Irish, and Welsh narratives of origins often laid claim to American lands and liberties through the supposed blood kinship or cultural similarities between Celts and Native Americans.

The second and related way in which migration contributed to a British Atlantic literature was thus through its representations of racial and regional identities within the United States. Late eighteenth- and early nineteenth-century settlers did not find the United States and its adjacent territories an empty wilderness upon their arrival, but instead sought to assimilate into a multicultural society including various European peoples, Native Americans, and African slaves. A number of the literary works I discuss in this book describe encounters among Celtic migrants and Indian tribes that cast Celts as mediators between the "savage" western frontier and "civilized" eastern settlements. In Britain, Celtic peoples had long been considered less civilized than the English. In the early republic, Celts often were depicted as physically, intellectually, and morally similar to Indians, and thus as especially suited to the hardships of life on the frontier. At the same time, their shared whiteness affirmed a bond between Celts and Anglo-Americans. Novelists and poets took advantage of this Celtic doubleness by incorporating racialized Celtic traits into the figure of the frontiersman to justify westward expansion and the marginalization or eradication of native peoples that it caused. While comparisons between Celts and Indians were frequent, those between Celts and Africans were relatively few, perhaps because Celtic people for the most part migrated voluntarily whereas slave migration was forced, but more likely because Celts—particularly Scots—were prominent enough among southern slaveholders to prevent such comparisons.[55] As Noel Ignatiev's controversial work suggests, even the poorest among early to mid-nineteenth-century Celtic immigrants may have attempted to assimilate into Anglo-American society by defining themselves against blacks, who occupied the lowest rung in the New World racial hierarchy.[56] To many observers, then, Celts and American Indians seemed to occupy a middle rung, above Africans and below Anglo-Americans.

The final and less immediately obvious way in which transatlantic migration shaped a British Atlantic literature was by encouraging writers to make connections, both rhetorical and literal, between and within the United States and the British archipelago. England had formed political unions with Wales in 1536 and with Scotland in 1707, and had maintained some degree of colonial government over Ireland since the Elizabethan era. Each of these relationships was unique, yet all required careful and continual negotiation of political and cultural interdependence and autonomy between England and its Celtic peripheries. When, in the years leading up to the American Revolution, tensions between the colonies and the British Parliament began to escalate, writers on both sides of the Atlantic looked to the history of

England's political relations with its Celtic peripheries for precedents in defining those between Britain and its American colonies. Following independence, American writers continued to look to the British archipelago for examples as they sought to mold culturally and geographically diverse regions into a unified nation-state, and to distribute power between a central federal government and localized state governments. For their part, Irish, and to a lesser degree Scottish and Welsh writers looked to American discourses of rights and liberties that had emerged in the years surrounding the War of Independence as they sought to assert their cultural difference, if not political independence, from metropolitan England.

The core of this study consists of three chapters devoted to writing by and about migrants from Ireland, Scotland, and Wales, respectively. These chapters offer a comparative rather than chronological perspective on British migration to the early American republic. Each covers the same span of years—roughly the 1780s through the 1820s—but examines the circumstances and stories proper to migrants from a specific region of the British archipelago. This approach allows me to demonstrate how American perceptions of migrants from each of the Celtic peripheries were determined largely by that periphery's unique relationship to England. Although these chapters occasionally draw on historical accounts, they are primarily concerned with literary representations of migrants and migration. I do not privilege non-literary texts as more true or authentic than imaginative works. Instead, I show that the supposedly factual and avowedly fictional representations of migrants and migration draw from a common set of conventions, rhetorical strategies, and ideological assumptions. Although genre is not, strictly speaking, a primary focus of this book, each of the three chapters examines how, as they circulated through the British Atlantic world, Celtic myths of origin were incorporated into literary genres including the Gothic novel, the historical novel, and lyric and epic poetry. Such acts of incorporation enabled writers on both sides of the Atlantic to subtly modify, or in some cases to dramatically revise, these narratives of origin to suit new contexts.

Chapter 2 examines how, during the 1790s and early 1800s, Irish resistance to British colonial rule stirred up hostility and fear towards Irish settlers in the United States. Drawing on Charles Brockden Brown's *Wieland* (1798) and *Edgar Huntly* (1799), and Maria Regina Roche's *Munster Cottage Boy* (1820), it argues that novelists used the language and conventions of the Gothic to represent Irish radicals in the United States and in Ireland as uncanny—at once foreign and familiar, homeless and at home. In the United States, Irish radicals recalled the nation's recent revolutionary past—a past of which Americans were proud—even while they were associated in the popular imagination with the foreign threats of Jacobinism, Catholicism, and the European Illuminati. *Wieland* and *Edgar Huntly* explore this uncanniness by featuring migrants from Ireland whose appearance in rural Pennsylvania coincides with apparently occult events. Yet in each case, the mysterious migrant's appearance only exacerbates pre-existing tensions caused by the early republic's xenophobic insularity. If Irish radicals in the nation's were unwanted reminders of Americans' revolutionary past, in Ireland these radicals manifested a patriotism that Britain had tried to expunge through centuries of colonial rule but that reappeared in ghostly, half-hidden forms to remind the Irish of their cultural heritage. By imagining the reintegration of Irish political émigrés into a reformed feudal hierarchy, *The Munster Cottage Boy* divests these migrants of their exilic ghostliness and depicts repatriation as essential to Ireland's economic prosperity and cultural integrity within the recently established United Kingdom.

Whereas Irish immigrants were regarded as threats to the political stability of the United States, Scots gained a reputation as among the most industrious and prosperous of immigrants. Chapter 3 explores the transatlantic creation of the myth of the successful Scottish migrant. Samuel Johnson's *Journey to the Western Islands of Scotland* (1775) and J. Hector St. John de Crèvecoeur's *Letters from an American Farmer* (1782) draw on eighteenth-century theories of racial difference to explain the value of Highlanders, particularly Hebrideans, to national strength and prosperity. While Johnson expresses concern that Scottish emigration might impoverish Britain morally and economically, Crèvecoeur incorporates the figure of the successful Scottish settler into an imperial American identity. Eighteenth-century writers including Johnson and Crèvecoeur tended to understand race as contingent and malleable; however, westward migration in the United States contributed to the hardening of racial categories. The second section of the chapter examines how James Fenimore Cooper's *Last of the Mohicans* (1826) employs the myth of the successful Scottish migrant together with the conventions of Walter Scott's Waverley novels to imagine an American identity formed through cultural rather than racial mixing. *The Last of the Mohicans* offers Scottish migrants' selective appropriation of Native American traits as a model both for Cooper's literary borrowings from Scott's works and for an American identity formed through cultural synthesis.

Although the Welsh migrated to the early republic in smaller numbers than the Scots or the Irish, they posed a challenge to dominant discourses of Anglo-American liberty that traced American national character to Anglo-Saxon origins. Chapter 4 examines the late eighteenth-century resurgence of a medieval myth describing the Welsh discovery of North America. The myth recounts the Welsh Prince Madoc's twelfth-century voyage to the Gulf of Mexico and his settlement further inland, where his people subdued and intermarried with native tribes. The resurgence of the myth in the 1790s coincided with westward expansion into the Ohio Valley, where settlers claimed to have seen the descendants of Madoc's Welsh Indians.

I explore the purposes that the Madoc myth might have served for three groups of people who shared claims to a British identity and an interest in westward expansion: the Welsh, the English, and the Anglo-American inhabitants of the early republic. The lyric poems of Iolo Morganwg suggest that the myth offered the Welsh the prospect of an American homeland during a period of economic depression and political oppression in Wales. At the same time, Robert Southey's epic poem *Madoc* (1795–1805) illustrates how the myth allowed the English to claim a continued interest in American settlement even following the loss of their colonies. Gilbert Imlay's novel *The Emigrants* (1793) demonstrates that for Americans, the myth legitimated westward expansion and the forced migration of native populations that this expansion caused.

While Chapters 2 through 4 offer detailed accounts of Irish, Scottish, and Welsh migration, the book's first and last chapters balance this depth with breadth by examining similarities and differences among Ireland, Wales, Scotland, and the United States from a British Atlantic perspective. Together, Chapters 1 and 5 suggest that the strongest resemblance and the greatest symbolic bond among the Irish, Welsh, Scots, and Americans may have been their shared sense of secondariness to the English in an Anglocentric British Atlantic world. Writers drew political and literary connections between these supposedly peripheral regions in response to pressures exerted by the metropolitan English center that threatened to efface Irish, Welsh, Scottish, and American cultural distinctiveness.

Chapter 1 examines the comparisons that Anglo-American writers drew among Ireland, Scotland, Wales and the American colonies in the years surrounding the War of Independence as they attempted to prescribe a balance between centralized imperial power on the one hand, and provincial or local forms of government on the other. Initially, efforts to configure the relationships between center and peripheries focused, somewhat ironically, on the definition of Englishness. Writers on both sides of the Atlantic questioned to what extent migrants to the colonies were entitled to English rights and liberties and thus to legislative representation. To answer this question, Edmund Burke, in his "Speech on Conciliation with America" (1775), and Samuel Johnson, in *Taxation No Tyranny* (1775), looked for historical precedents in moments when the Celtic peripheries had been granted or refused nominally "English" rights and liberties in exchange for political autonomy. In the wake of the War of Independence, American writers including John Jay and Alexander Hamilton similarly turned to England's government of Scotland, Ireland, and Wales in hopes of finding models through which to structure the balance of power between federal and state governments in the new United States. While anti-Federalist writers supported the decentralization of political authority and the distribution of the powers of government throughout a group of loosely affiliated states, Federalist writers hoped to perpetuate the relatively strong centralized power that characterized England's governance of its Celtic peripheries.

The struggles between centralized and local forms of authority by no means ended with the establishment of a United States government. While Chapter 1 examines these struggles in the political sphere, Chapter 5 explores their symptomatic manifestation in the literary realm. Chapter 5 reads the early nineteenth-century emergence of the literary sketch as a response to metropolitan England's continuing cultural and literary authority in the British Atlantic world. The literary sketch—a short, anecdotal narrative form—rose to popularity almost simultaneously in Scotland, Ireland, and the United States as a means of describing local color and preserving regional differences. Instead of taking metropolitan England as a standard of cultural value, Scottish and Irish literary sketches asserted the competing significance of regional cultures. American writers including Washington Irving, Lydia Sigourney, and Catharine Maria Sedgwick adopted the literary sketch to delineate the regional identities that developed within the United States as migrants from the British archipelago attempted to assimilate into an already racially and culturally complex American society. The popularity of the literary sketch in Ireland, Scotland, and the United States indicates its utility as a "decentralized" genre of writing—a form of fiction that lacks a unifying plot, and that privileges the local over the metropolitan.

A Parting Glance at England

In providing a literary history for a land that still considers itself a nation of immigrants, *Nation and Migration* complements recent literary and historical studies of other European immigrant groups to the early American republic, including the Spanish, German, and Dutch.[57] New arrivals in the American colonies and early republic experienced a historically unique form of cultural displacement because, as Barbara DeWolfe explains, "they were traveling in many different cultures mixed together and super-imposed on the remnants of an older, native culture that was in, but not of, that newer world of European transplants."[58] In the midst of all these peoples, however, the English undoubtedly exercised the largest influence over post-independence Americans' imaginations. Colonists of British descent were quick to assert their English rights and liberties before the Revolution and slow to distance themselves from English manners and mores afterwards.

Given England's centrality in the late eighteenth- and early nineteenth-century British Atlantic world, it may seem odd that a book on British migration does not include a chapter on English migrants. The reasoning behind this seeming omission is simply that we already have many books that examine the circulation of people and texts between England and North America in the eighteenth and nineteenth centuries.[59] *Nation and Migration* is intended as a counterpart to these numerous studies of Anglo-American literary exchange, and particularly to those such as Leonard Tennenhouse's *Importance of Feeling English*, which attends specifically to the impact of English migration on American cultural identity. Tennenhouse reads the literature of the early republic as the product of an exclusively English, rather than a broadly British, diaspora, arguing that Anglo-American settlers and their descendants attempted to remain English by reproducing in the United States aspects of English culture, including literary plots and conventions. If, as Tennenhouse suggests, Englishness in the early republic was culturally normative, then it makes sense that English émigrés are not marked in late eighteenth- and early nineteenth-century British and American writing in the same way that migrants from other regions of the British archipelago are. British and American writers rarely remarked upon distinguishing characteristics of Englishness—accents, dress, or behaviors—simply because those characteristics were the standard against which others were noted as deviations. Only towards the middle of the nineteenth century do we find an American writer pointing out a "most exquisitely marked specimen of the vulgar overbearing John Bull" in his territory.[60]

Yet if Anglo-Americans were generally keen to assert their cultural identity with the English, the English were reluctant to admit them to the privilege. English writers, for their part, made copious reflections upon American deviations from the implied norms of Englishness. Tilar Mazzeo has argued that these writers rejected a hybrid Anglo-American identity in favor of a "return to strategies of colonialism," or a re-Anglicization of post-Revolutionary America.[61] Although they may have imagined a distant cultural colonialism of sorts, English commentators on the United States seem to have been reluctant to settle there permanently. In the decades following independence, the vast majority of English writers on America were travelers passing through, or at best temporary residents.[62] Thus a second reason that this book does not include a chapter on English migrants is that the heyday of English migration to North America was the mid-seventeenth through the early eighteenth century. Although English influence on American literary culture remained significant, Scottish and Irish migrants were a more substantial presence in the late eighteenth- and early nineteenth-century United States than were English settlers.[63] When English migrants do figure in late eighteenth- and early nineteenth-century literature, they generally long to head home but are prevented by external obstacles such as war or familial prohibition, or internal conflicts such as knowledge of past misdeeds that they must confront if they return.

To illustrate these claims about representations of English migrants, I want to conclude with a brief reading of Charlotte Lennox's *Euphemia* (1790), a sentimental epistolary novel that incorporates the conventions through which Englishness is most often discussed in late eighteenth- and early nineteenth-century migrant fictions. The novel draws on Lennox's own experiences in Albany, New York, where her father held a military post, and where Lennox lived from approximately 1739 to 1743.[64] Written as a series of letters exchanged between the eponymous protagonist and her friend Maria, *Euphemia* is one of a number of late eighteenth-century sentimental novels in which a transatlantic crossing introduces the female protagonist to a new world of sorrows and suffering.[65] It foregrounds the distinctions between England and America by contrasting the experiences of Euphemia, in New York, with those of Maria, who remains in England and to whose romantic tribulations the entire second volume of the novel is devoted. *Euphemia*, like most fictional representations of English migration, is at bottom a sentimental novel in which migration constitutes one of the trials that the protagonist must endure. Euphemia marries Mr. Neville to please her dying mother only to discover that her new husband intends to emigrate to Albany regardless of Euphemia's desire to remain in England. Typically of fictional representations of English migration, Euphemia's removal to New York is a temporary measure rather than a step to permanent settlement abroad: Mr. Neville's uncle hopes that in Albany his dissipated nephew will acquire the discipline and steadiness necessary to run the estate that he stands to inherit upon his uncle's death. As the unfeeling Neville's dependent, Euphemia is homesick almost before she has left England, writing "We have now lost sight of land—all is sky and ocean; tremendous prospect! My mind feels its awful influence—my ideas are all solemn and sad."[66] Again, typically of accounts of English migration, the voyage to America entails loss rather than hope or opportunity.

Perhaps because English culture held a normative status in the early American republic, English transplants, whether historical, like William Cobbett and Frances Wright, or fictional, like Euphemia Neville, often function as a transparent or neutral lens that registers differences between the United States and England. Unmarked themselves, English characters serve to demarcate differences in others. Euphemia's harshest criticisms are reserved for the Dutch, who "keep up the customs and manners of their ancestors—the ancient settlers" (217). As a result of their failure to assimilate the more civilized ways of Anglo-Americans, "Their manners, their dress, their conversation, are so strange, so uncouth, so rudely familiar," Euphemia remarks, "that I am not surprised at the disgust they create" (229). Somewhat less disgusting are the "five nations of the Iroquois," who, with "unanimity, firmness, military skill, and policy . . . have raised themselves to the most formidable power in all America" (226). Although Indians are in many ways more foreign to Euphemia than the Dutch, her fellow Europeans, she finds in them many virtues to admire. Lennox's Indians demonstrate "a gentleness and humanity" that Mr. Neville and some of the novel's other Englishmen markedly lack (325). They are noble savages who have been corrupted by European vices.

When a group of intoxicated Mohawks annoys the pregnant Euphemia and her friends during a picnic, she remains confident that "if they had known who we were"—that is, English allies rather than French enemies—"they would have behaved with more civility" (258). Nonetheless, due to the fear that Euphemia experiences during the confrontation, her newborn son, Edward, bears "under his left breast the distinct mark of a bow and arrow, the arms born by one of these savages" (263). The trope of the unusual birthmark was commonplace in eighteenth-century British fiction, perhaps constituting an imaginative response to Britons' increasing geographic mobility. In Henry Fielding's *Joseph Andrews* (1742), for instance, baby Joseph is carried off by gypsies but is reunited with his father as an adult thanks to his strawberry-shaped birthmark, which authenticates his identity. In the context of transatlantic migration, which disperses family members across oceans and continents, the birthmark is an indelible sign that enables the recognition and reunion not simply of kin but also, symbolically, of the members of a diaspora.

Whereas Euphemia's role in the novel is primarily to report on the curiosities of life in the American colonies, Mr. Neville is one of a number of villainous English migrants who people late eighteenth- and early nineteenth-century Anglo-American fiction—from the dissipated soldier Belville in Susanna Rowson's *Charlotte Temple* (1791) to the self-interested aristocrat, Jasper Meredith, who toys with the affection of a virtuous but naïve New England girl in Catharine Maria Sedgwick's *Linwoods* (1835). These villains offer a critique of English masculinity. For, as Elisa Tamarkin has so aptly pointed out, they are not "bad English [characters], but characters who are badly English" due to their failure to embody English standards of honor, courage, and loyalty.[67] Mr. Neville's failures include not only "ill humour, and unjust reproach" towards his wife (265), but also neglect of their young son, Edward, whom Neville carelessly loses in the wilderness around Schenectady. Edward is presumed drowned, but is in fact adopted by the Hurons and educated by a French Jesuit in Montreal. His adoptive parents prove better than his own father; and when Edward is reunited with his mother, thanks to the identifying mark on his chest, Euphemia finds that he possesses an "air and manner, so unembarrassed, so polite, and even gallant, which, joined with a true English solidity of understanding, makes him pass for a prodigy" (387). Edward's childhood among the Hurons renders him far more civil and even chivalrous than his boor of a father, a contrast that offers support for Tim Fulford's claim that American Indians in late eighteenth-century Anglo-American literature often serve to reveal the deficiencies of English masculinity.[68] Edward embodies an English masculinity reinvigorated by Native American sensibility and honor.

A remarkable number of "good" English migrants in late eighteenth- and early nineteenth-century Anglo-American literature are rewarded with their return home, and Euphemia is no exception. Indeed, the alternative to returning home for fictional English migrants, particularly women, is death, which arguably restores these wanderers to a more permanent home. Thus the eponymous heroine of Rowson's *Charlotte Temple*, who cannot be reintegrated into English society after she is persuaded against her better judgment to run off with a soldier to New York, is relieved from her misery by death. Euphemia is rescued from her dependence upon her degenerate husband when Neville's uncle, disgusted by his nephew's self-interestedness, leaves his estate to her rather than to Neville. The estate will pass eventually to the virtuous Edward, and England will have assimilated into its own social order the best qualities—sensibility, chivalry, and honor—that the United States, through its indigenous peoples, has to offer. *Euphemia* is representative of literary renditions of English migration to the early republic in its ethnographic tendencies, its differentiation of virtuous from corrupt English masculinity, and in its portrayal of migration as a temporary, although nonetheless deplorable, measure.

Englishness is integral to *Nation and Migration* in ways that cannot be encapsulated in a single chapter on English migration. Perhaps the most important thing that Americans held in common with Scots, Irish, and Welsh people during the late eighteenth and early nineteenth centuries was the fact that they were not English at a time when metropolitan England was the center of cultural authority in the British Atlantic world. The next chapter examines how, during the 1760s and '70s, Englishness became a contested identity, as American colonists asserted their claim to English rights and liberties, and the English questioned whether emigrants retained such a claim. Participants in the debate over the American colonies' right to Parliamentary representation looked to Scotland, Ireland, and Wales for precedents in the extension of English rights and liberties beyond England's borders. Paradoxically, though, colonists could only retain what they considered English rights and liberties by declaring their political independence from Britain.

From English Empire to British Atlantic World

In 1765, after the Stamp Act initiated a transatlantic debate over the American colonies' right to Parliamentary representation in Britain, an anonymously written pamphlet titled *A Vindication of the Rights of the Americans* (1765) advocated the colonies' right to administer their own taxes by comparing colonial Americans to the peoples of the British archipelago. The writer points out that "our constitution is so tender of the Rights and Liberties of the Subject that the People of *England* have their Repr[esentative]s, the *Scotch* theirs, the *Welsh* theirs, the *Irish* theirs, the *Americans* theirs."[1] The constitution in question here is England's unwritten constitution—one that the American writer and his readers could for a few more years still consider "ours"—and his somewhat obfuscatory claim is that because this constitution allows Parliamentary representation of some sort to Scotland, Wales, and Ireland, so it should to the American colonies. *A Vindication of the Rights of the Americans* was hardly unique in using comparisons between the American colonies and England's Celtic peripheries to argue its case. Indeed such comparisons were made with increasing frequency by writers of all political stripes over the decade between the passing of the Stamp Act in 1765 and the outbreak of war between Britain and the colonies in 1775. Nor is this pamphlet's argument—that colonial assemblies should be granted quasi- or para-parliamentary status, with powers of taxation similar to those of the Irish Parliament—particularly original. This solution to the colonial conflict was suggested by Granville Sharp and Edmund Burke, among others. More unusual is the pamphlet's depiction of Americans as a distinct people, as different from the English as were the Scots, the Welsh, and the Irish, and as deserving of political representation on the basis of their collective identity.

The debates of the late 1760s and early 1770s primarily concerned the distribution of the powers of government between a centralized imperial authority—"the King-in-Parliament"—and local governing bodies.[2] This issue was complicated by Britain's status as what John Elliott terms a "composite monarchy," a monarchy whose power extended across more than one nation, each with its own distinctive forms of local government. Although England, Wales, Scotland, and Ireland shared a monarch, at the time of the colonial conflict only Ireland had a separate parliamentary body. Ireland's Parliament was subordinate to the British Parliament, which included representatives from Scotland and Wales.[3] This already complex distribution of power within Britain and Ireland was further complicated by Britain's possession of territory overseas. Elliott observes that "in general, imperialism and composite monarchy made uncomfortable bedfellows" because the extension of monarchical authority across distant regions of the globe encouraged patterns of domination and subordination among territories that were on principle supposedly equal.[4] The establishment of colonies in America not only raised questions about the distribution of power between a centralized British government and its possessions abroad; it also reintroduced the perennial question of whether Scotland, Ireland, and Wales were in fact equal partners with England, or subordinate, even colonized, English possessions.

Until the middle of the eighteenth century, the phrase "the English Empire" or, less often, "the British Empire" was used primarily to refer to the Celtic peripheries—Scotland, Wales, and Ireland—rather than to the American colonies or Britain's other overseas possessions.[5] In keeping with this usage, some historians have described the settlement of the American colonies as an extension of what Michael Hechter has termed internal colonialism: the practices through which an economically and politically powerful core—in this case metropolitan England—exploits its less economically developed peripheries.[6] According to these accounts, when Britons began to settle in North America, England attempted to transfer practices developed through the government of Wales, Ireland, and to a lesser extent Scotland, to its new possessions. However, extending the concept of internal colonialism to the settlement of the American colonies is problematic because it overestimates the strength of the imperial English center and underestimates that of the peripheries. Critics of the internal colonialism model have argued that, prior to Parliament's efforts to bring the American colonies more closely under its control in the wake of the Seven Years War, the British Atlantic world consisted of semi-autonomous regions of settlement that were only loosely tied to the putative imperial center.[7] Parliament's insistence upon tightening these ties impelled the colonies to declare their independence in 1776, after more than a decade of attempted negotiation and resistance. The War of Independence, in other words, was caused by the British Parliament's efforts to transform the colonies from semi-autonomous settlements into dependent peripheries.

It should not be surprising, then, that in the decade leading up to the American Revolution, writers on both sides of the Atlantic scrutinized England's political relationships with its Celtic peripheries, regarding them as precedents that might offer some hint towards a resolution of Parliament's conflicts with the American colonies. Those that hoped to consolidate some degree of British Parliamentary authority over the colonies looked to Anglo-Welsh, Anglo-Scottish, and especially Anglo-Irish relations for successful examples of how to balance centralized and local forms of government. Those that supported the colonies' bid for independence, by contrast, looked to England's government of its Celtic peripheries for cautionary tales of the misfortunes that might befall Americans if they did not succeed in throwing off British rule. Ireland loomed particularly large in these pre-Revolutionary debates both because it was a settler colony and because it had a subordinate parliament with powers of taxation, which was precisely what many colonial Americans claimed to want. In the years following independence, as Americans debated how best to distribute power in a nation comprised of thirteen discrete and heterogeneous entities, they again looked to the British archipelago as an example of a multinational state. Scotland figured most significantly in these post-Revolutionary debates because the 1707 Anglo-Scottish Union had ostensibly created an egalitarian political partnership of the sort that some Americans wanted to create among the states. Both before and after the Revolution, England's hegemonic government of, or putative partnership with, its Celtic peripheries seemed to contemporary observers to offer examples of how political authority might be exercised—in some cases successfully and in others less so—across a relatively large territory encompassing a variety of distinct cultures.

In fact, however, the Celtic peripheries' relationships to English imperial authority were as problematic and open to interpretation as were the colonies'. It was precisely this indeterminacy that enabled writers who took very different positions on the colonial crisis to find in Anglo-Celtic relations seeming precedents for British government of the colonies. English and American writers' comparisons between the American colonies and the Celtic peripheries had no real impact on the legislation that defined the powers of centralized and local forms of government in the British Atlantic world. Yet these analogies were not merely rhetorical. They provide insights into late eighteenth-century understandings of how the various pieces of the British Atlantic world fit together. By tracing late eighteenth-century writers' comparisons between the Celtic peripheries and the American colonies or states from the prewar to the postwar period, this chapter illuminates the unsettling of a politically and culturally Anglocentric British Atlantic world, as non-English regions of that world found potential sources of strength in their shared secondariness.

Johnson, Burke, and Colonial Englishness

In the 1760s and '70s, the question of whether certain political prerogatives resided in the colonial assemblies or in the British Parliament was often translated into the cultural realm, where it became a question of who counted as English. Did an Englishman lose his claim to Englishness upon migrating to the colonies? Or did he retain the same distinctively English rights and liberties as his kinsmen who remained in England? Paradoxically, participants in the debates over the colonies' rights often sought to answer these questions by looking not at England, but instead at its Celtic peripheries.

Englishness in the eighteenth century carried many connotations, but its primary association in the British Atlantic world was with liberty.[8] Bernard Bailyn and Caroline Robbins trace the association between Englishness and liberty to the writings of the seventeenth-century radicals who opposed the impositions of the Stuart monarchs.[9] For these commonwealthmen, liberty was guaranteed by England's constitution, understood as a set of "governmental institutions, laws, and customs together with the principles and goals that animated them."[10] Laura Doyle has explored the racial dimensions of this concept of English liberty, reminding us that seventeenth-century commonwealth thinkers attributed their pride in liberty to their Saxon descent and understood "freedom as a racial inheritance."[11] During the fifth century, the liberty-loving Saxons laid the foundations of the English constitution with their traditions of participatory government—traditions that persisted through repeated instances of oppression, from the Norman invasion to the religious tyranny of the Stuarts. Seventeenth-century English emigrants, many of whom left their country to escape religious oppression under the Stuarts, brought with them to the American colonies the racialized discourses of liberty that flourished during England's Civil War.

Yet migration and settlement in British North America also contributed to the mystification of English liberty and to the obfuscation of its racial origins, so that any white settler, whether of Saxon, Celtic, or other descent, could claim English rights and liberties. American colonists believed themselves, as much as the inhabitants of Great Britain, to be heirs to English liberty and to the English constitution that preserved it. They consequently perceived the Stamp Act, the Townshend Acts, the Tea Act, and the Coercive Acts—all of which were passed without their participation through elected representatives in the legislative process—as so many infringements upon their freedom and assaults upon their Englishness. However, Britons at home, even those who wished to avoid war with the colonies, were less certain that migrants retained their claims to English identity on the other side of the Atlantic.

While many little-known voices contributed to debates over whether American colonists were entitled to English rights and liberties, and thus to some kind of Parliamentary representation, I have chosen to focus here on the contributions of two of the best-known participants—Samuel Johnson and Edmund Burke—because their arguments can be taken to some extent as illustrative, respectively, of a metropolitan English and a peripheral Celtic perspective on the colonies' claims to participate in representative government.

Johnson, the son of a Litchfield merchant, never held political office, and likely never even voted, as the franchise was limited to the small minority of men who met the requisite property qualifications.[12] Nonetheless, *Taxation No Tyranny* (1775), Johnson's most thorough discussion of the colonial crisis, argues for the restriction of English rights and liberties to the British archipelago, and the centralization of political authority in the British Parliament. Johnson's support of Parliament's prerogative must have been well known, as he wrote *Taxation No Tyranny* at the request of North's administration. However, his scorn for the colonies' claim to local self-government must have exceeded the bounds of diplomacy, as he was asked to exchange the pamphlet's "bold language" for "milder terms" before it was published.[13]

In contrast, Burke, although he was a Member of Parliament, did not support the centralization of imperial government that Johnson desired. Instead, he advocated the re-establishment of a composite monarchy that would allow the colonies to retain local forms of self-government similar to those belonging to Ireland. Burke had witnessed first-hand the injustices of British colonial rule in his native Ireland and could sympathize with Americans' frustrations at the seeming curtailment of their customary rights.[14] He may have been sympathetic to the American cause in part because he saw colonists as ambitious outsiders like himself, anxious to share in metropolitan England's cultural capital as much as its political power.[15] Burke argued that since English rights and liberties had been extended so successfully in various forms throughout the Celtic peripheries, they ought to be extended similarly to the colonies. While Johnson could not entirely deny that the Celtic peripheries had been granted a version of English rights and liberties, he asserted that the colonies' political status simply was not comparable to the peripheries'. Despite their own efforts to regulate access to English rights and liberties, Burke and Johnson's disagreements suggest that Englishness was coming to be defined not so much by those at the center of the British Atlantic world, as by those who inhabited its outskirts.

Johnson's and Burke's most important contributions to the debate over the colonial crisis came relatively late in its development, with Johnson's *Taxation No Tyranny*—possibly "the most thunderous cannon of the whole anti-American campaign mobilized by Lord North's administration"—appearing only a couple of weeks before Burke delivered his "Speech on Conciliation with America" in Parliament on March 22, 1775.[16] By this point, the war that both Burke and Johnson wished to avoid was already looming, hastened by the inconsistencies and contradictions in the conciliatory proposals that North had outlined the preceding month. While North's plan reinstated the colonial assemblies' privilege of raising their own taxes for defense and administration, it did not renounce Parliament's right of taxation entirely and insisted upon Britain's continued right to regulate trade, leaving colonists afraid that Parliament might impose further punitive legislation upon them at any time.

Burke and Johnson recognized that the colonial crisis was not simply about taxation, but more broadly "about the rights and relations of colonies and mother-nations,"[17] and both favored what Thomas Curley has described as gradual and organic "constitutional evolution over political revolution."[18] Yet where Burke saw North's conciliation proposal as unnecessarily brutal towards the colonies, and feared it would irreparably alienate them from Britain, Johnson found it too weak, and adamantly upheld Parliament's right to tax the colonies. Although Burke acknowledged Parliament's fundamental right to legislate for the colonies, he argued that Parliament ought to maintain the harmony and unity of Britain's empire by renouncing that right and restoring to the colonies their prior privileges of levying their own taxes. For Johnson, the situation allowed no concessions: he maintained that Britain had the right to tax the colonies without granting them Parliamentary representation.

Johnson begins his defense of the consolidation of imperial authority in Parliament much as one would expect from the creator of the first English dictionary, by defining a colony. He proposes to examine "how a Colony is constituted, what are the terms of migration as dictated by Nature or settled by compact, and what social and political rights the man loses, or acquires, that leaves his country to establish himself in a distant plantation."[19] He divides the history of colonialism into two stages, ancient and modern. During "the migrations of the early world" (420), "one part of the community broke off from the rest" (419) and found a distant habitation where it "became another nation" (419). Early migrants, like the European peoples who settled Britain, made an irrevocable break with their communities of origin: "They looked back no more to their former home; they expected no help from those they had left behind" (419). But the centralization of government and the progress of the arts and sciences changed the character of migration. Individuals could no longer conquer lands or establish colonies on their own behalf; instead they acted as agents of the government that assisted their explorations (420). Modern colonialism thus succeeds only when the mother-country and its colonies share "one publick interest" (422). Yet Johnson goes on to explain that the welfare of the mother-country weighs more heavily than that of the colonies in calculating this shared interest. Resorting to the oft-used metaphor of the body politic, Johnson compares the mother-country to the torso and the colonies to its limbs, warning that "the body may subsist, though less commodiously, without a limb, but the limb must perish if it be parted from the body" (425).

Johnson's distinction between ancient and modern colonialism was important because it refuted the claims of those who grounded the colonies' right to self-government in a comparison of the American colonies and the much earlier settlement of England by the Saxons. *A Summary View of the Rights of British America* (1774), a document written by Thomas Jefferson for the delegates to the Continental Congress, asserts that "no circumstance has occurred to distinguish materially the British from the Saxon emigration." *A Summary View* develops the analogy between American and Saxon colonists, stating that

> our ancestors, before their emigration to America, were the free inhabitants of the British dominions in Europe, and possessed a right which nature has given to all men, of departing from the country in which chance, not choice, has placed them; of going in quest of new habitations, and of there establishing new societies, under such laws and regulations as to them shall seem most likely to promote public happiness. That their Saxon ancestors had, under this universal law, in the like manner left their native wilds and woods in the north of Europe; had possessed themselves of the island of Britain, then less charged with inhabitants, and had established there that system of laws which has so long been the glory and protection of that country.[20]

The pamphlet contends that just as the Saxons were under no obligations to those they left behind in their "native wilds," so Americans cannot be held accountable to the British government. By eliding any differences between the Saxon migration to England and the British to America, *A Summary View* establishes a precedent for the colonies which is all the more powerful because Americans claimed to have inherited their love of liberty from their Saxon ancestors. Johnson's distinction between ancient and modern forms of colonization refuses to acknowledge Jefferson's analogy between the Saxons and the American colonists, instead questioning the existence of a "universal law" that allows people to leave on a whim the country of their birth and establish a new society. British colonists settled America, he reminds readers, on behalf of their mother-country, to which they remained bound by mutual ties of obligation. Americans are "entitled to English dignities, regulated by English counsels, and protected by English arms," and in turn they must be "subject to English government, and chargeable by English taxation" (425).

Although Johnson acknowledges emigrants' conditional rights to certain English privileges and protections, he argues that colonists renounced their right to Parliamentary representation when they left Britain. In his *Journey to the Western Isles of Scotland* (1773), published just two years before *Taxation No Tyranny*, Johnson lamented that Highlanders, the vast majority of whom had no vote to renounce, were forced to emigrate by sheer scarcity of resources. In *Taxation No Tyranny*, by contrast, Johnson implies that emigrants to the colonies calculatingly choose to pursue the acquisition of property over the privilege of political participation. This contradiction might possibly be resolved if we assume that the imagined emigrant of *Taxation No Tyranny* is fairly affluent; nonetheless, even well-to-do colonists may have felt that for religious, political, or other reasons, they had little choice but to emigrate. *Taxation No*

Tyranny describes an emigrant who "left a country where he had a vote but little property, for another, where he has great property, but no vote. But as this preference was deliberate and unconstrained, he is still concerned in the government of himself" (430). Much as Burke would argue some fifteen years later in his *Reflections on the Revolution in France* (1790) that an Englishman's rights and liberties are "an entailed inheritance," Johnson suggests that an emigrant's renunciation of his vote is passed down to his descendants.[21] The present generation of rebellious colonists could acquire Parliamentary representation only by returning to Britain and exchanging its property for votes.

Richard Bland, a Virginia planter and statesman, countered Johnson's argument when he claimed that undertaking the hard work of colonialism for the benefit of their mother-country rendered Americans *more* deserving of English rights and liberties, including Parliamentary representation, than their countrymen at home. Bland declared that "if we are the descendants of Englishmen, who by their own consent and at the expense of their own blood and treasure undertook to settle this new region for the benefit and aggrandizement of the parent kingdom, the native privileges our progenitors enjoyed must be derived to us from them, as they could not be forfeited by their migration to America."[22] Johnson's refusal to grant emigrants the same rights as Britons at home perhaps reflects his skepticism of the commercial underpinnings of Britain's first empire and the national "aggrandizement" it promised.[23] He is particularly scathing towards slaveholders like Bland, asking derisively, "how is it that we hear the loudest *yelps* for liberty among the drivers of negroes?"[24] This indictment of the obvious hypocrisy of colonists who demanded liberty for themselves while participating in a slaveholding economy exposes the racism underpinning Bland's expenditure of "blood and treasure" on Britain's behalf.

Johnson further justifies the disenfranchisement of emigrants by comparing the American colonies to Wales and the former palatinates of Chester and Durham, all of which, over time, had been awarded Parliamentary representation and accorded English rights and liberties despite being geographically and politically marginal to England. The aim of Johnson's comparisons was to show that Wales, Chester, and Durham were in no way similar to the American colonies and therefore did not constitute precedents for allowing the colonies representation in Britain's Parliament. All comparatively distant from the seat of centralized English government, Wales, Chester, and Durham had been brought under the jurisdiction of England's Parliament only in the sixteenth century. Johnson describes the extension of Parliamentary representation to Wales, Chester, and Durham as compensation for the loss of their political autonomy. After they had been "reduced to the state of English counties, they had representatives assigned to them" (435). In contrast to the inhabitants of Wales and the palatinates, who were "reduced" or subdued by various forms of coercion, Americans voluntarily resigned their right to representation by emigrating (436). In Johnson's view they have been deprived of no preexisting political independence and therefore are owed no compensatory representation in Britain's Parliament.

Johnson is equally determined to deny the colonies' right to semi-autonomous assemblies of their own. Some writers, including Burke, looked to Ireland's Parliament, which was subordinate to the British Parliament, as a model for a decentralized form of colonial government.[25] Johnson has no good argument why the Irish Parliament shouldn't provide such a model except a rather circular claim that the legitimacy of any subordinate governing body must be "acknowledged by the Parliament of Britain" (435). However, even if the colonies were permitted to establish a subordinate assembly, their right to administer their own taxes could never, for Johnson, override or negate the British Parliament's right to tax them. Johnson argues that a colony is essentially no different from a parish: it can administer its own taxes, but it is also subject to any imposed "by superior authority" (432).

Johnson refuses to admit the colonies' resemblance to other peripheral regions under the political control of metropolitan England when to do so might imply that their claims were at least entitled to consideration; however, he is quite ready to acknowledge their similarities when doing so allows him to suggest the absurdity of the colonies' desire for independence. *Taxation No Tyranny* concludes with a parody of the Continental Congress's resolutions in which Johnson asks readers to imagine what would happen if Cornwall, "seized with the Philadelphian frenzy," determined "to separate itself from the general system of the English constitution, and judge of its own rights in its own parliament" (445). Johnson imagines a letter from the Cornish people to the members of the British Parliament in which they assert their power by threatening to "keep our Tin in our own hands," warning, "you can be supplied from no other place, and therefore must comply at last, or be poisoned with the copper of your own kitchens" (447). That the Cornish people's strongest argument in favor of independence is simply that they do not like how they are being governed indicates Johnson's complete contempt for the colonial cause (447). The comparison between Cornwall and the colonies is clearly meant to ridicule the latter's sense of importance, as Cornwall was by the end of the eighteenth century arguably the most Anglicized of England's Celtic peripheries, with the least grounds for claiming political independence.[26]

In Johnson's account, emigrants voluntarily renounce their claims to English rights and liberties even while they remain completely under the jurisdiction of Britain's Parliament. Johnson represents colonists as grasping and manipulative, out to get what they can from the mother-country while giving back as little as possible. Their self-interest is what has un-Englished emigrants in the first place, as they have chosen to pursue property and prosperity over political participation, demonstrating their lack of the public spirit that, for Johnson, is a definitive characteristic of Englishness. For Johnson, then, the American call for independence was morally repugnant, as well as politically unsound. Pointing out that "To love their country has always been considered as virtue in men, whose love could not be otherwise than blind, because their preference was made without a comparison," he professes never to have come across any people other than British Americans who have with such "blindness hated their country" (412).

What Johnson perceived as aggressive and misguided selfishness was for Burke a sign of the colonists' love of freedom and thus of their abiding Englishness. In his "Speech on Conciliation," Burke lists several reasons why Americans might be such strong advocates of liberty, including the predominance of Protestantism in the northern colonies, the existence of slavery in the south, and the sheer fact of their geographical distance from England. However, for Burke, the strongest source of their love of liberty is a kind of ideological heredity. Burke reminds his audience that the earliest emigrants left England in search of the religious freedom denied them by the Stuart kings. The descendants of these early emigrants "are therefore not only devoted to Liberty, but to Liberty according to English ideas and on English principles."[27] Burke figures Americans' love of freedom as an inherited trait when he reminds his audience that "the Colonies draw from you as with their life-blood, their ideas and principles" (121). The very act of resisting Parliament's authority to tax them is thus a sign of the colonies' Englishness; for as Burke points out, "the great contests for freedom in [England] were from the earliest times chiefly upon the question of Taxing" (120).

The writers of *The Declaration by the Representatives of the United Colonies of North America* (1775) employed similar rhetoric and reasoning to explain the colonies' decision to resist British tyranny, declaring that "While we revere the Memory of our gallant and virtuous Ancestors, we never can surrender those glorious Privileges for which they fought, bled, and conquered."[28] To submit to Parliament's authority ironically would demonstrate the colonies' un-Englishness, their lack of fidelity to their heritage. *The Declaration* further argues that shared blood and shared values require Britons to support the Americans' cause, claiming that "If the Humanity which tempered the Valour of our common Ancestors has not degenerated into Cruelty, you will lament the Miseries of their Descendants."[29] The authors of *The Declaration* here insinuate what some others asserted more boldly: that English virtues and liberties had degenerated in Britain, and now flourished only in the colonies.

Like Johnson, Burke is concerned not only with examining emigrants' claims to English rights and liberties, but also with defining the relationship between mother-country and colonies. Burke was easily as staunch a supporter of existing social hierarchies as Johnson, but he also believed that "subordination and liberty" are compatible principles of imperial organization.[30] Much earlier than his "Speech on Conciliation," Burke advocated the restoration of a decentralized system of government in which semi-autonomous colonial assemblies would be subordinate to the British Parliament, which, in its "imperial character ... superintends all the several inferior legislatures, and guides, and controls them all without annihilating."[31] In the "Speech on Conciliation," Burke further elaborates his vision of a British empire characterized "by a Unity of Spirit," manifest "in a diversity of operations" (136), a condition that can only be achieved through a careful distribution of power.[32] Subordinate legislatures like the Irish Parliament and colonial assemblies should "have many local privileges and immunities" but must all be accountable to "one common head," the British Parliament (132). Whereas Johnson declares the uselessness of England's colonial limbs without the national torso, Burke cautions that "England is the head; but she is not the head and the members too" (136), warning Parliament to allow the colonial "members" a substantial degree of local autonomy. To reconcile subordination and liberty, Burke proposes *to admit the people of our Colonies into an interest in the constitution* by restoring and legitimating colonial assemblies (136, italics in original).

Given the extended argument that Burke would later make in his *Reflections on the Revolution in France* in favor of building on tradition rather than beginning anew, it is not surprising that precedent also informs his plan for a decentralized system of colonial government. He finds four particularly relevant precedents in the cases of "Ireland, Wales, Chester, and Durham" (139). He endorses the formal institution of colonial assemblies through precedent when he notes that "Ireland has ever had from the beginning a separate, but not an independent, legislature; which, far from distracting, promoted the union of the whole. . . . This is my model with regard to America, as far as the internal circumstances of the two countries are the same" (158). In contrast to Johnson, who sought out differences between the political circumstances of the American colonies and the Celtic peripheries in order to argue that the latter could not be taken as models for the former, Burke assumes basic similarities between colonies and the peripheries, and implies that Parliament's treatment of the outlying regions of its empire should be, if not uniform, at least consistent.

The cases of Ireland, Wales, Chester, and Durham suggest to Burke that the extension of English liberties throughout the empire is more effective than force in securing the outlying regions' loyalties to Parliament, and, more broadly, to English rule. Commenting on centuries of colonial government in Ireland, Burke declares that "nothing could make that country English, in civility and allegiance, but your laws and your forms of legislature. It was not English arms, but the English constitution, that conquered Ireland" (140). Only after "English laws and liberties" were extended to Ireland were the wild Irish subdued (140). As in Ireland, so in Wales all efforts "to subdue the fierce spirit of the Welsh" failed until Henry VIII extended "all the rights and privileges of English subjects" to them. "From that moment," Burke claims, "as by a charm, the tumults subsided; obedience was restored; peace, order, and civilization followed in the train of liberty" (142). Burke adduces similar instances of the reconciliatory effects of extending English rights and liberties to Chester and Durham, glossing over the fact that the palatinates had never resisted English authority with the violence of Ireland, Wales, or the American colonies.[33] Indeed, the "Speech on Conciliation" perhaps emphasizes historical instances of Irish and Welsh resistance to English government in order to construe the American colonies' resistance as unexceptional and easily managed. In Burke's speech, all rebelliousness becomes a symptom of either residual or nascent Englishness.

By introducing into his argument the histories of Ireland, Wales, Chester, and Durham, Burke perhaps hoped to persuade his audience that by granting the colonies constitutional representation in the form of a subordinate parliament, Britain would regain the colonies' loyalties and quash their rebelliousness. He also sought to provide Parliament with what he saw as a valid reason to comply with the colonies' demands: that, in doing so, it would simply be following established precedent rather than admitting defeat. The precedents of Ireland, Wales, Durham, and Chester suggested that to confer political rights on the inhabitants of the peripheries was to confer Englishness upon them by encouraging them to become morally worthy of exercising these rights. Americans, however, had already demonstrated their Englishness through their insistence upon these rights. Burke thus questions, "if the doctrines of policy contained in these preambles, and the force of these examples in the acts of Parliament, avail any thing, what can be said against applying them with regard to America? Are not the people of America as much Englishmen as the Welsh?" (144). The answer for Burke, of course, is that Americans are at least as English as the Welsh. Johnson undoubtedly would have answered differently.

Burke's "Speech on Conciliation" urges Parliament to restore to the colonial assemblies their privileges of levying taxes not necessarily because it is right to do so, but because it is expedient, and more importantly, generous. "All government," he affirms, "is founded on compromise and barter" (164). Burke's fervent belief that granting the colonies' demands would forge between Britain and America "ties which, though light as air, are as strong as links of iron" (164) led Carl B. Cone to describe the "Speech on Conciliation" as a "great, futile appeal to reason, justice, humanity, commonsense, and the healing influence of time."[34] Yet, despite its considerable virtues, it is unlikely that Burke's plan to restore the colonies' privileges of taxation would have satisfied the Continental Congress or prevented the outbreak of war, as he was unwilling to concede Parliament's ultimate authority over the colonies. Burke might have considered Parliament's arbitrary exercise of that authority unwise and even unjust, but he acknowledged, along with Johnson, that it was legal.

Johnson and Burke were far from the only participants in the debates surrounding the colonial crisis to turn to draw comparisons between England's government of the colonies and of the outlying regions of the British archipelago. Their contributions to these debates demonstrate that such comparisons were not solely rhetorical gimmicks, but also attempts to delimit Parliament's authority over England's internal colonies and overseas empire. Their contributions also reveal that, at the moment of the colonial crisis, the English perceived the British Atlantic world as resembling the Galilean universe, symbolically if not geographically. England, and specifically London, occupied the center, and all other regions were defined in relation to it, with those farthest from the source of heat and light, or political authority, requiring the most compensatory legislation. From the perspective of those inhabiting the peripheries and colonies, Englishness was a desirable attribute not so much because of the cultural refinement it connoted (although that was not insignificant) as because of the political rights and liberties it implied.[35] When the United States declared its independence from Britain, Americans at once repudiated and embodied Englishness, demonstrating definitively that they would not submit to the infringement of their rights and liberties. Yet when the citizens of the new nation undertook the task of developing their own system of government, and of reconfiguring the balance between local and central forms of power, the British archipelago remained an influential model.

American Federalism and the Anglo-Scottish Union

Perhaps the biggest question that the creators of the American Constitution had to consider at the Philadelphia Convention in 1787 was how to distribute political power between state and federal governments. The attempt to develop a constitution "that would subordinate the states to the federal government without either consolidating them into a single government or depriving them of authority over their own internal affairs was merely a continuation of the ancient quest, dating back to the earliest history of the colonies, to find a workable allocation of authority between the center and the peripheries, between the national government and the states."[36] In the course of formulating the new Constitution, two distinct approaches to the issue emerged, with the Federalists favoring a strong central government and weak state governments, and anti-Federalists advocating a weak central government and strong state governments. On the one hand, Federalists tended to place little faith in civic virtue, believing that individuals are motivated by self-interest rather than by concern for the common good. They argued that, in a nation comprised of as many different peoples, cultures, and regions as the new United States, a strong central government would be necessary to adjudicate among the "various and interfering interests" that would emerge.[37]

On the other hand, the anti-Federalists recalled the problems that had led to the Revolutionary War, when Parliament, a strong, centralized political institution, attempted to govern the very distant and diverse colonies. Anti-Federalists feared that creating a strong federal government would simply reinstate a form of the tyranny from which the colonies had so recently freed themselves.[38]

To support their arguments, both Federalists and anti-Federalists looked to Great Britain, a multinational state formed through several different instances of political union, for precedents. Federalist John Jay declared the wisdom of looking to British precedents when he pointed out that "the history of Great Britain is the one with which we are in general the best acquainted, and it gives us many useful lessons. We may profit by their experience without paying the price which it cost them" (23). However, anti-Federalist responses suggest that the "useful lessons" to be derived from British history were a matter of interpretation. Whereas Ireland had dominated pre-Revolutionary comparisons between the American colonies and Celtic peripheries, Scotland featured particularly prominently in debates between Federalist and anti-Federalist writers. Ireland, although colonized by Scots and English settlers, possessed its own parliamentary body, albeit subordinate to the British Parliament, until 1800. In contrast, the 1707 Anglo-Scottish Union of Parliaments had consolidated the centralization of British government by absorbing Scotland's Parliament into England's, leaving Scotland at the mercy of a distant governing body in which English members outnumbered Scots by roughly twelve to one. The union was preceded by several years of debate in which some Scots had urged that Scotland should retain its own parliament while continuing to share a monarchy with England.[39] The 1707 Anglo-Scottish Treaty of Union thus raised questions about the distribution of power between central and local forms of government very similar to those faced by the creators of the American Constitution. While Federalist writers emphasized the benefits that parliamentary union had conferred on Scots, anti-Federalists pointed to Scotland's political disempowerment in a united Great Britain, suggesting that a strong national government would similarly disempower states, especially those farthest from the nation's political center.

The Federalist, a series of essays written by Alexander Hamilton, James Madison, and John Jay, aimed to encourage acceptance of the document created at the 1787 Constitutional Convention among "The People of the State of New York," to whom the essays were addressed. Along with Virginia, New York was one of the last states to withhold ratification of the Constitution, thanks to a strong anti-Federalist contingent. To avoid evoking personal animosities, *The Federalist* essays were published pseudonymously under the name Publius, an allusion to the founder of the Roman Republic, Publius Valerius Publicola. John Jay has been described as "the forgotten Publius" because he contributed only 5 of the 85 essays comprising *The Federalist*:

numbers 2 through 5 and number 64.[40] Jay's aim in numbers 2 through 5 seems
to have been to forge an association in readers' minds between federalism and
national unity, suggesting that one necessarily entailed the other. In *Federalist*
No. 2, for instance, he posits as already existing the unity that Federalists
hoped a strong central government would create. Publius observes that

> Providence has been pleased to give this one connected country to one
> united people—a people descended from the same ancestors, speaking the
> same language, professing the same religion, attached to the same prin-
> ciples of government, very similar in their manners and customs, and who,
> by their joint counsels, arms, and efforts, fighting side by side through-
> out a long and bloody war, have nobly established general liberty and
> independence. (9)

Here Jay dramatically overstates the ethnic homogeneity of the United States
in order to build a fiction of shared beliefs, values, traditions, and interests on
the putative foundation of shared ancestry. His vision of national unity was
undoubtedly "more prescriptive than descriptive."[41]

In *Federalist* No. 5, the "trope of union" that Robert A. Ferguson has traced
through Jay's contributions to *The Federalist* culminates in a discussion of
England's unions with Wales in 1536 and Scotland in 1707, both of which
Publius represents as historically inevitable events: "Although it seems obvious
to common sense that the people of such an island should be but one nation,
yet we find that they were for ages divided into three, and that those three were
almost constantly embroiled in quarrels and wars with one another" (9).[42]
Federal union, and the centralization of government that it entailed in Great
Britain, here is depicted as a means of resolving competing interests rather
than a potential source of contention among the peoples it unites, as was in
fact the case. Britain's island geography seems to naturalize the unification of
England, Wales, and Scotland; and *Federalist* No. 2 does its best to represent
"independent America" as a comparably discrete entity, made of "one connected, fertile, widespreading country" around which a "succession of navi-
gable waters form a kind of chain . . . as if to bind it together" (9).

Publius further argues that a strong central government will ensure to
Americans the benefits that the 1707 Treaty of Union offered to Scots—namely
harmony and security. The number opens with a long extract from a letter
written by Queen Anne, the monarch who oversaw the 1707 Anglo-Scottish
Union, to the Members of the Scottish Parliament, urging them to agree to
a union that would incorporate Scotland's Parliament into England's. The
Queen's letter describes this centralization of government as "the solid foundation of lasting peace" which will

> secure your religion, liberty, and property; remove the animosities amongst
> yourselves, and the jealousies and differences between your two kingdoms.

It must increase your strength, riches, and trade; and by this union the whole island, being joined in affection and free from all apprehensions of different interest, will be *enabled to resist all its enemies*. (23, italics in original).

In contrast to the Anglo-Welsh Union, which was brokered through England's conquest of Wales, the Anglo-Scottish Union purported to be an egalitarian partnership founded not just in economic and political interest, but also in affection. Publius thus takes the Anglo-Scottish union as an illustrative example to argue that unification under a strong central government would ensure the United States' internal harmony and render it less easily divided and conquered by external foes.

Lest his readers should miss the point of his analogy between a unified Britain and the United States, Publius warns that if "the people of America divide themselves into three or four nations" they will suffer the same types of conflicts that historically antagonized England, Scotland, and Wales: "envy and jealousy would soon extinguish confidence and affection, and the partial interests of each confederacy, instead of the general interests of all America, would be the only objects of their policy and pursuits" (23–24). These smaller republics would be continually "involved in disputes and war, or live in the constant apprehension of them" (24), and so would be unable to cultivate the learning and commerce proper to a civilized nation. Here, Publius introduces a straw man, as anti-Federalists did not in fact advocate the creation of several small republics instead of one nation. They merely sought a less powerful central government than the one outlined in the proposed Constitution, and a weaker alliance among the states, much like the already existing alliance established by the Continental Congress in the Articles of Confederation. "By turning division as the outcome to be expected from Confederation into his rhetorical reality," Ferguson explains, Jay's *Federalist* No. 5 "turned his opponents into betrayers of the *existing* union, as well as the foes of a stronger one."[43]

However, anti-Federalist responses to *Federalist* No. 5 in turn charged Publius with dramatically misrepresenting the Anglo-Scottish Union of Parliaments, and specifically with overlooking its impact on Scotland, as the less powerful of the two nations involved. Fittingly, the anti-Federalists ran a less systematic and coordinated campaign than the Federalists, and the label "anti-Federalist" implies a more coherent group than the disparate individuals whose reasons for opposing a strong centralized government varied widely.[44] The one point that anti-Federalists unequivocally agreed upon was that the proposed Constitution would establish a "consolidated government which would almost certainly swallow up the state governments, and which would attempt to impose uniform laws upon a people who were diverse and heterogeneous."[45] They also tended to believe, following Montesquieu, that republics function best when limited to a small territory in order to facilitate the people's participation in government.

It is understandable, then, that whatever their differences from each other, anti-Federalists would be inclined to see the Anglo-Scottish Treaty of Union as a dangerous precedent on which to model American government. James Winthrop, the anti-Federalist author of *Letters of Agrippa*, predicted that under a strong federal government, the mid-Atlantic states would come to occupy the position that metropolitan England had held for colonial Americans as the locus of commerce and government. Winthrop feared that northern and southern states would "in a very short time sink into the same degradation and contempt with respect to the middle state(s) as Ireland, Scotland, & Wales are in regard to England. All the men of wealth will resort to the seat of government, that will be [the] center of revenue, and of business, which the extremes will be drained to supply."[46] Much as the Anglo-Scottish Union of Parliaments drew Scotland's elite south to London, so the draw of a centralized American government situated in the mid-Atlantic would leave New England and the South culturally and economically impoverished.

"Scotland and England—A Case in Point," which appeared under the pseudonymous authorship of "An Observer" in *The New-York Journal* in December of 1787, also employed an extended comparison between the Anglo-Scottish Treaty of Union and federalism to argue against the ratification of the Constitution.[47] "An Observer" reminds readers that while the Anglo-Scottish Union may have benefited England, it effectively disempowered Scotland. The essay directly refutes the *Federalist* No. 5's representation of the economic, military, and civic outcomes of the Anglo-Scottish Union, declaring, "It must be obvious to everyone, the least acquainted with English history, that since the union of the two nations the great body of the people in Scotland are in a much worse situation now, than they would be, were they a separate nation" (13). The writer identifies anti-Federalists with Scotland's "most sensible and disinterested nobles, as well as commoners," who

> violently opposed the union and predicted that the people of Scotland would, in fact, derive no advantages from a consolidation of government with England; but, on the contrary, they would bear a great proportion of her debt, and furnish large bodies of men to assist in her wars with France, with whom, before the union, Scotland was at all times on terms of the most cordial amity. (12)

Although he does not makes the analogy explicit, the author implies that the strong central government outlined in the proposed American Constitution would similarly embroil individual states in wars and debts that did not immediately concern them. Whereas Federalists argued that a strong central government would prevent both foreign wars and internecine strife among states, their opponents feared that the inhabitants of New York might be asked to help put down slave insurrections in South Carolina, or those from Massachusetts to fight Indians tribes on the western border of Pennsylvania.

"An Observer" traces post-Union Scotland's woes specifically to its inadequate representation in the British Parliament—also, of course, the source of the colonies' unhappiness with Britain. With only 61 out of 764 Parliamentary seats, Scotland's beleaguered Members of Parliament must be always "immediately under the influence of the English ministry" and can give "very little attention . . . to the true interests of their constituency" (13). The author invokes recent memories of the colonies' taxation without Parliamentary representation to suggest that, under the proposed Constitution, Congress will be dominated by the representatives of the bigger, more powerful states, at the expense of the smaller, less powerful ones. From "the situation of Scotland," it concludes,

> surely no one can draw any conclusion that this country would derive happiness or security from a government which would, in reality, give the people but the mere name of being free. For if the representation, stipulated by the constitution, framed by the late convention, be attentively and dispassionately considered, it must be obvious to every disinterested observer . . . that the numbers is [sic] not, by any means adequate to the present inhabitants of this extensive continent, much less to those who will inhabit it at a future period. (13)

"An Observer" fears that a strong central government will gradually become ideologically, if not geographically, as distant from the people it governs as was Britain's Parliament from the colonies, and that it will leave many Americans, like the Scots in Britain, virtually unrepresented.

The event that an "An Observer" dreaded came to pass in September of 1788 when the ratification of the Constitution instituted the strong centralized government that Federalists desired instead of the loose lateral affiliations among states that anti-Federalists advocated. In both Britain and the United States the powers of centralized government would increase during the subsequent decades. To say that Federalist and anti-Federalist comparisons between the Anglo-Scottish Treaty of Union and the strong federal government defined by the Constitution provide a comprehensive account of the two parties' differences would be an overstatement; yet these comparisons do indicate, to a surprising degree, the major points of disagreement between them. Debates between Federalists and anti-Federalists over the distribution of power between federal and state governments also demonstrate the extent to which American efforts to create "new" forms of political organization were shaped, perhaps inevitably, by British models. On both sides of the Atlantic the process of nation formation required the careful distribution of power between centralized and local forms of government, and the reconciliation of national and local affiliations.

American independence may have created a politically autonomous nation-state, but it did not significantly transform the former colonies' cultural orientation, which remained strongly Anglocentric. Indeed, Elisa Tamarkin has argued persuasively that the early American republic's "Anglophilia," or its attachment to and emulation of English culture, was compensatory, a reaction to the severance of political ties.[48] Tamarkin's thesis gains additional support if, following the lead of mid-to-late eighteenth-century writers, we compare the United States to Celtic peripheries. American "Anglophilia" arguably was greater, and less vexed, than that of the Celtic peripheries, which remained politically subordinate to England. Late eighteenth- and early nineteenth-century writers situated in the Celtic peripheries were keen to assert their cultural differences from metropolitan England, and sometimes drew their nationalist rhetoric from the earlier struggles of the American colonies. American writers' efforts to create a national literature reveal greater deference to England, as they sought to rival English literary culture rather than to develop a distinctively different American literary culture.

Despite the differences in their attitudes towards English literary culture, writers situated in the cultural peripheries of the British Atlantic world—the United States, Ireland, Scotland, and Wales—shared in common the challenges of navigating an Anglocentric literary market. They looked to each other for inspiration as they adapted English literary forms to non-English contexts and developed strategies for addressing dual local and English readerships. In doing so, they contributed to an emerging British Atlantic literature. Also participating in very material ways to the creation of this literature were the hundreds of thousands of migrants who left Britain and Ireland for the United States in the wake of the Revolutionary War. Thanks in large part to the influx of these migrants, the United States began to expand westward and to develop its own internal system of urban centers—Philadelphia, Boston, and Charleston—and peripheral frontier lands. Irish, Scottish, and Welsh migrants brought with them to the United States alternative narratives of origin to the story of the Anglo-Saxon foundations of English rights and liberties, and these narratives contributed to the formation of American regional and national identities. The following chapters examine how these three migrant populations represented themselves, and how they were represented by Britons in the Old World and Americans in the New.

{ 2 }

The Irish Uncanny and the American Gothic

Hugh Henry Brackenridge's *Modern Chivalry*, which was published in install-
ments between 1792 and 1815, describes the picaresque adventures of Captain
John Farrago and his "bog-trotter" Teague Oregan, who has recently arrived
in the United States from Ireland. When the narrator comments in the first
chapter that he will "say nothing" of Teague's character "because the very
name imports what he was," Brackenridge invokes a transatlantic literary
and dramatic tradition in which the Irish were represented as ignorant buf-
foons with big aspirations.[1] "The character of the Irish clown," Brackenridge
explains to his readers, is already familiar from "the theatre in Britain," and
will be understood by "the midland states of America, and the western parts
in general, being half Ireland."[2] Although Brackenridge exaggerates here for
comic effect, the presence of Irish migrants in the early republic was substantial.[3] However, Brackenridge objects less to the sheers numbers of Irish
settling in the United States than to the traits embodied in Teague Oregan,
namely a "low education" coupled with "a great spirit of ambition."[4] Although
Teague can barely speak English, let alone read or write, he attempts in the
course of *Modern Chivalry* to become a congressman, a preacher, a member
of the American Philosophical Society, an excise officer, a lawyer, and a judge,
without great success.

Modern Chivalry reveals the rents in the early republic's social and political
fabric through Farrago's efforts to keep Teague out of positions for which he
is distinctly unqualified, but in which the general populace insist on install-
ing him. Farrago kindly explains to Teague that this pattern "is not the fault
of your nature, but of your education; having been accustomed to dig turf in
your early years, rather than instructing yourself in the classics, or in common school books."[5] Brackenridge's satire is directed less at Teague than at the
unthinking masses that fail to recognize how utterly ill-suited a "bog-trotter"
is for public office. Yet it is not quite the case that, as critics have claimed,
"Teague departs in no major way from the stage-Irish types that populated
the eighteenth-century stage at a time when Brackenridge was writing the

initial volumes of *Modern Chivalry*."[6] Teague, while still very much a figure of fun, poses a political threat in *Modern Chivalry's* American republic that his dramatic counterparts in Britain did not simply because they were barred from holding political office by their religion and their class. Thanks to American democracy, poor Captain Farrago is run off his feet trying to keep Teague in his natural place as a bog-trotter.

Teague's character is notable for what it reveals about changing perceptions of Irish migrants in the late eighteenth century. Within a decade of the publication of the first volume of *Modern Chivalry*, Irish migrants had come to be widely regarded as political threats—"wretches" "without property, without principles, without country and without character; dark and desperate, unnatural and bloodthirsty ruffians"—in short, a "restless, rebellious tribe."[7] In 1798, a coincidence of events in Ireland and the United States conspired to transform the way Irish migrants were perceived by many Americans. These two events—the United Irishmen's rebellion against British colonial authority in Ireland and the passage of the Alien and Sedition Acts in the United States—constituted the culmination of over two decades of intense political exchange between the two nations. Although in 1775 the Irish Parliament had voted to support Britain's war against the colonies, many in Ireland sympathized with the American cause and feared that the economic restrictions the British Parliament had placed on the colonies might be extended to Ireland. Thus an Irish Member of Parliament wrote, "here we sympathize more or less with the Americans, we are in water colour what they are in fresco."[8] The success of the American Revolution inspired the United Irishmen to seek the reform, if not the end, of British rule of Ireland.

Even as Irish republicans adopted the former American colonies' revolutionary spirit, Americans, in the wake of the French Revolution and under the influence of a Federalist government, began to express anxieties about political radicalism and distrust of foreigners.[9] Irish radicals who fled to the United States during the 1790s in hopes of finding an ideological home, a nation sympathetic to their principles, found instead that the revolutionary fervor of 1776 had been replaced by a much more cautious approach to political reform. Theobald Wolfe Tone, a leader of the United Irishmen who fled to the United States after he was implicated in a plot against the English government, was disappointed when he arrived in Philadelphia to find the city's inhabitants "a churlish, unsocial race, totally absorbed in making money."[10] Tone had looked to the United States as an example for Ireland to follow, and was discouraged to find that only twelve years after the end of the War of Independence, an elite mercantile class had taken the place of the British aristocracy in the New World's social order.

David A. Wilson estimates that of the approximately 60,000 Irish immigrants who arrived in the United States during the 1790s, only about 3,000 had fled Ireland because of their involvement in radical politics.[11] Nonetheless,

Irish immigration during this decade and the first decade of the nineteenth century was politicized to an extent that far exceeded the real impact of the rebellion. Irish immigrants, radical or not, found themselves subject to suspicion and hostility simply because of their nationality. One Irish victim of nativist sentiment complained bitterly: "Is a man an alien? Does he meddle with politics? If so, he is told, and with few exceptions he is universally told that, being an alien, he has no right to speak, much less to write, on our political concerns. Native opposition to alien meddling extends much further. Emigrants, settled with their families and fortunes for ever, and naturalized by all the forms of the law, are always considered, and by all parties treated, as foreigners. . . . Against foreigners by birth and citizens by adoption, universal prejudice has formed an universal conspiracy."[12]

Whether or not they had been involved in radical politics at home, Irish migrants "swiftly became both politically conscious and politically active" in the United States.[13] Their swelling numbers, and their tendency to support republicanism at a time when deep differences were forming between political parties, led Harison Gray Otis, a Federalist congressman from Boston, to warn in 1796 that "If some means are not adopted to prevent the indiscriminate admission of wild Irishmen & others to the right of suffrage, there will soon be an end to liberty & property."[14] The "means" adopted included the passing of the 1798 Naturalization Act, which increased the residency requirement for citizenship and suffrage rights from five to fourteen years, and the Alien and Sedition Acts, which, among other stipulations, authorized the deportation of any resident alien deemed "dangerous to the peace and safety of the United States" or suspected of any "treasonable or secret machinations against the government thereof."[15]

Although these Acts were technically aimed at *all* aliens, some immigrant groups were perceived as more alien than others, and the Irish arguably were regarded as the most alien of all. The rebellion against British colonial rule in Ireland, rather than evoking Americans' sympathy, led them to suspect Irish migrants of "treasonable or secret machinations" against the American government. William Cobbett's *Detection of a Conspiracy, Formed by the United Irishmen, with the Evident Intention of Aiding the Tyrants of France in Subverting the Government of the United States of America*, which was published in May of 1798, while the Alien and Sedition Acts were being debated in Congress, asked readers in hysterical tones whether Irish settlers "can possibly have any other object in view than an insurrection against the government of America."[16] The United Irishmen were widely believed to be affiliated with not only French Jacobins, but also European societies of Freemasons and Illuminati, groups that embodied what Nigel Leask has described as "the paradox of conspiracy—the cultivation of secrecy to win revolutionary enlightenment."[17] Perhaps the most troubling aspect of the Irish threat to American political stability for Cobbett was that fact that "Great numbers of these wretches ... are what are called CITIZENS; so that no alien laws will touch them."[18] Not only are aliens difficult to distinguish from citizens, Cobbett warns; citizenship is not a guarantor of political allegiances. Whether genuine or assumed, citizenship might serve to protect those who harbor the feelings and opinions of aliens. Ironically, if anyone embodied the difficulty of distinguishing between alien and citizen, it was Cobbett. Although a recent—and as it transpired, temporary—immigrant from England, Cobbett felt entitled to claim a citizen's right to political involvement in a way that many Irishmen perhaps did not.

Both in the United States and in Ireland, writers turned to the language and conventions of the Gothic novel to represent Irish migrants. They did so, I argue, because, in the wake of the American and French Revolutions, Irish migrants evoked the uncanny—a sense of anxiety or fear caused by something that is at once familiar and strange.[19] During the 1790s and early 1800s, Irish radicals were at once foreign and familiar, homeless and at home, whether they were in the United States or in Ireland. With their belief in liberty and equality, and their opposition to British colonial rule, politically radical Irish migrants recalled the United States' recent revolutionary past—a past of which Americans were proud. Yet at the same time, the Irish were associated in the popular imagination with Jacobinism, Catholicism, and the European Illuminati—all of which were distinctly foreign and threatening. The Gothic novel, which originated in the mid-eighteenth century as a "quintessentially English domestic product," conflates the foreign and supernatural in order to foreground "the legibility of Englishness as the not-foreign and the not-wild."[20] Once exported to the United States and Ireland, the Gothic similarly served to define the boundaries of national belonging. In both contexts, Gothic writers associated Irish migrants with supernatural sounds, sights, and events. They used Gothic conventions—fantastical plots, haunted dwellings, doubled characters, sinister and often foreign villains, spotless heroines, strange landscapes that seem almost alive—to represent Irish migrants as the uncanny.[21]

Charles Brockden Brown's *Wieland; or The Transformation: An American Tale* (1798) and *Edgar Huntly; or, Memoirs of a Sleepwalker* (1799), two of the earliest American Gothic novels, explore Irish uncanniness by featuring as seeming villains migrants from Ireland whose appearance in rural Pennsylvania coincides with apparently occult events.[22] However, in both novels, the mysterious migrant's appearance only exacerbates already existing problems that are the real source of the seemingly occult happenings. In *Wieland* the mysterious Carwin's arrival from Ireland coincides with the advent of disembodied voices heard at Mettingen, the farm outside of Philadelphia where Theodore Wieland lives with his wife Catharine and sister Clara. After Wieland murders his wife and children, claiming to have heard God's voice commanding him to do so, Clara learns that Carwin is biloquial—that he can throw his voice and imitate others' voices—and holds him responsible for manufacturing the voice that instructed Wieland to kill his family. Carwin becomes a scapegoat for the murders caused by Wieland's own flawed reasoning and the isolated insularity of Mettingen. Similarly, in *Edgar Huntly* Clithero, an Irishman who emigrated after attempting in a fit of madness to kill his employer, becomes a scapegoat in Edgar's attempt to solve the mystery surrounding his friend Waldegrave's murder. Clithero's unconscious midnight wanderings provoke Edgar's own somnambulism and his murder of five Indians, including the one who in fact killed Waldegrave. In both *Wieland* and *Edgar Huntly*, then, the mysterious outsider turns out not be the cause of seemingly supernatural happenings which are instead traced to familiar and domestic sources of conflict.

Brown does not simply make the trite point that people are not always what they seem. *Wieland* and *Edgar Huntly* ask how we are to judge the truth of another person's self-representations in a society comprised of deracinated and rootless individuals who lack communal knowledge or authoritative guidance on which to base their judgments. These novels seek an epistemology for a nation of immigrants, taking Irish, or seemingly Irish, migrants as test cases simply because, more so than any other immigrant group except possibly the French, the Irish epitomized moral and political ambiguity for post-Revolutionary Anglo-Americans. The Irish novelist Maria Regina Roche suggests in *The Munster Cottage Boy* (1820) that Irish migrants were uncanny for different reasons, and in different ways, in Ireland than they were in the United States. If Irish radicals in the United States were at once familiar and threatening reminders of Americans' revolutionary past, in Ireland these radicals were manifestations of an Irish patriotism that Britain had tried to expunge through the Anglo-Irish Union of 1800 but that reappeared in ghostly or uncanny forms to remind the Irish of their political heritage. In *The Munster Cottage Boy*, Glenmore, an Irish nobleman, is wrongfully accused of participating in the United Irishmen's uprising and flees to the United States. When he secretly returns home many years later to find his daughter, his presence is manifest in the lights seen and sounds heard in his crumbling ancestral estate. By imagining the reintegration of Irish political émigrés into a reformed social order, *The Munster Cottage Boy* divests these migrants of their exilic ghostliness and depicts repatriation as essential to Ireland's economic and cultural rehabilitation.

Wieland, Edgar Huntly, and *The Munster Cottage Boy* share a complicated transatlantic genealogy of genres, stemming most immediately from British political and Gothic novels of the 1790s. Pamela Clemit has traced Brown's debts to the former, showing how Brown followed the radical William Godwin in relying on "the power of allegory and fable, rather than elaborately plotted, more naturalistic modes of representation" and eschewing the courtship plot for tales of flight and pursuit in which "the protagonists are constantly changing roles."[23] Brown's contemporaries also perceived these similarities; for, much as American critics dubbed James Fenimore Cooper "the Scott of America," Brown was described in the British press as "the Godwin of America."[24] Christopher Looby and Peter Kafer, among others, have argued that Brown's adaptations of the conventions of British Gothic fiction—including structural devices such as found manuscripts, frame narratives, and fragmented stories; and thematic concerns with the supernatural, doubles, confinement or imprisonment, dreams, and incest—offered him a "conceptual grammar" through which to examine issues of "political legitimacy, social solidarity, and cultural coherence."[25]

If *Wieland* and *Edgar Huntly* are heirs to British political and Gothic novels, they are also, as W. M. Verhoeven has suggested, progenitors of the national tale, a genre of fiction that flourished during the early nineteenth century in Ireland, Scotland, and Wales.[26] National tales such as Roche's *Munster Cottage Boy* played an important part in the emergence of cultural nationalism in the Celtic peripheries, as they countered metropolitan English representations of Ireland, Scotland, and Wales, and asserted the Celtic peripheries' cultural distinctiveness against English attempts to homogenize the British archipelago.[27] Similar to Irish, Scottish, and Welsh national tales, *Wieland* and *Edgar Huntly* participate in imagining an identity for a formative American nation; but in Brown's novels, the national tale's project is disturbed and even undermined by the conventions and discourses of Gothic and political novels. Whereas national tales generally attempt to render a Celtic people comprehensible and sympathetic to a metropolitan English readership, Gothic and political novels of the 1790s tend to emphasize the limits of human sympathy and the unreliability of our perceptions and judgments. And whereas the national tale aims to consolidate a national identity, promoting the incorporation of disparate groups into a national community bound by affective or sentimental ties, Gothic and political novels reveal the schisms, corruption, and exclusions upon which nations are founded. These genres call into question the possibility of the affective communities represented in national tales, instead depicting the formation of what Leonard Tennenhouse terms a "paranoid community," composed "of disparate individuals by means of a process that disarticulates and parodies the sentimental ending."[28] By incorporating the conventions of Gothic and political novels with those of the national tale, *Wieland*, *Edgar Huntly*, and *The Munster Cottage Boy* reveal an ambivalence towards the project of nation formation, emphasizing the repressions and exclusions it requires.

Irishness and Insularity in *Wieland* and *Memoirs of Carwin the Biloquist*

Wieland and *Edgar Huntly* each introduce into a relatively small and insular social circle a mysterious stranger with Irish connections whose appearance coincides with seemingly supernatural effects for which natural causes are later revealed. In each case, too, the stranger initially is of interest to others not so much because of his Irish connections as because his antecedents are largely unknown. For instance, when Edgar Huntly comes across Clithero Edny—an Irishman with a very un-Irish name—wandering around the large elm tree where Edgar's friend Waldegrave recently had been murdered, Edgar begins to suspect Clithero of the crime even though Clithero has hitherto seemed "a pattern of sobriety and gentleness."[29] Although "there was nothing in the first view of his character calculated to engender suspicion," Edgar relates, "I perceived that the only foreigner among us was Clithero" (14). It might seem surprising that Clithero's foreignness would be cause for suspicion given that Pennsylvania, where both *Edgar Huntly* and *Wieland* are set, was the most ethnically diverse state in post-Revolutionary America. But if, according to Looby, "Philadelphia was where ethnic diversification and economic modernization first registered as crucial problems for the nation-in-formation," then these problems became even more critical as ethnic diversification spread from the city to surrounding areas, which were dotted with small, often ethnically homogeneous communities in which all the inhabitants were intimately known to each other.[30] Clithero is a "foreigner" not only because he comes from another country, but because he comes from beyond Norwalk, a community where, Edgar explains, "each farmer was surrounded by his sons and kinsmen" (14).

While Clithero's history is unknown to the inhabitants of Norwalk, they do know that he is "an emigrant from Ireland" (14). In contrast, the origins of Carwin, *Wieland*'s mysterious stranger, remain indeterminate for much of the novel and are fully explained only in its unfinished "prequel," *Memoirs of Carwin the Biloquist*, which Brown published serially in *The Literary Magazine* between 1803 and 1805. By situating readers in the unknowing position of the novel's narrator, Clara, *Wieland* questions how we can form accurate judgments about others in a nation of immigrants, where little can be known about their origins and history. The novel rejects sensory perception and abstract reasoning as adequate grounds for judgment, but it offers no clear and easy answers to the question. However, Brown does suggest that insularity—a lack of exposure to the unfamiliar—increases the possibility of misjudgment. *Wieland* thus reflects what Bryan Waterman has described as Brown's concern with creating a nonpartisan and secular sphere of intellectual exchange that would further the "disinterested transmission of correct and useful knowledge" in the United States.[31] Brown shared the belief of William Godwin, whose literary and political works he had read and admired, that "knowledge, such as we are able to acquire it, depends in a majority of instances, not upon the single efforts of the individual, but upon the consent of other human understandings sanctioning the judgement of our own."[32] That Brown may have had Godwin's definition of knowledge as communal consensus in mind when writing *Wieland* is suggested by *Memoirs of Carwin the Biloquist*, which he began at the same time as *Wieland* and which makes more explicit reference to Godwin's ideas. While *Wieland* implies that exposure to the foreign and unfamiliar is important to the development of accurate judgment, *Memoirs* explores how absolute secrecy on one hand and complete revelation on the other can determine the boundaries between the foreign and the familiar, and between insiders and outsiders.

Although Carwin's past remains obscure in *Wieland*, the Wieland family's history is fully explained in the novel's opening pages. Clara and Theodore's tendency to dwell, sometimes morbidly, on their family's German origins renders their status as Americans almost as ambiguous as Carwin's. The Wielands are descended from a "native of Saxony" who was renowned as "the founder of the German Theater."[33] Theodore Wieland is heir to the family's domains in Lusatia; and his friend Pleyel, who feels a "partiality to the Saxon soil, from which he had likewise sprung, and where he had spent several years of his youth" (42), unsuccessfully attempts to persuade Wieland to claim his inheritance. Wieland refuses to leave an agrarian republic for a feudal state that he associates with tyranny and barbarism, claiming that "no spot on the globe enjoyed equal security and liberty to that which he at present inhabited" (43). Looby has argued that Clara's account of the Wielands' ancestry reveals Brown's "anxiety concerning the apparent groundlessness of American political legitimacy" and his desire to root American agrarian republicanism in "a determinate and authoritative Saxon origin"—namely the fantasy of "the unconstrained deliberations of German warriors gathered in the forest" to which the English traced their political institutions.[34] Yet Theodore's allusion to Saxon brutality not only foreshadows his own violence towards his wife and children, but also suggests that "Saxon soil" constitutes a dubious foundation for "American political legitimacy." While many late eighteenth-century Americans did trace their rights and liberties back through England to Germany, Brown deliberately evokes Germany's more sinister and tumultuous associations with the Gothic.

Despite their supposedly shared Saxon origins, Anglo-Americans regarded German immigrants with mixed feelings. During the eighteenth century, German immigration operated through a system of sponsorship. Established settlers assisted individuals from their home region in migration and settlement. As a result of this sponsorship system, German migrants tended to settle in clusters that amounted to "segregated ethnic enclaves."[35] The region outside of Philadelphia, where the Wielands live, was one such enclave, with German settlers providing a buffer between the city and "the wild, disruptive, and factional violence to the west" in counties settled primarily by Irish and Scottish immigrants.[36]

German settlements were regarded with some resentment and suspicion because of their insularity. Benjamin Franklin, for one, objected to German immigrants' practice of "herding together," asking, "why should the *Palatine Boors* be suffered to swarm into our Settlements, and by herding together establish their Language and Manners to the Exclusion of ours? Why should *Pennsylvania*, founded by the *English*, become a Colony of *Aliens*, who will shortly be so numerous as to Germanize us instead of our Anglifying them, and will never adopt our Language or Customs, any more than they can acquire our Complexion."[37] Despite his shrill tone here, Franklin did not want to outlaw German immigration entirely. Fearing the political power of a German voting bloc, he hoped to distribute Germans throughout the colonies so that they would not outnumber the English in any given region. Always one to put his beliefs into action, Franklin helped to run a transatlantic charity that, as its founders explained, sought "effectually to civilize, and incorporate" German immigrants "with the *British* inhabitants, amongst whom they reside" by providing German communities in colonial Pennsylvania with bilingual clergymen and schoolmasters. The charity aimed to create among German and British settlers "that sameness of interest, and conformity of manners, which is absolutely necessary to the forming them into one people, and bringing them to love, and peaceably submit to the same laws and government."[38]

While Wieland's political allegiance to the British Crown is never in question in Brown's novel, he does claim to obey divine rather than human law when he kills his wife and children. Moreover, the Wieland family estate at Mettingen is by no means integrated with surrounding communities, but instead prides itself on its self-sufficiency. We learn that Clara and Theodore's father, who migrated from Germany to Pennsylvania by way of an apprenticeship to a London merchant, regarded isolation as essential to his religious practices, believing that "devotion . . . must be performed alone" (12). After their father mysteriously burns to death during his solitary religious devotions—an event that Clara and Theodore construe as a divine punishment—they are raised by their aunt in Philadelphia. There, they become firm friends with Pleyel and his sister Catharine, the latter of whom Wieland soon marries and the former of whom Clara loves. Clara relates that the four friends "gradually withdrew ourselves from the society of others" (23) and were "left to the guidance of our own understanding" (24). Their subsequent errors in judgment suggest that their "own understanding," divorced from general consensus or received wisdom, was a poor guide at best. Thanks to Mettingen's isolation, Wieland becomes obsessed by thoughts from which exposure to others' ideas might have distracted him. Clara explains that "Those ideas which, in others, are casual or obscure, which are entertained in moments of abstraction and solitude, and easily escape when the scene is changed, have obtained an immoveable hold upon his mind" (39–40). Mettingen's insularity also fosters a Gothic ambience that colors its inhabitants' intellectual pursuits. The shadow of the elder Wieland's mysterious death hangs over the estate; and although Clara and Wieland transform the scene of their father's religious devotions into a site of music and conversation, their interest in German literature does nothing to dispel the pervasive gloom. Their grandfather's Gothic dramas offer up "scenes of violence and carnage . . . wildly but forcibly pourtrayed" (63); and the strange events leading up to Wieland's murder of his wife and children begin when the friends gather to act out a German tragedy describing "a chain of audacious acts, and unheard-of disasters" (89)—an apt metafictional description of what the novel's characters soon will encounter in their own lives.

Brown encourages readers to consider the national implications of the Mettingen circle's isolated insularity through the question that Wieland and Pleyel discuss early in the novel: whether Cicero, in his speech *Pro Cluentio*, misled his listeners in making "the picture of a single family a model from which to sketch the condition of a nation" (34). While Brown thus invites us to read Mettingen as a microcosm of the early republic, he also asks us to question just how representative this community is, or ought to be. The practice of taking the family as a model of the nation has a long history among novelists; and it was particularly prominent in the national tale, which often figured the consolidation of a national identity through the bonds of marriage or blood kinship. In Brown's hybridization of the national tale and the Gothic, by contrast, the Wieland family's dissolution suggests the fissures and flaws in a formative American identity. As a microcosmic model of the nation, Mettingen is threatened by its own inwards-looking homogeneity.

Mettingen's insularity leaves its inhabitants susceptible to the deceptions and manipulations of outsiders such as Carwin, whose appearance, confusingly, does not seem to reflect his character. Carwin looks like a farm laborer, with "rustic" garb, "aukward" posture, and an "ungainly and disproportioned" body (57); yet his voice is unusually "mellifluent and clear," and his sentiments and manners are refined (58). Carwin's novelty renders him a perpetual topic of conversation at Mettingen: "Not a gesture, or glance, or accent, that was not, in our private assemblies, discussed, and inferences deduced from it" (82). Clara and her friends conclude from these conversations that Carwin will make "an inestimable addition to [their] society" and before long he is "regarded as a kind of inmate of the house" (87). Even after he has been so rapidly incorporated into their domestic circle, however, Carwin avoids "all mention of his past or present situation" (82), so that his new acquaintances remain stymied by "the inscrutableness of his character" (87). The only insight they have into Carwin's history comes from Pleyel's chance encounter with him some years earlier in Spain, where Carwin's "garb, aspect, and deportment, were wholly Spanish" (77). Pleyel's encounter perhaps should have indicated to Clara the extent of Carwin's talent for disguise, as he could appear "indistinguishable from a native [of Spain], when he chose to assume that character" (79), and yet no traces of this identity remain.

The Wielands begin to view the newcomer with suspicion only after the mysterious voices engineered by Carwin have caused fear and dissension at Mettingen, and only after sources outside their community alert them to his dangerousness. Pleyel learns from a newspaper advertisement that Carwin has "escaped from Newgate prison in Dublin" (147) and is generally believed to be "the most incomprehensible and formidable among men…engaged in schemes, reasonably suspected to be, in the highest degree, criminal, but such as no human intelligence is able to unravel" (149). Carwin's past residences in Spain and Ireland imply connections with Jesuits or Freemasons—connections that *Memoirs of Carwin the Biloquist* confirms. The newspaper's account of Carwin's past is immediately endorsed by the first person Pleyel encounters in Philadelphia, a coincidence that suggests the Wielands would have done well to ask around before admitting a stranger into their domestic circle.

That Carwin turns out to be a "double-tongued deceiver" (278) might seem to imply Brown's support for the Alien and Sedition Acts, which encouraged Americans to view foreigners as potential threats to national stability and security. Ultimately, however, it is Wieland's, Pleyel's, and Clara's misjudgments that lead to the dissolution of the Mettingen circle, suggesting that such threats can lie in the familiar as easily as in the foreign. The most devious of Carwin's plots concerns Clara, perhaps because, as an unmarried woman, she is the most vulnerable, and, to Carwin, the most interesting, of the group. Clara is the center of the Mettingen community, drawing its members together almost too closely. Not only does Wieland's affection for her verge on the incestuous, as Shirley Samuels has noted, but Pleyel and Carwin also become implicit rivals for her love.[39] A typical Gothic heroine, Clara is known among her friends as the most virtuous, courageous, and self-sufficient of women. Even as she attempts to determine whether Carwin's "fellowship tended to good or to evil" (87), she also, for propriety's sake, tries to avoid revealing too readily her love for Pleyel. Clara is awakened to the "impenetrable veil of [Carwin's] duplicity" when she catches him hiding in her chamber, seemingly with the intention of raping her (107). Realizing that Clara's discovery must inevitably render him unwelcome at Mettingen, Carwin determines to enjoy "the sweetest triumph" possible under the circumstances by leading Pleyel to doubt Clara's virtue. Hiding under the cover of darkness, he imitates Clara's voice so that Pleyel believes that he has overheard an amorous rendezvous between Carwin and Clara.

Clara's initial failure to recognize Carwin's "duplicity" is matched by Pleyel's and Wieland's errors of judgment. Each man relies too much on his own perceptions, privileging them over consensual knowledge or shared beliefs. Pleyel, who considers himself the epitome of rationality, persists in considering "the testimony of his senses" (126) more reliable than Clara's long history of unblemished conduct. Clara feels that Pleyel "has drawn from dubious appearances, conclusions the most improbable and unjust" (120), and hopes that "reason" and "argument" will persuade him of her innocence (160). Yet Pleyel refuses to consider the possibility that Clara's "voice had been counterfeited by another" even though the "casual or concerted resemblance of the voice" was at odds with the sentiments it expressed, sentiments "denoting a mind polluted by groveling vices" (134). Pleyel insists on privileging his own sensory perceptions over consensual knowledge—in this case, Clara's well-established reputation for virtue. Wieland repeats Pleyel's mistake when he seems to hear God's voice commanding him to kill his wife and children. Rather than questioning the "testimony of his senses" when it comes into conflict with common belief about God's intentions, Wieland assumes that this voice is an "unambiguous token of [God's] presence" and an "audible enunciation of [his] pleasure" (189). Whereas Clara is only temporarily the victim of Pleyel's error, Catharine and her children are irrevocably the victims of Wieland's.

Clara acknowledges in retrospect that "the evils" her narrative describes "owed their existence to the errors of the sufferers" (278)—that is, to Wieland's, Pleyel's, and her own errors in judgment. Yet Carwin bears the blame for these errors because he is an outsider. Clara, who initially assumes that Carwin must have murdered Catharine and her children, continues to believe him "the enemy whose machinations had destroyed us" even after Wieland readily acknowledges having committed the deed himself (217). When Carwin confesses responsibility for the mysterious voices heard at Mettingen, Clara is certain that he must also be responsible for the voice that commanded Wieland to kill his family. Carwin admits that the effects of his biloquism exceeded his intentions and that his vocal exploits may have undermined Wieland's ability to distinguish between real and imagined voices; but he argues that the decision to commit the murders, to act upon the commands of the mysterious voice even when they conflicted with common sense, was Wieland's own. Indeed, in earlier conversations with Carwin in which the question of the mysterious voices overheard at Mettingen had arisen, Carwin had always encouraged his new friends to believe that "human agency" and "known principles" must have a role in producing them (85). Clara's uncle, whose credibility and rationality are established early in the narrative, and who represents the views of those outside Mettingen, also exculpates Carwin. He points out that auditory "illusions" like Wieland's "are not rare" (202), and notes that his own father (Clara's maternal grandfather), plunged off the edge of a cliff to his death at the behest of a voice unheard by any of his companions (203). This, in conjunction with the elder Wieland's religious mania and mysterious death, suggests a suitably Gothic predisposition to madness in the Wieland family that Carwin's biloquism may have exacerbated, but for which he cannot be blamed.

The "transformation" of *Wieland's* subtitle is usually understood to refer to Theodore Wieland's transformation into a deluded murderer.[40] But it might also refer to the transformation of Mettingen, or of the family estate that stands for the nation. Largely as a result of its insularity and isolation, the peaceful community at Mettingen dissolves into a scene of carnage and desolation, destroying itself from within. To the extent that Carwin does play a role in Mettingen's devastation, his claim to foreignness is dubious at best. Het turns out to be neither Spanish nor Irish, but rather exactly what he appeared to be when Clara first laid eyes on him—a farm boy from rural Pennsylvania. If he was indeed a threat to the stability and security of the Mettingen community, he was a domestic, rather than a foreign one. *Wieland* situates the newly formed United States in a nexus of transatlantic migration and suggests that a strong and resilient nation must cultivate heterogeneity by opening itself to foreign ideas, influences, and individuals. Through the transformation of Mettingen, the novel suggests that threats to the nation's stability and security are not external to its borders, but instead originate within them, in homogeneity and insularity. By creating an environment hostile to the foreign and unfamiliar, Brown warns, the Alien and Sedition Acts will only produce an inwards-looking nation that may eventually destroy itself through its own exclusivity.

While the Alien and Sedition Acts were repealed in 1800, the xenophobia to which they had contributed was again exacerbated in 1803, when the French took possession of the formerly Spanish colony of Louisiana.[41] And it was in 1803 that Brown returned to his unfinished *Memoirs of Carwin the Biloquist*, which he had begun along with *Wieland* in 1798, perhaps inspired by this resurgent xenophobia to reconsider Carwin's foreign connections. While some critics regard Carwin's role in *Wieland* as less that of a fully developed character than a Gothic plot device—"a mischievous wanderer with a special talent for projecting voices"[42]—the unfinished *Memoirs* provide Carwin with a history that retroactively transforms him from an ambiguous outsider into an American youth whose revolutionary tendencies stem from his attempts to infiltrate a secret society closely resembling the United Irishmen. His general foreignness in *Wieland*, in other words, acquires very particular dimensions in the *Memoirs*. According to his *Memoirs*, Carwin, the son of a boorish Pennsylvania farmer, discovered his biloquial talents while herding cattle. In search of an education, Carwin escaped to Philadelphia, where he made the acquaintance of a wealthy Irishman, Ludloe, who invited Carwin to return to Ireland with him. There, Carwin enjoyed a period of "studious leisure, and romantic solitude" (310) before spending three years in Spain, where he learned enough of the "language, habits, and religion" (311) to pass as a native, as Pleyel notes in *Wieland*. Upon Carwin's return to Ireland, Ludloe offered to introduce him into a secret society, the existence of which he must conceal on pain of death, but the initiation into which requires Carwin to relate his complete history without any lies or omissions. The fragment ends with Carwin's first failed attempt at such a complete revelation.

The *Memoirs* extends *Wieland*'s epistemological concerns, asking not only how we tell true identity from false appearances, but also how we recognize a whole truth from a partial or incomplete one. In this "prequel" to *Wieland*, Brown further explores the social and political implications of these epistemological questions, examining how concealment and disclosure delimit boundaries between insiders and outsiders, and between the foreign and familiar. The events of *Wieland* show that Carwin's biloquism gives him power over others only so long as it remains secret. In his *Memoirs*, Carwin explains that he developed the habit of telling lies in order to preserve the secret of his "biloquial faculty" (314), as he calls it, from detection. He notes in retrospect that a lie's "direct consequences may be transient and few, but it facilitates a repetition, strengthens temptation, and grows into habit" (293). While in Spain, he has no compunction about the "profound and deliberate" deceit he practices in order to learn the secrets of the Castilian Jesuits because his biloquism already has hardened him "to the frequent practice of insincerity" (312). Carwin comes to believe "that the value of sincerity, like that of every other mode of action, consisted in its tendency to good, and that, therefore, the obligation to speak truth was not paramount or intrinsical . . . and that, since men in their actual state, are infirm and deceitful, a just estimate of consequences may sometimes make dissimulation my duty" (312). Carwin's vaguely utilitarian attitude towards truthfulness contrasts with Ludloe's belief that complete truthfulness is a paramount duty that, "once introduced into the manners of mankind, would necessarily bring every other virtue in its train." Ludloe, a "eulogist of sincerity" (312), echoes William Godwin's *Enquiry into Political Justice* (1793) in arguing that a society of perfectly truthful individuals would be entirely just, free, and harmonious.[43]

Carwin's differences from Ludloe imply a critique of some of Godwin's principles; but upon one of these principles Carwin agrees with his mentor, namely, "that man is the creature of circumstances: that he is capable of endless improvement: that his progress has been stopped by the artificial impediment of government" (316). Under Ludloe's tutelage, Carwin not only pursues his own self-improvement but also begins to envision longingly a society that would allow its members to attain moral and intellectual perfection.[44] Carwin believes that his "native country, where a few colonists from Britain had sown the germe of populous and mighty empires" has come closer to realizing this ideal than any other society throughout history (317). He dreams of improving upon the United States with "a moral political structure" that would embody "pure wisdom" (318–319). From certain "hints and ambiguous allusions" that his mentor makes, Carwin becomes convinced that Ludloe's secret brotherhood is already in the process of establishing "a new model of society, in some unsuspected corner of the world" (323), a conviction that increases when he discovers among Ludloe's papers a map of "two islands, which bore some faint resemblance, in their relative proportions, at least, to Great Britain and Ireland" but which appear to be located in uncharted regions of the south Pacific (343). Familiar in shape but displaced in space, the islands on Ludloe's map are geographically uncanny.

Ludloe's map recalls the colonial schemes of Theobald Wolfe Tone and, as Nigel Leask has argued, suggests that the brotherhood to which Ludloe belongs might harbor revolutionary ideals similar to the United Irishmen's. Tone proposed his plan for "a colony in one of Cook's newly discovered islands in the South" to William Pitt in 1788, suggesting that a strategically positioned colony might help Britain to keep Spain's imperial ambitions in check.[45] In his *Memoirs*, Tone hints only half-jokingly that the establishment of this colony might have prevented the 1798 United Irishmen's uprising when he claims that "instead of planning revolutions in our own country, we might be now, perhaps, carrying on a privateering war . . . on the coasts of Spanish America," and adds threateningly, "Perhaps the minister may yet have reason to wish he had let us go off quietly into the South Seas."[46] The resemblance of the islands on Ludloe's map to Great Britain and Ireland similarly poses colonialism and revolution as alternative means of social change. We can only infer that either Ludloe's brotherhood has established its own colony in the South Seas as a new and improved version of the British archipelago or that the map's geographical displacement of the archipelago is an attempt to disguise through transposition the brotherhood's plans for reforming Great Britain and Ireland.

Because the *Memoirs* is unfinished, readers never learn the meaning of the mysterious map, and neither does Carwin. It is unclear why Brown did not finish the *Memoirs*, but, in a work that explores how concealment and revelation function to create boundaries between insiders and outsiders, the limitations on our knowledge created by the *Memoirs'* unfinished state is ironically appropriate. Through Carwin's attempts to gain admission to Ludloe's secret society, Brown asks whether principles of absolute truthfulness and transparency tend to promote perfect liberty and equality or tyranny and paranoia. Before Carwin can be admitted to the brotherhood, he must agree to two seemingly contradictory mandates: complete concealment and utter revelation. Accustomed to hiding his biloquial abilities, Carwin is unperturbed by "the task of inviolable secrecy" (322) concerning the society's existence. However, he is shaken by the demand that he must "disclose every fact in his history, and every secret of his heart" (324). Confession, Carwin realizes, would entail disempowerment, as the "efficacy" of his biloquism—the power it gives him over others—"depended on its existence being unknown" (325). Carwin's biloquial manipulations of Clara, Pleyel, and Wieland depend upon his ability to disguise his person and his voice, and to resist or confound the interpretations of others by keeping his past carefully concealed. The continual confession required by Ludloe's brotherhood promises, as Godwin's *Political Justice* suggests it would, to render government unnecessary.

The internalized mandate of absolute revelation replaces external forms of authority, as the individual's knowledge that his every thought and deed must be reported in full becomes a check on his actions.[47]

If we understand Ludloe's secret society as Brown's imagining of the United Irishmen—a strange blend of Godwin, the Illuminati, and Wolf Tone—then, to become a member, Carwin paradoxically must give up the disguises, tricks, and concealments that in *Wieland* marked his Irish connections. Brown leaves unanswered the question of which is preferable, a fallen society in which deception is possible but so are self-fashioning and self-determination, or a pristine utopia in which transparency and sincerity might become an internalized form of tyranny. The Alien and Sedition Acts, as an attempt to prevent disguise and deception in newcomers to the United States, ironically pushed the nation closer to the image of the Irish brotherhood depicted in Carwin's *Memoirs*, precisely the type of conspiratorial, paranoid society against whose influence the Acts were intended to guard. Together, *Wieland* and *Memoirs of Carwin the Biloquist* question whether attempting to expunge possibly dangerous foreign influences from the United States is really the best way to create a stable and secure nation, or whether such insularity and homogeneity might simply leave citizens unable to recognize and respond appropriately to real threats. *Wieland* and the *Memoirs* at once exploit and explode the popular associations between Irishness and underground revolutionary plots forged by William Cobbett and others.

Rebellious Ghosts in *Edgar Huntly* and *The Munster Cottage Boy*

Charles Brockden Brown's fiction entered a transatlantic literary marketplace within which it contributed to the development of new genres of Romantic fiction. Eve Tavor Bannet has recently shown that William Lane's Minerva Press facilitated this process by bringing Brown's novels to an English readership.[48] The Minerva Press specialized in what we might now call genre or formula fiction, and particularly in Gothic and sentimental novels written by women. While critics have tended to assume that Brown wrote his novels for a relatively elite, educated readership, Bannet reminds us that American writers' and readers' tastes were shaped primarily by literature imported from Britain, including Minerva Press novels, which were immensely popular in the United States. Brown strategically borrowed "generic situations, plots and devices" from Minerva Press fiction and adapted them "to the contemporary manners, sentiments, concerns and scenes of his native land."[49] In turn, all six of Brown's novels were published on the Minerva Press between 1800 and 1807, suggesting that Brown's adaptation of the genres for which the press was famous helped him to win an English readership.[50] Here I draw on Brown's second novel, *Edgar Huntly*, and *The Munster Cottage Boy*, written by the Irish novelist Maria Regina Roche and published on the Minerva Press in 1820, to examine how the figure of the revolutionary Irish migrant functioned in this transatlantic literary culture.[51] My aim in doing so is not to suggest that Roche was directly influenced by *Edgar Huntly*, although it is quite possible that, living in London and writing for the Minerva Press, she may have read Brown's works. Instead, I have paired these novels because they so clearly demonstrate how the radical Irish migrant became a Gothic convention, a ghost that haunted early nineteenth-century novels of nation formation on both sides of the Atlantic.

In the preface to *Edgar Huntly*, Brown differentiates his novel explicitly from the European Gothic, and implicitly from the popular fiction of the Minerva Press. In place of the "puerile superstition and exploded manners; Gothic castles and chimeras" that European novelists used for "calling forth the passions and engaging the sympathy of the reader," *Edgar Huntly* substitutes "incidents of Indian hostility, and the perils of the western wilderness" (3). In Brown's Americanized Gothic, Indians arouse not only the implied reader's passions, but also those of the eponymous protagonist. Edgar Huntly's vehement hatred of Indians stems from their violent massacre of his parents when he was a child.[52] During his wanderings through the wilderness of rural Pennsylvania, Edgar begins to resemble the bloodthirsty savages he abhors as he invokes retributive justice to sanction his own bloody deeds—the single-handed killing of five Indians. Remarking upon his usual "antipathy to scenes of violence and bloodshed" (185), he attributes his uncharacteristic actions to a kind of out-of-body experience. During his wilderness wanderings, Edgar claims, he was "not governed by the soul which usually regulates [his] conduct," but instead by a "spirit vengeful, unrelenting, and ferocious" (184). Much as Edgar's passing propensity for violence renders him the Indians' double, his temporary self-alienation transforms him into the double of Clithero, an Irishman whose seeming radicalism turns out to be insanity.[53]

Although Brown identifies American Indians as performing in *Edgar Huntly* the functions fulfilled by supernatural phenomena in European Gothics, it is in fact Clithero who is consistently described as "haunting" the wilderness (91) and as himself "haunted" by diseased thoughts (276). Clithero's narrative figuratively haunts Edgar's own story, revealing similarities between the two men. We are invited to trace Clithero's ghostliness to his exile from Ireland for deeds that, as Luke Gibbons has argued, render him a figure for the United Irishmen, and thus also for the radical Irish immigrants whose presence in the United States influenced the passage of the Alien and Sedition Acts.[54] Clithero, whose "parents were of the better sort of peasants," would have "spent [his] life in the cultivation of their scanty fields" (36) had not Euphemia Lorimer, a wealthy widow, recognized his natural intelligence and taken him into her household in Dublin. There, his "views were refined and enlarged by history and science," and he acquired "a thirst of independence, and an impatience of subjection and poverty" (37). Clithero eventually rose to become the steward of Mrs. Lorimer's estate and the betrothed of her niece. His luck runs out when, in self-defense, he kills Mrs. Lorimer's evil twin brother, whose death, she believes, must portend her own. Overcome with guilt at his seeming ingratitude towards his benefactress, Clithero determines in a state of "phrensy" that the kindest course of action would be to kill Mrs. Lorimer too (74). Gibbons reads Clithero's attempt to murder Mrs. Lorimer while she is asleep as the revolt of an upwardly mobile peasant against the aristocracy. Insofar as Clithero describes his attempted murder of Mrs. Lorimer as "perverse and rebellious" (83), and decides in consequence to leave an Ireland that is "lapsing fast into civic broils" (267), this reading of Clithero as an Irish revolutionary is persuasive. Yet Clithero describes his murder of Mrs. Lorimer as an act of temporary insanity, in which he, like Edgar in his murder of the Indians, was governed by a spirit not his own. If Clithero is a rebel, then he seems to be at best a half-hearted and remorseful one.

Gibbons and Jared Gardner have shown that *Edgar Huntly* establishes parallels between Indians and Irishmen as un-American savages only to illustrate Edgar's own similarities to both of these classes of "aliens."[55] Notably, though, Edgar is much readier to acknowledge his similarities and to extend compassion to Clithero than to the Indians, a preference which suggests that not all aliens are similarly un-American. Edgar perceives Clithero as a misguided outcast whose intentions are virtuous, and who might be recuperated and transformed into an American: "The magic of sympathy, the perseverance of benevolence, though silent, might work a gradual and secret revolution, and better thoughts might insensibly displace those desperate suggestions which now governed him" (107). The revolutionary Irish immigrant might, through a psychological "revolution," become a law-abiding and productive American citizen.

Clithero's ghostly haunting of the wilderness and of Edgar's narrative, I suggest, might be explained through this potential for recuperation and transformation, a potential that Edgar cannot find in the nameless and faceless Indians who also serve as his doubles. Although Clithero insists upon living "unsocial and savage state," thanks to Edgar's kind ministrations, his "gloomy thoughts seemed to have somewhat yielded to tranquillity" (276), and he acknowledges that Edgar's kindness has prevented him from committing suicide (261). When Edgar learns that Clithero's frenzied attempt on Mrs. Lorimer's life was unsuccessful and that she is alive and well in the United States, he hopes that this information will "cure [Clithero's] diseased intellects, and restore him to those vocations for which his talents, and that rank in society for which his education had qualified him" (277). Instead, however, the news reawakens in Clithero "the tumult and vehemence of phrensy," as he dramatically declares his intent to kill her (280). Clithero's reaction confirms for Edgar that the Irishman is not in fact recuperable, but is at the very least a "maniac" (280), if not, as Gibbons has argued, a rebel. While Edgar's savagery is temporary and contextual, Clithero's "phrenzy" is unpredictable and to some degree permanent. Clithero's disappearance after he throws himself off the ship carrying him to a lunatic asylum leaves open the possibility that he may not have drowned, but merely "forced himself beneath the surface" of the water until the ship passed and he could "gain the shore" (285). The indeterminacy of Clithero's death only adds to his ghostliness, leaving open the possibility that he may return to haunt Edgar and Mrs. Lorimer in the future. His disappearance into the Atlantic Ocean, the vast body of water separating Ireland from the United States, fittingly figures his exclusion from both countries.

Roche's *Munster Cottage Boy* also takes an exiled Irish revolutionary as its ghost, but Glenmore haunts his family's decaying estate in Ireland rather than the American wilderness to which he has been banished. Glenmore, who escaped to the United States to avoid hanging after he was wrongly "accused of the double crime of rebellion and murder," has returned home to Ireland to find his daughter, Fidelia.[56] While he searches for her, he hides himself in the partially ruined Castle Glenbower, a property he rightfully should have inherited. Fidelia, who was raised by foster parents and is unaware of her noble ancestry, hears strange sighs when she visits Glenbower, and receives mysterious epistolary communications from the castle's "ghost." A local innkeeper's wife traces the apparent haunting of Castle Glenbower to the depopulation of the Irish countryside, which, she claims, has ruined the estate and unsettled ancestral spirits. The old woman remarks that "'tis enough to trouble the poor souls in their graves, to think of this place they were so proud of being let to go all to ruin. But this comes of people settling in foreign parts, and deserting their own natural homes" (2: 187). As the old woman's complaint suggests, emigration in *The Munster Cottage Boy* is represented as not simply unfortunate, but unnatural. The supernatural phenomena at Glenbower reflect the disturbance of the natural economic and affective ties binding the Irish people to their land.

Irish emigration rates soared during the 1820s, as Ireland fell into a major economic depression following the end of the Napoleonic Wars. Roughly 800,000 to one million Irish people migrated to the United States between 1815 and 1845—twice the number that had left during the preceding 200 years.[57] These migrants also belonged to a different demographic from earlier expatriates. During the eighteenth century, Irish migrants tended to be relatively educated and prosperous: they were farmers, merchants, or artisans who viewed emigration as a means of upward mobility and generally left Ireland by choice. Early nineteenth-century migrants, by contrast, tended to be sub-tenants or farm laborers with little or no education; a number of them were Catholic and Gaelic-speaking. These people tended to experience emigration as banishment against their will, or, as it is figured in *The Munster Cottage Boy*, as a form of disinheritance that divested them of an ancient birthright.

The Munster Cottage Boy's concern with emigration is notable because Irish fiction written in the early decades of the nineteenth century tended to explore Ireland's longstanding conflicts with and connections to Britain and Continental Europe to the exclusion of its somewhat more recent affiliations with the United States. Indeed, migration to the United States really only became a common theme in Irish fiction during the 1840s, in the years leading up to the Great Famine—for instance in William Carleton's *Black Prophet: A Tale of Irish Famine* (1846) and *The Emigrants of Ahadarra* (1847). *The Munster Cottage Boy*'s emigrant is by birth an aristocrat, although he was raised by peasants in a cottage in Munster. Given his associations with the peasant class, it is perhaps not surprising that Glenbower's frequent laments for his homeland should resemble those expressed in popular songs of the early nineteenth century such as "The Exile of Erin" and "The Exiled Irishman's Lamentation." Similar to *The Munster Cottage Boy*, these songs feature migrants who are forced to leave Ireland for political rather than economic reasons. They also tend to represent emigration as form of dispossession instead of a choice. In "The Exile of Erin," for instance, the exile mourns that in contrast to "the wild deer and wolf," he has "no refuge for famine or danger, / A home and a country remain not for me":

> Ah! Never again, in the green shady bowers,
> Where my forefathers liv'd, shall I spend the sweet hours,
> Or cover my harp with the wild woven flowers,
> And strike the bold numbers of Erin go Bragh.
>
> O, Erin my country! tho' sad and forsaken,
> In dreams I revisit thy sea-beaten shore;
> But alas! in a far foreign land I awaken,
> And sigh for the friends who can meet me no more.[58]

In its emphasis on what migrants lose, rather than on what they gain, by leaving Ireland for America, *The Munster Cottage Boy* echoes popular early nineteenth-century emigration songs and reflects the changing demographics of and attitudes towards emigration in Ireland following the end of the Napoleonic Wars.

Although Roche's novel foregrounds the emotional or affective aspects of the emigrant experience, *The Munster Cottage Boy* is also concerned with the more pragmatic aspects of emigration, representing it as both a cause and an effect of Ireland's political and economic distresses. Similar to Brown, Roche adapts Gothic conventions to suit the conditions of the nation about which she is writing, using ruined castles to represent the economic and political devastation of Ireland, and the wanderings of her spotlessly innocent heroine to illuminate the sufferings of Irish expatriates. Through these adaptations, Roche suggests that only by restoring Ireland's ancient feudal hierarchy—the country's natural social order—will the unnatural flow of people from the nation be staunched.

The Munster Cottage Boy's language is wildly overwrought, and its plot is unimaginably complicated; but, aesthetic flaws notwithstanding, it is perhaps Roche's most politically topical novel, as it explores the political and economic dispossession that motivated Irish emigration during the late eighteenth and early nineteenth centuries. Although Roche's most well-known novel, *The Children of the Abbey* (1796), was set partially in Ireland, she only began exploring in depth Irish landscapes, problems, and peoples during the 1820s. Quite possibly, as Natalia Schroeder suggests, the "resounding successes of Maria Edgeworth, Lady Morgan and other 'Irish novelists'" may have encouraged the financially struggling Roche "to put her acquaintance with her own country to better use."[59] *The Munster Cottage Boy* offers evidence for Clare Connolly's claim that Irish-authored novels of the 1820s "are notably concerned with experiences that exist on the borderline between existence and extinction."[60] As an exile, Glenmore, much like Clithero, inhabits precisely such a state between life and death, unable either to renounce his Irish past or embrace an American present. Connolly draws a connection between "ghostly fiction and expatriate authorship," suggesting that Irish writers who, like Roche, lived in London and wrote about Ireland for an English readership themselves occupied a liminal or ghostly position.[61] For English readers, the value of these writers' works rested in their "autochthonous relationship to Irish culture," a relationship that emigration necessarily attenuated.[62] While Glenmore's ghostliness in *The Munster Cottage Boy* may well reflect Roche's own liminality as an Irish author writing for an English audience, it more obviously reflects what Roche regarded as the unnaturalness of emigration.

Written only twenty years after the Anglo-Irish Union of Parliaments recast Britain's colonial government of Ireland as a political partnership, *The Munster Cottage Boy* offers a very cautious depiction of the United Irishmen's uprising of 1798. Glenmore might be described as a rebel twice removed. He sympathizes with the United Irishmen's cause, but does not participate in the rebellion. However, he does give refuge to his foster-father, who also did not participate in the rebellion but who is wanted for harboring fugitive rebels (hence the two removes). When government officials arrive to apprehend his foster-father, Glenmore shoots one of them. Although Roche will not allow her aristocratic hero to dirty his hands in a political uprising, she introduces minor characters whose participation in the United Irishmen's uprising indicts Britain for creating the oppressive conditions that encouraged the rebellion in the first place. One of these characters is Terence Dullaney, a Catholic who was prohibited by the penal laws from serving in the British military, despite repeatedly offering his services to "his king and country" (2: 235). In 1798, Terence was invited take a "high command" among the United Irish forces, but he rejected the offer "with scorn" and instead once more "pressed to be allowed to enlist under the banner of his king" (2: 236). When he was again turned away by the British army, "in a paroxysm of resentment and despair," he joined the United Irishmen and ever since has "led a dangerous and desultory life, at the head of a band of wandering insurgents, so impressed with a sense of his wrongs as to reject availing himself of the act of amnesty that was at last past [*sic*]" (2: 237). Political dispossession has left Dullaney, similar to Glenmore and Fidelia, a wanderer. While Roche stops short of sanctioning rebellion, *The Munster Cottage Boy* is otherwise fairly pointed in its indictment of British government of Ireland, singling out "tyranny"—both of Britain over Ireland and of a corrupt aristocracy over the Irish peasantry—as the cause of widespread poverty, political unrest, and most importantly, emigration.[63]

The Munster Cottage Boy draws attention to the plight of migrants through Fidelia's own wanderings around Ireland and England. Throughout the novel, Fidelia is persecuted by various people who either suspect that she is of noble parentage and hope to exploit her connections for their own ends, or simply want to take advantage of a beautiful and unprotected young woman. She repeatedly meets with "insulting rudeness" and "mysterious estrangement" (4: 50), until she fears she must be "destined for ever to be disappointed, for ever to find herself the sport of fortune—driven from place to place, without any certainty of protection or shelter" (4: 279). Fidelia's wanderings as she flees her persecutors allow Roche to illustrate the economic problems of rural and urban regions of Ireland. The wretched conditions in which Fidelia finds farm laborers living as a result of absenteeism was by the early nineteenth century the standard stuff of travel narratives. More unusual is Roche's depiction of the landscape just outside Dublin:

> Large buildings . . . in ruins, built for different businesses and manufactories, gave a deplorable idea of the distress that had in a degree fallen upon the country—a distress which it did not require one to be a profound politician to be able to account for, namely, to the arrangement that rendered indispensable the partial emigration of the chief people of the kingdom, and of course, with them, the voluntary abandonment of it by those not only connected with them, but who liked to follow where fashion led the way. (2: 166–167)

Describing the defection of the landowning class to London as a kind of "partial emigration," Roche implies that absenteeism is responsible both for economic depression, as the wealthy spend their money abroad, and for the emigration of the lower classes, which, in leaving Ireland, are only following the example set by their betters. The upper echelon's "voluntary abandonment" of Ireland contrasts with Fidelia's own forced mobility, as she crisscrosses between Ireland and England in hopes of finding a permanent refuge from degrading dependency on one hand and poverty on the other.

Glenmore's and Fidelia's migrancy reveals that emigration is devastating not only economically, for Ireland, but emotionally, for the individuals who must leave their homes. *The Munster Cottage Boy* represents leaving one's homeland, whether by choice or through force, as a profoundly unnatural thing to do. Even when Glenmore, having revealed to Fidelia that she is "the child of an outlaw—a proscribed being" (4: 74), invites her to return to the United States with him, he discourages her from taking this momentous step unless she has absolutely no other prospects of survival. Speaking of his own homesickness, he warns, "I strongly advise you against migrating from your native clime, if in it you behold any prospect of permanent felicity; for, alas! Too well, from sad experience, do I know what it is to tear ourselves away from the scenes of early attachment and interest" (3: 13). Fidelia's prospects of economic security, let alone happiness, had never "seemed to her more vague or uncertain; yet still her heart died within her at the thought of quitting her native country" (3: 13). The strength of Fidelia's repugnance towards the mere idea of exile, albeit in the company of her newfound father, suggests the unnaturalness of emigration. Fidelia has been repeatedly "renounced, despised, forsaken by all whom she loved" in Ireland and admits that she has nothing "to attach her to the spot she so tenaciously clung to" (4: 240). Nonetheless she feels "as if she could grasp the very sods of the earth—cling to the very fibres of the rocks" (4: 240) rather than leave Ireland for the United States. Glenmore understands her attachment, revealing that during all his years in exile with "other persecuted beings like [him]self" he has never stopped thinking of "the dark brown heath—the mountains shrouded in mist—the narrow vales, with their cold blue streams winding along them" (2: 7). His attachment to his homeland transforms his literal haunting of the Glenbower estate into a more symbolic emotional haunting of Ireland. Even when he is not there in body, he is there in spirit.

The sheer strength of Fidelia and Glenmore's attachment to Ireland also indicates their nobility. More so than common peasants, they belong to Ireland as much as the dirt and rocks to which Fidelia longs to cling. Glenmore's repatriation and reappropriation of his family's estates not only affirm his and Fidelia's inherent connection to Ireland; they also herald the restoration of an ancient social hierarchy that will discourage the migration of the lower orders by rendering them content and prosperous at home. In a scene reminiscent of Edgar Huntly's revelation that Clithero did not in fact kill Mrs. Lorimer, Glenmore learns that the man he shot while attempting to protect his foster-father did not die from his wound. Thus he is "no longer a proscribed being" and "might again meet the light of day without shrinking—again encounter his fellow-men without apprehension" (4: 230). However, during his long absence his estates have been usurped through a conspiracy headed by an English steward, and Glenmore finds himself again deprived "of all hope or expectation of future independence in his native country—of there returning, after all his long and painful wanderings, and being in peace at last" (4: 231). Only the restoration of his estates and his rightful social position can end Glenmore's exile. Happily this is effected by Fidelia's suitor Grandison, who shares all the chivalrous virtues of his Richardsonian namesake, and who has long suspected that Fidelia might be of noble birth. The marriage of Grandison and Fidelia, and the political alliance between Glenmore and Grandison, promise to restore order and prosperity to the country. Given his many years of homesickness, it is not surprising that Glenmore eschews absenteeism, choosing to rehabilitate Glenbower Castle. Grandison, also the heir to a large Irish estate, dreams of "advocating the cause of his countrymen . . . and gradually leading [them] to that emancipation that would permit those whom worldly policy had tempted to apostatize from the faith of their ancestors to quiet their consciences by returning to it" (1: 168–169). Grandison's support of Catholic emancipation, along with Glenmore's plans for improving the lives of his tenants, suggest that "progress" in Ireland requires the restoration of an earlier social order, before the Protestant Ascendancy came to power, before Catholics were stripped of their rights, and before widespread absenteeism caused economic ruin and disaffection among the lower classes.

As an Irish national tale that incorporates the conventions of the Gothic, *The Munster Cottage Boy* completes a transatlantic literary circuit whereby the politicized Irish migration of the late 1790s informed Brown's *Wieland* and *Edgar Huntly* which in turn influenced the development of the Irish Gothic. Indeed, Roche was not the only early nineteenth-century Irish writer whose fiction bears the mark of Brown's influence. For instance, Charles Maturin's *Melmoth the Wanderer* (1820) shares *Wieland*'s concern with religious mania as a source of national fragmentation or dissolution, while Sidney Owenson's adaptation of Gothic conventions to comment on and consolidate national identity in *The Wild Irish Girl* (1806) recalls Brown's aims in *Edgar Huntly*. Yet rather than attempting to trace a direct line of influence from Brown to Irish writers including Roche, Maturin, and Owenson, it is perhaps more accurate to regard these writers as subject to common influences and heirs to shared traditions. For a start, all of them wrote for two audiences—one at home, whether that was Ireland or the United States, and one situated in metropolitan England. As Brown remarked in his "Sketch of American Literature" (1807), "the American states are, in a literary view, no more than a province of the British empire. In these respects we bear an exact resemblance to Scotland and Ireland."[64] The sense of self-division created by writing for two quite disparate audiences was a virtually inescapable part of the American and Irish novelist's experience in the late eighteenth and early nineteenth centuries. Furthermore, Irish and American novelists both inhabited nations that had, in living memory, experienced the hardships of colonial oppression and the resulting ravages of war, albeit on very different scales. It is not surprising that although their fictions participated in consolidating a national identity, Brown, Roche, and their Irish and American contemporaries also explored the violent forms of exclusion and regulation on which nations are founded.

In the Romantic-era Irish and American Gothic, the Irish migrant becomes a symbol of displacement and alienation. Irish migrants appear ghostly or supernatural because they are rootless, cut off from the past and without a home to which they can return. These migrants accrue a weight of meaning that far exceeds their literal status as representations of the many people who left Ireland during the late eighteenth and early nineteenth centuries. In his analysis of writing about Ireland's Great Hunger, the famine of the mid-nineteenth century, Ian Baucom suggests that the Irish only became Irish when they left Ireland. Launching into the Atlantic allowed them to acquire the geographical and cultural distance from Ireland necessary to envision themselves as a distinct people. Baucom sees this entry into a wider Atlantic community as empowering, and to some extent it may have been so.[65] Yet for those on the shores on either side of the Irish migrant's transatlantic crossing, the Irish migrant became a figure of loss and alienation whose wanderings threatened the stability and cohesiveness of the nation.

Scots and Scott in the Early American Republic

In his *Tour through the Whole Island of Great Britain* (1724–1727), Daniel Defoe remarked that one of the most important effects of the 1707 Anglo-Scottish Union of Parliaments was to open "the door to the Scots in our American colonies." If Scottish emigration were to continue at its current rate, he added, "Virginia had rather be called a Scots than an English plantation."[1] Defoe was an early observer of what Eric Richards has described as a Scottish emigrant ideology consisting of "values and techniques appropriate to overseas settlement, and a lessening attachment to native soil."[2] By opening up England's colonies to Scots, the 1707 Union encouraged those of the mercantile, professional, military, and even the landed classes to look abroad for the economic and political opportunities they could not find at home in Britain. Tenant farmers and artisans left Scotland with the more modest aim of making a living, impelled by the eighteenth-century collapse of local industries such as linen manufacturing and kelp processing, precipitous rises in rent, and the enclosure of farmland for pasturage.[3] Scots played a disproportionately large role in settling, defending, and governing Britain's overseas territories in the eighteenth century. Richards argues that by the end of the eighteenth century, "Scots had conquered their sense of provincial inferiority" through their "muscular seizure of opportunities . . . throughout the Atlantic world."[4] Even Highlanders, although culturally, linguistically, and economically marginalized within Britain, turned the militarization of the Highlands to their advantage by using the army as a stepping stone to a more prosperous and stable life in North America.[5]

Letters written by Scottish emigrants to their friends and family in Scotland often support Richards' triumphalist account of Scottish migration, suggesting that it not only offered Scots the prospect of greater prosperity, but also allowed them to lay claim to a British identity that they could not assert at home. Alexander Cumine migrated from Aberdeenshire to Charleston, South Carolina, in 1763, where he apprenticed himself to a Scottish tobacco merchant in the hopes of eventually starting his own firm. A few months after his arrival, Cumine wrote to a friend that in Charleston "the Scots are very numerous and are extremely industrious & sober by which means they are become the principall Merchants in the place[,] there being three Scotch Merchants here to one of any other Nation[,] and they have been extreamely lucky in trade & making Connections." It is because Scots "generally do well," he adds, that "the Natives dislike them, and bear them [so?] much Envy."[6] James Campbell, a Scottish storekeeper working in Maryland for the Glasgow-based firm of Finlay, Hopkirk, and Co., similarly remarked in 1772 that while American-born inhabitants of the region "in general are too lazy & indolent" to make good use of the Chesapeake's natural resources, "our Countrymen do well—Many who left their country in the year 1715 being now in a very thriving and prosperous way."[7] Even Scots who were transported for their participation in the 1715 Jacobite rebellion, or who began life in the colonies as indentured servants, seemingly managed to rise above their initial disadvantages.

Cumine and Campbell attributed Scots' success in North America to precisely the "muscular seizure" of colonial opportunities that recent historians of Scottish emigration have described. Yet Cumine's and Campbell's letters are paradigmatic Scottish examples of what David Gerber and Stephen Fender have identified as the "America letter," a genre that, while it may also have conveyed the writer's personal news, was at least in part "a guidebook to the processes of emigration and resettlement . . . often motivated by the desire to inspire others to emigrate."[8] The conventions of the America letter encouraged writers to censor feelings of frustration, disappointment, and homesickness in order to represent emigration as a "travail through which one moved to a higher state of existence."[9] While it is tempting to regard letters as relatively transparent historical documents, they are arguably as mediated and convention-bound as other more recognizably literary works.[10] This is not to say that Cumine's and Campbell's letters offer untrue or inauthentic accounts of Scots' experiences in North America, merely that they offer partial ones. Education, occupation, gender, place of origin, political party, and reasons for leaving Scotland, among other factors, all shaped Scottish migrants' success in the New World.

The myth of the successful Scottish migrant has a history that precedes its transatlantic manifestation, perhaps originating in Scottish migration south to London after the 1603 Union of Crowns under James I/VI. Certainly, by the time the 1707 Union of Parliaments created the British state, comparisons between Scots in London and swarms of locusts were commonplace, as Scots began to occupy positions that were thought to belong rightfully to the English. It is difficult to say whether most Scottish migrants did in fact attain the upwards mobility that English observers attributed to them.[11] They certainly posed enough of a threat to inspire the publication of John Wilkes's Scotophobic newspaper *The North Briton* (1762–1763) and collections of anti-Scottish propaganda including *The British Antidote to Caledonian Poison* (1762) and its sequel, *The Scots Scourge: or, Pridden's Supplement to the British Antidote to Caledonian Poison* (1763). However, their turn to the colonies suggests that Scots found greater opportunities, or perhaps just fewer obstacles, in their pursuit of social integration and economic mobility beyond Britain.

This chapter examines the transatlantic racialization of the myth of the successful Scottish migrant. It is concerned not so much with the historical successes or failures of actual Scottish migrants as with examining the functions that this myth performed in American and British culture and literature. Accordingly, it focuses mainly on writing *about* Scottish migrants rather than writing *by* them. Eric Richards' and Barbara DeWolfe's examinations of Scots' first-person accounts suggest that migration to the colonies allowed Scots to share in an imperial British identity and that these migrants retained a primary loyalty to Great Britain. However, writers situated in the American colonies and early republic were anxious to claim Scottish migrants' purported talents and abilities for their own country, and incorporated the figure of the successful Scottish migrant into their construction of an imperial American identity. I argue here that transatlantic representations of the successful Scottish migrant drew on and contributed to the changing ideas about race that made possible the literary imagining of a racially pure but culturally mixed United States.

To explain the adaptive characteristics of Scots, and especially of Highlanders, eighteenth-century writers often resorted to the climatic and stadial theories of race that, according to Roxann Wheeler, "provided the most important rubric for thinking about human differences in the eighteenth century."[12] Climatic theory, which prevailed among French *philosophes* such as Montesquieu, traced a people's distinctive characteristics to variable environmental factors like soil quality and temperature. Climate, or environment, for these thinkers, was the primary determinant of a people's economic and political institutions, and thus also of their cultural customs and moral beliefs. Stadial theory, which was formulated by Scottish thinkers including Adam Smith and William Robertson, located the source of a people's distinctive traits and behaviors in their progress along a teleological continuum from savagery, through feudalism, to commercial civilization. Stadial theory posited that all peoples move through discrete stages of social development, albeit at variable rates, and that all peoples in a given social stage share similar traits.[13] Climatic and stadial theories of difference were compatible, as environmental factors could determine a society's rate of development. Both theories understood national or racial characteristics to be contingent and malleable. Eighteenth-century Scotland, with its relatively prosperous commercial Lowlands and barren semi-feudal Highlands, was invoked as evidence in climatic and stadial accounts of racial difference, as it seemed to demonstrate that the harsh conditions of life in the north had retarded Highlanders' socio-economic development and cultural refinement compared to their southern neighbors.

The myth of the successful Scottish migrant informed and was informed by Enlightenment theories of racial difference. The first part of this chapter compares Samuel Johnson's *Journey to the Western Islands of Scotland* (1775), which employs stadial theory to argue against the depopulation of the Hebrides, with J. Hector St. John de Crèvecoeur's *Letters from an American Farmer* (1782), which uses climatic theory to explain why Hebridreans tend to flourish as settlers in the American colonies. For Johnson and Crèvecoeur, Hebrideans stand in for the inhabitants of the Scottish Highlands and Islands more generally; but, as the *Journey* and the *Letters* illustrate, the Hebrides provided an ideal test case for exploring a range of theories about the causes and effects of migration precisely because of their isolated location off the west coast of Scotland. Johnson's and Crèvecoeur's accounts of Hebridean migration represent ethnic difference as malleable and contingent, allowing that Highlanders might eventually become Britons or Americans. Yet the accounts of non-European peoples produced by those involved in European global exploration, including westward migration in the United States, led some of Johnson's and Crèvecoeur's contemporaries to reconceptualize human difference as innate and intransigent.[14] This reconceptualization led to the divergence of two terms, "nation" and "race," that hitherto had often been used more or less synonymously to refer to a lineage or genealogy.[15] The distinction between race—now a biological category—and nation—a political and cultural community—figures importantly in James Fenimore Cooper's efforts to imagine a racially pure but culturally diverse American identity. The second part of the chapter examines how Cooper's *Last of the Mohicans* (1826) employs the myth of the successful Scottish migrant and the conventions of Walter Scott's Scottish Waverley novels to imagine an American identity formed through cultural rather than racial mixing. As mediators between "primitive" Native America and "civilized" Anglo-America, Cooper's Scottish migrants enable the formation of an American identity that incorporates Native American skills and values while excluding their persons and their blood.

Colonial Doubling in Johnson's *Journey* and Crèvecoeur's *Letters*

Although Johnson's *Journey to the Western Islands of Scotland* and Crèvecoeur's *Letters from an American Farmer* might seem to have little in common, they are companion texts of sorts: the former laments Scots' departure from the Highlands and Islands, and the latter celebrates their arrival in the American colonies in the most extravagant terms. Both the *Journey* and the *Letters* aimed to introduce a metropolitan English reading public to regions of the globe with which most readers were unfamiliar, but in which England held a kind of proprietary interest. Johnson undertook his journey to Scotland in 1773, but decided to publish an account of it only in 1775, perhaps motivated by the increasing political tensions between Britain and the American colonies, where many Highland emigrants settled. Crèvecoeur, a French soldier who remained in the colonies after the Seven Years War and became a naturalized British citizen, had completed the *Letters from an American Farmer* by 1776, only a year after Johnson's *Journey* was published. But thanks to the vagaries of war, the *Letters* did not appear in print for another six years, most of which time Crèvecoeur spent on the run or in prison for suspected treason. It was finally published in London in 1782.

Despite their contrary views on the desirability of Scottish emigration, Johnson and Crèvecoeur both trace its cause to the vestiges of feudalism in the Highlands. They were hardly alone in this assessment. Virtually every writer who commented on Scottish migration during the late eighteenth and early nineteenth centuries attributed it to the Highlands' crumbling feudal system. For instance, *A Candid Enquiry into the Causes of the Late and the Intended Migrations from Scotland* (1771), one of the most substantial of these commentaries, claimed that Highlanders had long been kept in a state of "indeterminate subordination" by their chieftains that was "in fact no better than real slavery."[16] The enclosure of land and raising of rents made even this "slavish condition" insecure, as tenants were "liable to be turned out of their poor farms whenever the haughty and capricious master shall think fit."[17] Lowland migration patterns were also altered by the demise of feudal bonds between chieftain and clansmen, as landless laborers in "indigent circumstances" sought work in "already overcrowded" towns and villages.[18] However, the relatively speedy and inexpensive passage from the West of Scotland to the eastern American seaboard meant that Scots need no longer endure these hardships at home. The anonymous author of *A Candid Enquiry* prophesies that, instead, Highlanders "will act like peaceable Indians, who, when they are oppressed by Europeans, avail themselves of the wideness of the country, and remove to a greater distance from them."[19] Emigration promises to elevate Highlanders from near-slaves to "peaceable Indians," and the depopulation of Highland estates becomes a presage of Indian removal in the United States. The analogy between Highlanders and Indians problematically blurs the distinction between voluntary and forced migration. During the late eighteenth century, Highlanders often did emigrate voluntarily (though not without mixed feelings), but the suggestion that easygoing Native Americans similarly "chose" to move west rather than fight over land with European settlers is questionable.[20]

In attributing emigration to the Highlands' lingering feudalism, late eighteenth- and early nineteenth-century writers framed their discussions of population in racial as well as economic terms. Feudalism, an economic adaptation to the scarcity of arable land in the Highlands, shaped Highlanders' distinctive racial characteristics. Johnson and Crèvecoeur turn to feudalism to explain the traits that make Scots valuable workers, whether at home in Britain or abroad in the American colonies. Although Johnson sympathizes with Highlanders' economic and cultural frustrations, his mercantilist understanding of political economy leads him to oppose emigration as a solution to their problems. He suggests instead that government subsidies might assist the modernization of agricultural practices in the north and enable Highlanders to remain in the land of their forefathers. In contrast, Crèvecoeur argues that the Highlands' cruel climate and vestigial feudalism have prepared Highlanders to prosper in an agrarian republic. However, he too advocates government intervention in migration, suggesting that the Hebrides might be most beneficially used as the site of a penal colony. Together, the *Journey* and the *Letters* position the Scottish Highlands and the American colonies as transatlantic doubles, bound by the passage of people and the distant control of English government.

Johnson has been taken to task for the prejudicial baggage he brought along on his travels through Scotland with James Boswell; but his concern about the causes and effects of large-scale emigration was genuine and marked.[21] He comments repeatedly on the "general dissatisfaction, which is now driving the highlanders into the other hemisphere."[22] Like many of his contemporaries, Johnson traced feudalism's decay to the Parliamentary legislation enacted in the wake of the 1715 and 1745 Jacobite rebellions to bring the wayward northern periphery more firmly under the centralized authority of British government. This legislation initiated the building of roads, the stationing of troops, and the implementing of judicial assizes throughout the Highlands. It prohibited traditional clothing in order to undermine Highlanders' sense of collective identity, and banned the ownership of weapons to prevent another uprising. For Johnson, the most lamentable effect of the "last conquest, and the subsequent laws" (73) was the weakening of the ties of obligation and loyalty that had bound chieftain and clansmen for centuries. With the substitution of English political and military power for the chieftains' ancient authority, the "adherence, which was lately professed by every man to the chief of his name" (101) was replaced by "the desire of growing rich" (95). Yet the sluggish growth of the Highland economy, Johnson observes, has failed to keep pace with the intellectual emancipation of Highlanders, so that their "ignorance grows every day less, but their knowledge is yet of little other use than to shew them their wants" (97).

Johnson's analysis of Highlanders' plight implicitly relies on stadial theory, according to which feudalism should have been gradually and organically superseded by a more diverse economy if Parliamentary legislation had not disrupted this development by undermining feudal institutions before agriculture and trade were sufficiently developed to supply Highlanders' needs. If, as Karen O'Brien has suggested, Johnson did not share the Whiggish attachment to progress common to Enlightenment thinkers like Adam Smith and William Robertson,[23] neither did he simply idealize the past. He regrets the demise of feudalism not because of its inherent virtues, but because "a once effective if severe system of government in the Highlands has undergone sudden and severe disruption without any viable alternatives being offered in its place" (69). Emigration has become an attractive option for Highlanders because it offers them an escape from this state of economic and cultural limbo at a moment "when the clans were newly disunited from their chiefs, and exasperated by unprecedented exactions" (101). After all, it should not be surprising if "he that cannot live as he desires at home, listens to the tale of fortunate islands, and happy regions, where every man may have land of his own, and eat the product of his labour without a superior" (101). While Johnson is clearly skeptical of the hyperbolic depictions of American opportunity circulated by emigration agents, he sympathizes with the frustration that leads Highlanders to credit their reports.

But Johnson is arguably concerned less with the happiness of Highlanders than with the economic stability of Great Britain. He shares "the mercantile assumption that 'people are the wealth of the nation': the belief that density of population would both power production and drive up prices."[24] Charlotte Sussman has shown that mercantilism informs much eighteenth-century writing about population and political economy, from Jonathan Swift's *Modest Proposal* for the commodification and consumption of babies to Oliver Goldsmith's *Deserted Village*, which observes that "The man of wealth and pride / Takes up a space that many poor supplied."[25] Johnson similarly argues that "to make a country plentiful by diminishing the people, is an expeditious mode of husbandry; but that abundance, which there is nobody to enjoy, contributes little to human happiness" (96). Much as a landowner who creates plenty by ridding himself of tenants cannot, from the tenants' perspective, be called a good landlord, a government that "hinder[s] insurrection, by driving away the people" and "govern[s] peaceably, by having no subjects" cannot be called a good government (103). For Johnson, government is for the people, although certainly not by the people, and one of its aims is therefore to maintain population. He holds the nobility and landed gentry responsible for sustaining Highlanders at home on the principle that "population should be run by the state as a merchant runs his business."[26] Thus one of the very few practical suggestions he makes for preventing emigration and improving the Highland economy is that tenants' rents be kept low artificially through government subsidies until they begin to benefit economically from agricultural improvements and can afford to pay higher rents (103).

Johnson acknowledges that the economic modernization of the Highlands would be no quick or easy task. On the contrary, during his visit to the Hebrides, he is quick to observe in islanders a tendency towards laziness and prevarication; but he sees these traits as the product of their circumstances rather than as innate and ineradicable flaws. He attributes their refusal "to endure a long continuance of manual labour" and their willingness to "endure many inconveniences, which a little attention would easily remove" to force of habit and lack of knowledge (93). The introduction of new modes of labor and of civilized conveniences would, in time, remedy these undesirable traits. If the partial improvement of the Highlands has caused the demise of feudalism, only the unlikely restoration of a feudal order on the one hand or further modernization on the other can quiet the "epidemical fury of emigration" (75). Johnson credits the 1707 Union of Parliaments with initiating the improvement of Lowland Scots, before which, "the culture of their lands was unskilful and their domestic life unformed" (51). Ever since Lowland Scots "have known their condition was capable of improvement," he admits, "their progress in useful knowledge has been rapid and uniform," and signs of "elegance and culture" are, by 1773, readily visible even among Highland lairds and clergyman (52).

Journey to the Western Islands aims to convince readers that the initial improvements introduced by the 1707 Union are not far-reaching enough. While Johnson blames Highland landowners, to some extent, for their tenants' unhappiness, he ultimately suggests that it is the British government's duty to remedy the "dissatisfaction" causing Highlanders to emigrate. He acknowledges that if Highlanders simply long for "the pleasures of happier climates" (102), their migration cannot be prevented, but warns that "if they are driven from their native country by positive evils, and disgusted by ill-treatment . . . it were fit to remove their grievances and quiet their resentment" (103). Britain's loss, Johnson warns readers, will be the colonies' gain; and if Highlanders "have been hitherto undutiful subjects, they will not much mend their principles by American conversation" (103). Highlanders' recent history of rebellion might predispose them to sympathize in the colonial agitations that, when the *Journey* was published in 1775, were about to erupt into war.

Crèvecoeur's tale of Andrew the Hebridean, who has arrived from Barra to settle in Pennsylvania, suggests that Johnson's warning was apt. While Johnson's *Journey* can be read as part travelogue, part anti-emigration tract, Crèvecoeur's *Letters* was perceived by some of its earliest readers as a "transatlantic imposition" intended to drain Britain's resources by encouraging emigration to the colonies.[27] English critic Samuel Ayscough accused Crèvecoeur of exaggerating the colonies' attractions, and of trying to "poison" "the young mind, unstable in its opinions, warm in its enterprises" with the belief that emigrants would inevitably find greater wealth and happiness in America.[28] The *Letters* resembles the "America letter" not only in its overblown rhetoric, but also in its intended audience of Britons unfamiliar with life in North America. Commenting on the popularity of the *Letters* upon its publication in 1782, Albert E. Stone explains that Crèvecoeur's book "provided two generations of Europeans with their chief impressions of the American colonies," with editions appearing in Dublin, Belfast, Leipzig, Leyden, Paris, and Maastricht by the end of the century.[29] The popularity of the *Letters* perhaps was due in part to the naïve charms of its narrator, Farmer James, a third-generation American of English descent who shares his author's uneasy mix of agrarian republicanism and loyalty to British rule.[30] Unlike the cosmopolitan Crèvecoeur, however, Farmer James is a kind of native informant, whose accounts of colonial life supposedly are uncorrupted by European book learning, and who aims to "describe our American modes of farming, our manners, and peculiar customs" to his correspondent, the "enlightened Englishman," Mr. F. B.[31]

Ralph Bauer and Grantland Rice have shown that, despite his naïve pose, James's letters demonstrate a familiarity with European discourses of natural history, including, I would add, climatic theories of race.[32] In his letter titled "What Is an American?" James suggests that environmental factors play a key role in transforming new settlers from Europeans into Americans. This process occurs over generations, as the children and grandchildren of immigrants become secularized and deracinated. In the colonies, Farmer James explains, "individuals of all nations are melted into a new race of men" that will be further differentiated "by the power of the different climates they inhabit" (70). Indeed, the colonies encompass such a diversity of climates that Europeans must "become, in the course of a few generations, not only Americans in general, but either Pennsylvanians, Virginians, or provincials under some other name" (73).

However, not all immigrants succeed in becoming Americans. Only "the sober, the honest, and the industrious" (84) can endure the hardships of settlement, and some immigrants have been better prepared by their native environments than others to exercise the sobriety, honesty, and industry necessary to succeed. The Irish, James claims, suffer from the detrimental effects of England's "ancient conquest" of their kingdom and "do not prosper so well" as other groups (85). In contrast, Scottish immigrants, who are accustomed to "high, sterile, bleak lands . . . where everything is barren and cold" tend to be "industrious and saving; they want nothing more than a field to exert themselves in, and they are commonly sure of succeeding" (85–86).

To show how the hardships of daily life in northern Scotland prepare migrants to prosper in the colonies, James relates the story of Andrew, "an honest Scotch Hebridean" who illustrates "in epitome what the Scotch can do wherever they have room for the exertion of their industry" (86). Andrew, a Gaelic-speaking man from Barra, arrives in Philadelphia with his wife and son, and eleven guineas. After working as a farmhand for two years in order to save money and learn the customs of the country, he leases "a hundred acres of good arable land" and begins to farm it (101). James rejoices to see "honest Andrew . . . become a freeholder, possessed of the vote, of a place of residence, a citizen of the province of Pennsylvania" (102). The answer to Crèvecoeur's question, "What is an American?" would seem to be "a Hebridean." Andrew's achievement of Crèvecoeur's ideals of prosperity, contentment, and republican virtue is intended to suggest that in the colonies anyone, however ignoble his origins, can improve his lot through hard work. The tacit caveat, though, is that conditions in the immigrant's homeland must have prepared him for that hard work.

In one of the contradictions that riddle the *Letters*, James claims that an immigrant must renounce his native culture to become an American, but suggests at the same time that Andrew's country of origin has prepared him particularly well to thrive in the colonies.[33] The *Letters* asserts that "*He* is an American, who, leaving behind him all his ancient prejudices and manners, receives new ones from the new mode of life he has embraced, the new government he obeys, and the new rank he holds" (70). An immigrant does not so much make himself anew as allow himself to be made anew by the environment in which he finds himself—one that includes laws, institutions, and social conventions different from those to which he is accustomed. The settler participates in this transformation through his renunciation of his native culture. Yet despite this active forgetting of the past, an immigrant's successful assimilation is to a large extent influenced by his country of origin. Farmer James attributes Andrew's successful settlement in Pennsylvania to two factors: the inhospitality of Barra's climate, and, echoing Johnson, the inadequacy of its semi-feudal economy to meet Hebrideans' basic material needs. Thanks to the inhospitality of northern Scotland's climate, Highlanders' "constitutions are uncontaminated by any excess or effeminacy, which their soil refuses" (97), and they already possess the fortitude and endurance necessary to prosper in the colonies. Added to these Spartan conditions are the exigencies of a semi-feudal economy. Andrew explains that although his landlord Mr. Nieil was kind to his tenants, "the land is thin, and there were too many of us" to prosper on the island. Whereas Johnson believed that the difficulties of eking out a living under such conditions made islanders lazy and apathetic, Crèvecoeur suggests that these obstacles cultivate a stoic industriousness. On another point, however, Johnson and Crèvecoeur are in agreement: the inequities of feudalism and the harshness of existence in the Highlands ensure migrants' loyalty to their new home in the colonies. Farmer James asks, "What attachment can a poor European emigrant have for a country where he had nothing?" (69); and Johnson claims that "a common highlander has no strong attachment to his native soil; for of animal enjoyments, or of physical good, he leaves nothing that he may not find again wheresoever he may be thrown" (105).

Crèvecoeur clearly considers the agrarian republicanism of the American colonies preferable to the feudalism of the Scottish Highlands; yet the *Letters* represents the Hebrides and the colonies as doubles insofar as the land and population of each are at the disposal of a government situated in the English metropolis. Johnson found the depopulation of the Hebrides particularly unfortunate because "in more fruitful countries, the removal of one only makes room for the succession of another: but in the Hebrides, the loss of an inhabitant leaves a lasting vacuity, for nobody born in any other part of the world will choose this country for their residence" (102). As if in answer to Johnson, Farmer James proposes a means of replacing Hebrideans lost to emigration. He recommends that "the English government" should transform the Hebrides into a penal colony and reserve "good lands" in the lush middle colonies like his own Pennsylvania for "the honest primitive Hebrideans," where they might settle "as a reward for their virtue and ancient poverty" (88–89). Describing the Hebrides as "the hell of Great Britain, where all evil spirits should be sent" (89), James asserts that "the severity of the climate, the inclemency of the seasons, the sterility of the soil, the tempestuousness of the sea, would afflict and punish" criminals appropriately (88). At best, these trials might also reform Britain's criminals, and by cultivating their fortitude and courage, prepare them to reap the rewards of colonial settlement later on. The hell of the Hebrides would punish convicts, and the fertile middle colonies in turn would reward Highland emigrants—but possibly to their detriment. After all, the preservation of the Hebrideans' distinctive virtues is dependent upon environmental conditions. James muses on the Hebrideans: "I wish we had a colony of these honest people settled in some part of this province; their morals, their religion, seem to be as simple as their manners. This society would present an interesting spectacle could they be transported on a richer soil. But perhaps that soil would soon alter everything; for our opinions, vices, and virtues are altogether local: we are machines fashioned by every circumstance around us" (98). An infusion of Hebrideans might for a time improve the aggregate American character; but, once settled on the "richer soil" of the middle colonies, this colony of virtuous Highlanders might gradually degenerate into a bunch of lazy good-for-nothings.

James's proposal to turn Barra into a prison camp is mildly amusing in its ethnocentric ideas of what constitutes punishment; yet his representation of Hebrideans and convicts as interchangeable populations may not have seemed at all peculiar to contemporaries like Johnson. In demonstrating how the science of demography developed in tandem with colonial practices, Sussman explains that eighteenth-century population theorists tended to count people "for the purposes of moving them around" to places where they might be needed to carry out the work of colonization.[34] The greater mobility of geographically and socially marginal populations, whether Highlanders or felons, "allowed England to define itself against the subaltern populations of the rest of its empire."[35] Crèvecoeur's vision of a colony of Hebrideans suggests that American settlers may have shared the British tendency to regard "subaltern populations" as moveable resources, even though these same settlers, or their ancestors, might quite recently have been similarly marginal.

Crèvecoeur and Johnson each brought to bear on the issue of Highland migration new theories about the relationship between political economy and ethnic difference; and, in doing so, they participated in the racialization of the myth of the successful Scottish migrant. Both writers saw Highlanders as a potentially valuable national resource whose difference from other populations was relatively fluid and malleable, determined largely by the vestiges of feudalism in northern Scotland. Johnson suggests that if Hebrideans could be prevented from emigrating, their counterproductive habits might gradually be remedied through the economic development of the Highlands and Islands. Crèvecoeur depicts Hebrideans as already well suited to thrive under the hardships of colonial settlement in America, although he acknowledges that, over time, their adaptive qualities might be undermined by the colonies' comparatively less austere environmental conditions. For Johnson, then, Hebrideans' material prosperity and intellectual liberation were merely theoretical possibilities, while they were for Crèvecoeur immanent but contingent realities.

During the late eighteenth and early nineteenth centuries, however, European exploration and imperial expansion, including westward migration in the United States, contributed to the hardening of racial categories. The emerging biological sciences configured human difference as innate and unalterable. Moreover, these inherent differences were believed to render racial amalgamation or hybridization through marriage unnatural, if not actually impossible.[36] James Fenimore Cooper's representations of Scottish and Native American migration reflect these changing understandings of race. While Cooper does not represent race as entirely intransigent, he suggests that some peoples, like Highlanders, have through historical or environmental circumstances become more adaptable than others. Those races that, like the Mohicans and Iroquois, are less adaptive, are destined to diminish or even die out. In *The Last of the Mohicans* Cooper employs the figure of the successful Scottish emigrant to distinguish race, which is relatively fixed, from culture, which is malleable. Comparing Scottish and Indian migrants allows Cooper to imagine an imperial American identity that is at once racially pure and culturally mixed, and that combines Scots' courageous chivalry with American Indians' shrewd self-control.

Scottish Americans and the American Scott

If Scots played a disproportionately large role in settling British North America, the novels of Walter Scott played an equally sizeable part in the history of American literature. Emily Todd explains that "even though Scott was not an American writer and never visited the United States," thanks to the immense popularity of his novels, "he participated in the nineteenth-century

American literary marketplace, and helped to shape practices of publishing and reading in nineteenth-century America."[37] James Fenimore Cooper famously was first dubbed "the Scott of America" in an 1822 issue of the *North American Review*.[38] Although Cooper resented this label, subsequent critical comparisons between the two authors, such as George Dekker's 1967 study *James Fenimore Cooper: The American Scott*, suggest that it carries a certain accuracy: Cooper adapted and modified for an American context the conventions of the historical romance that Walter Scott had employed to perform the work of British nation formation.[39] Yet, as these comparisons have demonstrated, Cooper was no mere imitator of Scott; instead, as Ian Dennis has claimed, he "engage[d] in a conscious, critical, even at times resentful dialogue with his great model and rival."[40] In *The Last of the Mohicans* Cooper comments on his literary relationship to Scott by adapting the myth of the successful Scottish immigrant perpetuated by Defoe, Johnson, Crèvecoeur, and others. While critics generally have overlooked the Scottish descent of the primary non-Indian characters in *The Last of the Mohicans*—Colonel Munro; his two daughters, Alice and Cora; and Major Duncan Heyward—and often describe them as English, Anglo-American, or even Anglo-Saxon, I argue that their Scottishness is far from incidental to Cooper's account of American nation formation.[41]

The Last of the Mohicans suggests that Scots' historic experiences of colonial migration and settlement might have encouraged them to adopt the prudence and self-control that Cooper attributes to the Mohican Indians, and enabled them to supersede temporarily North America's native populations as bearers of an American identity characterized on one hand by chivalrous sentiment and on the other hand by stoic self-command. The novel sets Cora and Alice Munro's captivity under the French-allied Iroquois against the French victory over, and the Iroquois massacre of, Colonel Munro's British troops at Fort William Henry in 1757. By emulating the prudence of the eponymous Mohican, Uncas, Duncan Heyward succeeds in rescuing his betrothed, Alice, but only at the expense of Uncas's and Cora's lives. Heyward's marriage to Alice consolidates a racially pure American identity, while his friendship with and emulation of Uncas offers a model of cultural hybridization that brings together the best of Scottish and Indian traits.

A striking number of mediators between Native Americans and the British and American governments during the colonial era were of mixed Scottish and Indian descent, including John Norton, Alexander MacGillavray, and John Ross.[42] Yet *The Last of the Mohicans* ignores the cultural and racial mixing that occurred historically among Scots and various Indian tribes. It also eschews the literary hybridization described by Tim Fulford, through which "ancient Celts and contemporary Native Americans were imaged in terms of each other over and over again" in late eighteenth- and early nineteenth-century British and American works.[43] Although Cooper's Mohicans may at some level derive from Scott's Highlanders, which in turn may be drawn from accounts like James Adair's *History of the American Indians* (1775), *The Last of the Mohicans* assigns Indians and Scots to contiguous rather than identical stages on the developmental path from savagery to civilization. Cooper accords Scots a feudal chivalry that is an improvement over the tribal savagery of Indians, exploiting the romantic connotations of feudalism that Crèvecoeur, and to a lesser extent Johnson, overlook. *The Last of the Mohicans* situates its male characters along a gendered continuum of national identities that runs from brutish masculinity to overcivilized effeminacy. Cooper contrasts the savage violence of the Iroquois with the sophisticated hypocrisy of the French to imagine an American masculinity whose primary representatives in the novel are the Mohican Uncas and Duncan Heyward, a southerner who is "half a Scotsman."[44]

As Uncas, the most civilized of the novel's savages, teaches the refined and romantic Heyward the fortitude and prudence necessary to survive in the wilderness, Heyward progresses toward a deracinated American identity that unites aspects of Scottish chivalry and Indian savagery to overcome the challenges of westward expansion. The cultural appropriation through which Heyward becomes American offers a model for the literary relationship between Cooper's and Scott's historical romances. The Leatherstocking Tales borrow selectively from the Waverley Novels, rejecting their valorization of feudal chivalry while incorporating their representation—itself drawn from Enlightenment historiography—of cultural appropriation as a mechanism of teleological social development.

By incorporating characters of Scottish ancestry into *The Last of the Mohicans*, Cooper not only traces the formation of an American identity marked by sentiment and self-command but also explores the transformation of Britain's North American colonies into the United States, a nation with its own colonial projects. Post-Union Scotland arguably shared the American colonies' political and economic dependence on England. Yet Cooper's comparisons of Scottish Americans and Native Americans reveal the limitations of recent characterizations by historians and literary critics of Scots as colonial subjects.[45] While both Scots and Native Americans in *The Last of the Mohicans* are exiled or alienated from their respective homelands, only Scots have the opportunity to assimilate into a formative European-American society. Moreover, the colonial migrations of Scots, according to Cooper, are a direct cause of the exile and eradication of Native Americans. In a nascent American nation, Scots themselves become colonizers.

While Cooper follows Johnson and Crèvecoeur in tracing Scottish migration to the demise of feudalism, he is less interested in a feudal economy's effects on the oppressed lower orders than in the chivalric sense of honor it cultivated in the landowning classes to which Heyward and Munro belong. Both characters' migrations seem to have been dictated to some extent by the Jacobite rebellions of 1715 and 1745, which Scott explores respectively in *Rob Roy* (1817) and *Waverley; or 'tis Sixty Years Since* (1814). Scott suggests that the Jacobites' attempts to reinstate the Scottish Stuart monarchy on the British throne were motivated by a desire to recover Scotland's pre-Union independence and to preserve the values and institutions of feudal society. The anti-Scottish prejudices exacerbated by the unsuccessful rebellions further limited the already restricted participation of Scots in a nominally British government and perhaps inspired the colonial drive that Cooper attributes to them in *The Last of the Mohicans*. Heyward and Munro unite this forward-looking colonial ambition with the feudal ideals of honor and chivalry they have brought from Scotland.

Scots represent for Cooper a strange blend of exilic adaptability and Old World feudalism. The scant but pertinent details that Cooper provides about Duncan Heyward's family history suggest that he is descended from some of the approximately two thousand Scots transported to the American colonies following the 1715 Jacobite rebellion. Like most of these exiles, Heyward's family was from the landed classes, formerly "an ornament to the nobles of Scotland" (157). Further like these Jacobites, who tended to settle south of the Chesapeake Bay, Heyward's family has established prosperous plantations in the American South.[46] Munro, in contrast, represents those "ancient and honourable" Scottish families that were not transported, but that were left impoverished by the Jacobite rebellions and so forced to rebuild their fortunes in the colonies (159). As a young man, Munro left Scotland "in the service of [his] king" and eventually settled in the West Indies because he was too poor to marry his beloved Alice Graham. Munro explains: "it was my lot to form a connexion with one who in time became my wife, and the mother of Cora. She was the daughter of a gentleman of those isles, by a lady, whose misfortune it was . . . to be descended, remotely, from that unfortunate class, who are so basely enslaved to administer to the wants of a luxurious people" (159). After his first wife's death, Munro returned to Scotland with Cora, where the wealth he had accrued on his West Indian plantation allowed him to marry his still-unwed childhood love, who died giving birth to his second, purely Scottish daughter, Alice.

Munro's history illustrates the ambivalent relationship of Scots to metropolitan England and its colonies. His passive phrasing in speaking of his first wife—"it was my lot"—allows him to disclaim responsibility for forming a "connexion" with a mulatto. Instead, he attributes his interracial union to Scotland's prior "unnatural union with a foreign and trading people," or to the Anglo-Scottish Union that gave Scots access to England's colonies (159). Again refusing personal culpability, Munro describes slavery as "a curse entailed on Scotland" by England, implying that Scots participate in the oppressive institution of plantation slavery only because they themselves have been oppressed by the English. As Munro discovers in the West Indies, and as Heyward's family's southern plantation further illustrates, empire offered Scots material prosperity at a moral cost. The history of the political and economic disempowerment of Scots within Britain perhaps makes Munro and Heyward each more keenly aware that his colonial affluence depends upon the even greater disempowerment of non-European peoples. Yet this recognition does not prevent either Munro's embarrassment at admitting his "connexion" with a woman of African descent, or Heyward's revulsion at the thought of marrying the racially mixed Cora. Similarly, although Munro and Heyward are exiles of sorts, they show little concern about the displacement of Native Americans from their lands. In fact, *The Last of the Mohicans* situates the colonial migrations of Scots as a cause of Native Americans' unfortunate but, for Cooper, seemingly inevitable eradication, as Heyward's appropriation of Uncas's prudence and fortitude renders Uncas extraneous to a formative American nation.

The Last of the Mohicans defines American identity in opposition to a savage, brutish masculinity, on one hand, and an overcivilized effeminacy, on the other hand. The novel's primary representative of unrefined savagery is Magua, one of the Iroquois or Hurons whom Leatherstocking describes as "a thievish race" of "skulks" and "vagabonds" (37). In contrast to Magua's "knavish look" (39), the Mohican Uncas resembles a finely chiseled Grecian statue "of the noblest proportions" (53). Cooper invites readers to attribute Magua's moral degeneracy to his "mongrel" or mixed blood (39), while Uncas's moral nobility and unmixed ancestry are embodied in his "high, haughty features, pure in their native red" (53). Magua and Uncas respectively embody the stereotypes of the ignoble and noble savage that, according to Robert F. Berkhofer, Jr., have "persist[ed] from the era of Columbus" onward.[47] Cooper gave these stereotypes new life by drawing on early nineteenth-century theories of race that posited possibly immutable and inherent connections between physical appearance, moral attributes, and purity of blood.

Magua and Uncas differ from each other most markedly in their capacity for sympathy and, as a result, in their treatment of women. Enlightenment historians including Adam Smith, William Robertson, and John Millar employed stadial theory to argue that a people's capacity for sympathy indicated its progress from barbaric tribal origins toward the historical telos of commercial civilization. In *The Theory of Moral Sentiments* (1759), for instance, Smith claims that "the savages in North America" regard "the weakness of love, which is so much indulged in ages of humanity and politeness . . . as the most unpardonable effeminacy."[48] While these savages possess a "heroic and unconquerable firmness," a "humane and polished people . . . have more sensibility to the passions of others."[49] Smith theorizes that savage peoples must cultivate courage, fortitude, and self-command in order to endure the hardships of their daily existence. Civilized peoples enjoy the prosperity, security, and leisure necessary to cultivate more refined virtues, including sympathy.

Smith's student John Millar developed this argument in his *Origin of the Distinction of Ranks* (1771) by suggesting that a people's civility could be gauged by their valuation of refined, "feminine" virtues like sympathy and, accordingly, by their treatment of women. Millar concurs with Smith that when men must exert "their utmost efforts to procure the bare necessaries of life," they are incapable "of feeling the delicate distresses and enjoyments of love, accompanied with all those elegant sentiments, which, in a civilized and enlightened age, are naturally derived from that passion."[50] Romantic passion—a particular type of sympathy—thus emerges only as a society progresses from tribal savagery to feudalism, when continual war over property and power creates "the high notions of military honour, and the romantic love and gallantry, by which the modern nations of Europe have been so much distinguished."[51] Feudal society, in which men and women occupy very different spheres, is "naturally productive of the utmost purity of manners, and of great respect and veneration for the female sex."[52] Smith's and Millar's accounts of the stadial development of sympathy and love reveal the extent to which Cooper's constructions of masculinity not only draw upon Enlightenment history but also depend upon women. Female characters in *The Last of the Mohicans* are touchstones by which the civility—and Americanness—of male characters can be measured.

Magua regards both Mohicans and Europeans as effeminate precisely because of their chivalric respect for women. He declares that "the pale faces make themselves dogs to their women" and that the Mohicans, who have adopted European ways, "are content to be called women" (42, 50). Magua, by contrast, regards Alice and Cora as a means through which he can revenge himself against their father, Munro, who once had whipped Magua "like a dog" for his drunkenness (103). Magua's canine imagery distinguishes his own emasculation from the voluntary subservience of European men. Magua hopes to reassert his masculine prerogative by keeping Cora as his captive and wife, so that "when the blows scorched the back of the Huron, he would know where to find a woman to feel the smart" (105). Although Cora acknowledges her father's "imprudent severity" in beating Magua, she is horrified to discover that her captor might "revenge the injury inflicted by Munro, on his helpless daughters" (103, 104). Magua's desire for vengeance not only emphasizes his arguably justifiable lack of sympathy for Munro, but also illustrates his lack of chivalry. Gary Dyer has argued that Cooper challenges Scott's valorization of chivalry by showing that chivalry rests on "an economy governed by desire."[53] Because Magua feels no sexual desire for Cora and Alice, he feels no impetus to protect them. However, Cooper does not, as Dyer suggests, represent all Indians as uniformly impervious to either sexual desire or chivalric ideals.

While Magua remains resistant to the civilizing influence of feminine virtues, Uncas is evidently so deeply impressed by Cora's charms that his haste to rescue her renders his efforts, in Leatherstocking's words, "more like that of a curious woman, than of a warrior on his scent" (120). Cooper invites readers to attribute the Mohicans' relative politeness and sophistication in comparison to the Iroquois to their earlier contact with Europeans. They have had more time to acquire the relatively refined morals and manners of the settlers. Uncas's comparative civility is evident in his silent joy when he and Heyward succeed in tearing Cora and Alice from Magua's clutches: "The manhood of Heyward felt no shame, in dropping tears over this spectacle of affectionate rapture; and Uncas stood, fresh and blood-stained from the combat, a calm, and, apparently, an unmoved looker-on, it is true, but with eyes that had already lost their fierceness, and were beaming with a sympathy, that elevated him far above the intelligence, and advanced him probably centuries before the practices of his nation" (115). Although Uncas does not weep unabashedly, as does Heyward, neither does he remain "a stranger to any sympathy" (112), as does the temporarily defeated Magua. Even as Uncas's "blood-stained" appearance relegates him to the realm of savagery, his furtive appreciation of Alice and Cora's joy and relief reveals his civility. Cooper makes it clear that Uncas's union of refined sympathy with stoic courage is unusual; his "beaming" eyes represent "centuries" of progress from savagery toward civilization. Yet Cooper does not go so far as to suggest that Uncas's "instinctive delicacy" is unnatural (115). Although sympathy is contrary to his "habits," it is compatible with his "nature" (114).

In contrast to both Magua's indifference to suffering and Uncas's stoic sensibility, the French general, Montcalm, reveals his overcivilized effeminacy in displays of false feeling and affected sympathy. He embodies the xenophobic stereotypes of French sophistication that were common in late eighteenth- and early nineteenth-century British and American literature. Montcalm's "insinuating polish" and great attention to "the forms of courtesy" persuade Munro that "if the truth was known, the fellow's grandfather taught the noble science of dancing" (162, 153, 151). Montcalm conquers through cunning rather than courage. He extorts surrender from the "commanding and manly" Scotsman (162) not by defeating the British troops in battle, but instead by intercepting a letter from Munro's superior, General Webb. Munro bitterly contrasts Montcalm's cunning to the true "dignity" that he associates with the Scottish Order of the Thistle, "the veritable *nemo me impune lacessit* of chivalry" to which Heyward's ancestors belonged (157). Much as Munro regards Montcalm's affectations as representative of all French military officers, he is highly conscious that his own actions reflect on Scotland's virtues as well as on his personal honor. He regards his decision to surrender as an act of humanity intended to save the lives of his troops, declaring that "it would but ill comport with the honour of Scotland, to let it be said, one of her gentlemen was outdone in civility, by a native of any other country on earth!" (152). During their meeting, Montcalm exposes his own lack of

civility when he claims to need a translator to negotiate with Munro and subsequently reveals that he has understood perfectly Heyward's and Munro's
conversation in English. More crucially, Montcalm demonstrates the empti-
ness of his reputation "for courage and enterprise" in his refusal, or inability,
to prevent the Iroquois' massacre of British soldiers, women, and children
following Munro's surrender (94). Although Montcalm maintains that courage "as strongly characterizes the hero" as humanity (153), his own cowardice
renders Munro's humanity toward his troops worthless.

Whereas Magua embodies savage masculinity and Montcalm represents
overcivilized effeminacy, Heyward and Uncas, as characters that unite prudence and compassion, fall somewhere between these two extremes, with
Heyward somewhat closer to Montcalm's refinement, and Uncas closer to
Magua's savagery. Magua and Uncas, the ignoble and noble savages, obviously
are foils; yet Uncas and Duncan, as their names suggest, are also doubles,
and they share a sympathetic bond that transcends their cultural differences.
This bond is formed during a skirmish with Magua's band of Iroquois, when
Heyward's "slight sword was snapped" and Uncas intervenes to save his life
(71). After the encounter, "the two young men exchange[d] looks of intelligence, which caused Duncan to forget the character and condition of his
wild associate" and to vow that he "never will require to be reminded of the
debt he owes" to Uncas (73). It is significant that Uncas saves Heyward's life
not through "bodily strength," of which Heyward possesses a good deal, but
rather "in the coolest and readiest manner" through the careful judgment
that Heyward markedly lacks (71, 73). Indeed, as Forrest G. Robinson and Ian
Dennis have noted, Heyward's imprudence makes him a less than competent
hero despite his chivalric ideals. During the first half of the novel, Heyward
falls asleep when he is meant to be keeping watch, attracts the Iroquois'
notice by firing his gun at inopportune moments, and rushes into battles
from which others must extricate him. When Alice playfully greets him as a
"recreant knight! he who abandons his damsels in the very lists!" she elicits
Heyward's "chagrin" because her mockery is perhaps a little too close to the
truth (149). But if Heyward is, as Robinson has described him, "a little thick,"
or somewhat lacking in the reasoned judgment and self-command that we
might expect of a hero, he is hardly, as Dennis would have him, a "criminally
inept" parody of one of the passive protagonists in Scott's Waverley novels.[54]

Unlike the eponymous hero of Scott's *Waverley* (an Englishman initially
enthralled by the primitive customs of Scottish Highlanders), Heyward does
not encounter savage society only to retreat thankfully to the safety of civilization. Instead, he recognizes the usefulness of Uncas's cautious self-control
in frontier warfare and begins to emulate it. His prudence is put to the test
when he determines to infiltrate an Iroquois camp in which Alice is imprisoned. As Heyward prepares for his mission, Leatherstocking warns him: "You
will have occasion for your best manhood, and for a sharper wit than what

is to be gathered in books, afore you outdo the cunning, or get the better of the courage of a Mingo! . . . remember, that to outwit the knaves it is lawful to practise things, that may not be naturally the gift of a white skin" (229). Chivalrous courtesy will get Heyward nowhere with the Iroquois, so he must fight fire with fire, by employing what Leatherstocking elsewhere calls "red gifts"[55]—sharp wit, prudence, and "presence of mind"—to find and free Alice (233). While Heyward, disguised as a traveling conjuror, is seeking clues to Alice's whereabouts, Uncas is chased into the camp by Iroquois warriors. Rather than jumping impulsively into the fray to save his friend, as he might have done previously, Heyward saves Uncas from a "fatal blow" by subtly sticking out his foot to trip up the most menacing of the Mohican's pursuers, thereby "precipitat[ing] the eager savage, headlong, many feet in advance of his intended victim" (238). In saving Uncas's life, Heyward does not simply repay his debt and prove his friendship; he also demonstrates his newfound ability to think on, and with, his feet.

Even as Heyward saves his life, then, Uncas becomes, in the novel's logic, an expendable character. Of course to many of Cooper's early readers, Uncas's race automatically would have rendered him disposable, even though the novel's title suggests that he is its most important character. But while Uncas's function in *The Last of the Mohicans* thus far has been to protect Heyward and the Munro sisters from the Iroquois' cunning attacks, Heyward becomes increasingly, although not entirely, capable of undertaking this task himself. Heyward has acquired his double's judgment and self-command, and in doing so he has checked his own tendencies toward overcivilized effeminacy. Despite Uncas's growing capacity for compassion, his death at the end of *The Last of the Mohicans* prevents him from cultivating this American masculinity, which consequently is identified exclusively with white settlers. Whereas Heyward demonstrates the ability of Scots to adapt to the hardships of frontier warfare while maintaining civilized values, the Mohicans' progressive refinement ends not in civilization, but in eradication. Significantly, it is Magua who deals Uncas's death blow. Scottish appropriation of the noble savage's skills renders the Mohicans superfluous, while the ignoble savage's violence ideologically justifies for Cooper the westward removal of Native American tribes that was occurring as he wrote.

While literary critics generally have agreed upon the centrality of masculinity to the construction of national identity in early nineteenth-century America, the character they most often identify as Cooper's model of a distinctively American masculinity is not Heyward but Leatherstocking, also known variously as Hawkeye and Natty Bumpo.[56] As a frontiersman, Leatherstocking has mastered the selective appropriation of Native American traits that Dana D. Nelson terms "playing Indian."[57] Leatherstocking not only speaks to the Mohicans in their own language, but he also shoots as sharply, listens as acutely, and endures suffering as patiently as do Uncas and his father, Chingachgook. At the same time, he displays "through the mask of his rude and nearly savage equipments, the brighter, though sunburnt and long-faded complexion of one who might claim descent from a European parentage" (28). Leatherstocking's identification with Mohican customs prevents him from reassimilating into the European settlements, but his aversion to racial mixture prevents him from integrating through marriage into the Mohicans' tribe. Leatherstocking's solitary self-sufficiency illustrates Nelson's claim that "playing Indian is often associated with claiming a notably isolated manly independence";[58] yet this is not the manliness that Cooper associates with an American identity defined by chivalric sentiment and savage fortitude. Although Leatherstocking possesses the self-control and presence of mind that Heyward must cultivate, he evidently cannot develop the heterosexual passion—or the reverence for women and feminine virtues—essential to chivalry. This indifference to female charms suits Leatherstocking for the hardships of frontier life so antithetical to domestic comforts, but it also unfits him for participating in the population and civilization of the American wilderness.

Leatherstocking's apparent incapacity for romantic love or heterosexual desire highlights women's reproductive importance to American nation formation while also revealing what Donald Davie has called the "murkiest most unsavoury element" in *The Last of the Mohicans*, Cooper's much-remarked-upon antipathy to miscegenation.[59] Leatherstocking, who proudly describes himself as a "man without a cross," or without the racial admixture that taints Cora, says skeptically: "I have heard that there is a feeling in youth, which binds man to woman, closer than the father is tied to the son. It may be so. I have seldom been where women of my colour dwell" (265). *The Last of the Mohicans* suggests that heterosexual desire cannot, or at least should not, cross racial boundaries, conceived of broadly in terms of light and dark, European and non-European, blood. Thus Cooper invites us to attribute Uncas's and Cora's mutual attraction to their dark blood, and Duncan's preference for Alice over Cora to Alice's pure Scottish parentage. If, for Cooper, like must attract like, then European newcomers cannot acquire the Native American traits necessary to successful settlement through interracial marriage. They can, however, acquire these traits through homosocial bonds like the friendships between Uncas and Duncan, and between Chingachgook and Leatherstocking; or through the paternal and filial love uniting Leatherstocking and Uncas. These bonds join like with like in gendered rather than racial terms and enable the transmission of traits through cultural appropriation rather than racial mixing. While Leatherstocking professes a complete incomprehension of heterosexual desire, he understands the tie between father and son, and cannot conceive of a stronger feeling than his paternal love for Uncas. When Magua kills Uncas, Leatherstocking and Chingachgook's friendship grows stronger through their shared grief: "Chingachgook grasped the hand that, in the warmth of feeling, the scout had stretched across the fresh earth, and in that attitude of friendship, these two sturdy and intrepid woodsmen bowed their heads together, while scalding tears fell to their feet, watering the grave of Uncas" (349).

Uncas's death reminds us that although friendships between men in *The Last of the Mohicans* certainly are not "entirely without social significance," as Nina Baym has claimed, they can produce no offspring.[60] While the process of cultural appropriation through which Leatherstocking and Heyward learn to play Indian is crucial to the formation of an American identity combining prudence and sympathy, it is not in itself sufficient to create an American people. However, Heyward demonstrates that homosocial and heterosexual bonds are not mutually exclusive. During his stint in the Iroquois camp, Heyward finds that, "in addition to the never-ceasing anxiety on account of Alice, a fresher, though feebler, interest in the fate of Uncas, assisted to chain him to the spot" (244). Heyward proves his newfound strength of mind in an attempt first and foremost to rescue Alice, but secondarily to help Uncas, the friend from whom he has learned caution and self-command. When Heyward plays Indian, he goes all out; but unlike Leatherstocking, he performs his part only for a short time and for the explicit purpose of rescuing a woman. Heyward's union of chivalrous sentiment and savage fortitude may be as short-lived and incomplete as his performance in the Iroquois camp, yet it is Heyward, rather than Leatherstocking, who advances America toward Cooper's masculine ideal, quite simply because the heterosexual desire informing the codes of chivalry means that Heyward will marry and reproduce, thereby assisting in the peopling of a new nation.

The Last of the Mohicans represents the work of American nation formation in gendered terms, assigning to men the task of cultural appropriation and to women that of racial reproduction. Similar to that in Scott's *Waverley*, the romance plot in *The Last of the Mohicans* compares the desirability of fair and dark heroines, with fair heroines representing passivity and domesticity, and dark ones representing an adventurousness that "chafe[s] against the bonds of decorum."[61] The dark heroines in both *Waverley* and *The Last of the Mohicans* are stronger and seemingly more capable of enduring adversity than their fair counterparts. Although in both cases the dark woman's self-sufficiency evokes the hero's ardent admiration, it fails to elicit the stirrings of a chivalrous desire to protect and cherish her. Such women arguably are too "savage"—too robust and resilient—to function as the heroines of chivalric romance. Thus Cora, with her Creole ancestry, is much better suited to surviving the trials of life in the American wilderness than her faint-hearted Scottish sister Alice, whose limbs are more or less useless when it comes to holding her upright. For instance, when Cora and Alice are captured by Magua, Cora demonstrates the "fortitude and undisturbed reason" that Heyward often lacks (82), while Alice turns to Cora "with infantile dependency" (108). Cora is a substitute protector whose native endurance enables her to support Alice throughout their travails in the wilderness, until Heyward is prepared to assume this task.

Cora's heroism wins the admiration of Magua, Uncas, and Heyward, yet insofar as Cooper invites us to trace her fortitude to her dark blood and its traces of savagery, Cora is not accountable for her virtues, which figure as a kind of perversion of normative gender traits. Alice, by comparison, has no distinguishing qualities other than her Scottish fairness, her appropriately womanly weakness, and her adoration of Heyward. She functions to evoke chivalric sentiment from Heyward and to provide him with occasions to test his judgment. Cooper acknowledges the possibility of marriage between Cora and Heyward only to reject it firmly as, if not entirely repugnant, then undesirable and unnecessary to the process of American nation formation. When Munro accuses Heyward of "scorn[ing] to mingle the blood of the Heywards, with one so degraded" as Cora, Heyward claims moral superiority to "a prejudice so unworthy of [his] reason," instead pleading Alice's sweetness and beauty as the cause of his lack of interest in her sister (159). Yet it is Cora's "degraded" blood that renders her too self-sufficient and even too masculine to be an object of Heyward's chivalric passion. Although marriage between Heyward and Cora might have symbolically effected the union of prudence and chivalry that Cooper valorizes, the marriage also would have tainted the racial purity of a formative American identity. Heyward's emulation of Uncas's virtues achieves the same purpose while avoiding racial admixture.

The Last of the Mohicans constructs a genealogy of American identity determined by cultural appropriation rather than by blood inheritance. This appropriative model of historical change and identity formation perhaps also illuminates Cooper's understanding of his own relationship to Walter Scott. The Leatherstocking Tales, Cooper suggests, do not emulate, and perhaps fall short of, the Waverley Novels; instead, they selectively borrow and diverge from their Scottish predecessors. Thus, in an 1831 letter to the editor of the *New Monthly*, Cooper objects to being called "the 'rival' of Sir Walter Scott." He declares: "Now the idea of rivalry with him never crossed my brain. I have always spoken, written and thought of Sir Walter Scott (as a writer) just as I should think and speak of Shakspeare—with high admiration of his talent, but with no silly reserve, as if I thought my own position rendered it necessary that I should use more delicacy than other men."[62] While acknowledging his influence, Cooper rejects the suggestion that he is peculiarly indebted to Scott. Moreover, by comparing Scott to Shakespeare rather than one of their esteemed contemporaries like Byron or Austen Cooper arguably relegates Scott to the literary past. Similarly, by writing Scots into his novels, Cooper represents both savagery and feudalism as stages through which America has passed, and Scott as an author for the Old World rather than the New.

Much as Cooper adapted Scott's plots, characters, and historiography to an American context, William Joseph Snelling challenged Cooper's insistence on the impossibility of interracial love by reworking the characters and plots of the Leatherstocking Novels. Snelling's "The Bois Brulé," the centerpiece of his collection, *Tales of the Northwest; or Sketches of Indian Life and Character* (1830), challenges Cooper's insistence on racial purity through its Scots-Indian protagonist William Gordon, whose father is Scottish and whose mother is Assinneboine. Snelling, who had spent seven years as a fur trader and interpreter at Fort Anthony in Minnesota before returning to his home in Boston to write, hoped his *Tales of the Northwest* would counter the misrepresentations of frontier life perpetuated by the "Indian tales, novels, etc. which teem from the press and circulating libraries."[63] Snelling's revision in "The Bois Brulé" of *The Last of the Mohican*'s representations of interconnected Scottish and Indian diasporas suggests that Cooper's novel may well have been one of the misleading "Indian tales" he had in mind.

"The Bois Brulé" is set between 1814 and 1820, when the land west of the Mississippi "was the scene of bitter contention and fierce strife, between two rival trading companies" (85), the Hudson's Bay Company and the Northwest Company. It describes the Scottish Earl of Selkirk's misguided attempt to establish a colony on the Red and Assiniboine rivers near the border between present-day Manitoba in Canada and North Dakota in the United States. Selkirk, who gained control of the Hudson's Bay Company in 1810, intended the agricultural settlement of Assiniboia—or as Snelling spells it, Ossinneboia—as a temporary refuge for fur traders in search of food and shelter, and a permanent refuge for Highlanders who had been forcibly evicted from their land. Selkirk peopled Assiniboia with Scottish emigrants like Duncan Cameron, who, in "The Bois Brulé," has been chose "to superintend [the] infant colony, and to instruct the new comers in the mysteries of husbandry" (97). Cameron's daughter, Flora (whose name of course recalls the Jacobite heroine of Scott's *Waverley*), has fallen in love with the Gordon, but her proud father predictably will not consent to their marriage. Cameron declares, "The blood of Lochiel and Sir Evan Dhu runs in my veins, and it shall not be contaminated with my consent. The boy is a good boy, and the Gordons are an ancient and noble race, but his mother is an insuperable objection" (94).

Snelling makes it clear from the beginning of the story that Cameron's prejudices against Gordon's "Indian blood" (91) are, if not positively ignorant, at least misguided. Gordon has been educated in Quebec, and like *The Last of the Mohican*'s Heyward, he is a model of chivalry. Unlike Heyward, however, Gordon is a perfect hero from the beginning of the narrative, and must only convince Cameron that he is worthy of Flora. He thus spends the story performing feat upon feat of derring-do, all of which demonstrate his courage and refined manners. For instance, while Gordon is hunting buffalo with the

Assinneboine, the hunters come across a lone woman, identified only as the "wife of Wawnhaton" who belongs to an enemy tribe. The hunters plan to kill the woman, but Gordon takes charge of her, explaining, "I do not wish to see her blood spilled. Have charity for her, my brethren. She is but a woman, and cannot hurt you" (114). Gordon's rescue of Wawnhaton's wife from his savage kinsmen indicates the depth of his capacity for romantic love and chivalric honor, and hence his worthiness of a white wife.

Like Cooper, however, Snelling suggests that most Indians are incapable of Gordon's refined feelings. When "a band of roving Yanktons" attacks the colony, wounding Cameron and carrying off Flora as their captive, Gordon seeks Wawnhaton's aid. While Wawnhaton is willing to repay Gordon's kind treatment of his wife by helping him to rescue Flora, he does not understand Gordon's love for the Scotswoman: "In the opinion of the Indian, a woman was but a kind of slave, or beast of burthen. He might prefer one to another on account of superior beauty or industry, or because she was the mother of his children; but he had no more conception of such love as Gordon's than the most abstruse problem in Euclid" (174). After Gordon rescues Flora, Cameron at last agrees to their marriage, and deeply repents having "listened to the voice of pride and vain glory rather than to natural affection" (183), and the Earl of Selkirk, who has been a supporter of Flora and Gordon's love from the first, congratulates Flora "on the gallantry and perseverance of her lover, who, he said, had fairly won her in the fashion of the days of chivalry" (185).

In Gordon and Flora's marriage, culture triumphs over race in a manner that Cooper might not have believed possible, as Flora seems to love Gordon every bit as much as he loves her. Gordon's very existence as one of "the off-spring of intermarriages of the white traders, and their subordinates, with Indian women" implies that there is no innate repulsion between Europeans and Indians, or at least between European *men* and Indian *women* (85). Even Snelling will not go so far as to suggest that a white woman could actively desire a full-blooded Indian man. Indeed, Flora does not learn of Gordon's mixed race until after he has proposed to her, even though Gordon wonders at her mistake, claiming, "I never sought to deceive: I thought my descent was as plainly stamped on my features as the mark on the brow of the first homicide" (91).

While Gordon and Flora's marriage suggests that interracial desire is possible, it does not hold out interracial marriage as the foundation of a viable American identity. For a start, Gordon differs from the general run of half-breeds, a dif-ference that the story invites us to attribute to his Scottish blood. The other half-breeds in "The Bois Brulé" are of French descent, and although they "are physically a fine race of men," "in manners and morals, they are on a par with the Indians" (85). When these half-breeds join the Yanktons in attacking Assiniboia, they "fully proved their claim to Indian birth. Their savage kinsmen could not have behaved with more barbarity" (166).

Gordon's Scottish blood raises him above these "bois brulé" or individuals of mixed French and Indian descent, endowing him with refined chivalry in place of their blunt savagery. That Flora and Gordon's marriage takes place against the general demise of Selkirk's colony further suggests that interracial marriage, for Snelling, holds no great promise for the regeneration of frontier life. Even before the Yanktons attacked the settlement of Ossinneboia, its crops had failed, and "everything wore the garb of poverty. The colonists were ragged, and their sunken faces and hollow eyes told a tale of dearth and distress" (147). Soon after the marriage, "Lord Selkirk returned to Scotland, and his colony died a natural death" (195). Flora and Gordon also go to Scotland at the command of Gordon's hitherto-neglectful father. In proving himself worthy of Flora's hand—and evidently of his Scottish father's recognition—Gordon effectively transcends his mixed blood, becoming an honorary Scot. The narrator informs us that Gordon, who had never before visited his father's country, "now resides on the banks of the Esk with his wife, and has a large family of sons and daughters" (195). While Alice and Heyward's union participates in the peopling of the United States, Snelling situates Flora and Gordon's happy and prosperous marriage in the Old World rather than the New.

In contrast to Johnson and Crèvecoeur, who, despite their differences, both represent Highland migrants as an immediately available national resource, "The Bois Brulé" and *The Last of the Mohicans* represent the intrepid and resourceful Scottish migrant as a figure belonging to the past. While the transatlantic myth of the adaptable and ambitious Scot persisted into the nineteenth century, it claimed to describe a figure that had existed several decades ago. To some extent, this is historically accurate: the more educated and prosperous Scots who had migrated to the colonies before the War of Independence were replaced in the nineteenth century by poorer and less skilled migrants, many of whom left their homes only because they could see no alternative.[64] Yet the early nineteenth-century literary relegation of the ambitious Scottish migrant to the United States' past also resembles the similar relegation of the Indians to whom Scots had so often been compared and with whom they had interacted so extensively on the western frontier. In exploring various forms of Scottish and Indian hybridity and interchangeability, Cooper's and Snelling's fictions reveal the racial origins of a frontier identity defined by chivalry and cunning, courtesy and prudence. By suggesting that this identity was historically situated—a stage along the way to commercial refinement—they render disposable the Scots and Indians from whom it was derived. The myth of the successful Scottish migrant thus offered an alternative genealogy of American identity to the Anglo-Saxon narratives that accompanied the Welsh migrations discussed in the following chapter.

Wales and the American West

In comparison to Ireland, Scotland, and England, Wales contributed relatively few people and resources to the settlement of British North America. Some historians have questioned the existence of a Welsh diaspora, arguing that for all intents and purposes, eighteenth- and early nineteenth-century "Welsh migration can be accounted part of the broader English movement. From similar backgrounds and leaving for similar reasons, Welsh migrants . . . went to America alongside thousands of their English contemporaries, and, apart from (in some cases) distinctive surnames, are largely indistinguishable from them."[1] Yet, Wales's cultural contribution to the Romantic-era lore of migration and settlement was disproportionately large. Wales offered British migrants the legend of Prince Madoc, who, in the twelfth century, left his home in war-torn Wales and sailed to the Gulf of Mexico, where his people subdued, and in some tellings, mixed with, native tribes. While the figure of Madoc has been traced to medieval Welsh poetry, the myth effectively entered history in late sixteenth-century works such as Richard Hakluyt's *Principall Navigations* (1589), which described Elizabethan efforts at colonial settlement in the New World.[2] Over time, the myth was shaped "by the ebb and flow of imperialism, trade rivalry, and colonial settlement" so that late eighteenth-century versions located Madoc's tribe in the Midwest, between the Mississippi and the Missouri rivers, where "all the rival imperialisms of the continent—American, British, Spanish, and the ghost of the French—were inexorably coming to a focus."[3] The Madoc myth thus figured significantly among the narratives of origins that legitimated the United States' westward expansion during the 1790s.

The resurgence of the Madoc myth at the end of the eighteenth century coincided with the first major wave of westward migration into the Ohio Valley. Frontiersmen claimed to have seen Madoc's descendants, often referred to as Welsh Indians because of their supposed intermingling with Native American tribes, in the regions that would become Kentucky, Tennessee, and Ohio. Accounts of the Welsh Indians appeared in a diverse

range of late eighteenth- and early nineteenth-century works on both sides
of the Atlantic, from John Filson's *Discovery, Settlement and Present State of
Kentucke* (1784) in the United States, to Robert Southey's epic *Madoc* (1805)
in Britain. A series of essays that appeared in the *Gentleman's Magazine* in
1791 offers a standard account of the Welsh Indians assembled from numerous sources, describing them as fair-skinned and red-haired, as speaking a
pure, and thus to eighteenth-century Welshmen, a largely incomprehensible,
version of Welsh, and as retaining some vestiges of primitive Christianity.
These "insulated Cambrians" had inhabited the southeast coast of North
America until "about one hundred and thirty years ago," when they began
to move "into such interior parts" of the continent "as were unpossessed by
the natives, as the European Colonists spread over the maritime countries."[4]
The Gentleman's Magazine situates Madoc's descendants culturally between
American Indians and European colonizers, neither savage nor civilized,
natives nor newcomers. Geographically, the Welsh Indians were less easy to
locate. By the end of the eighteenth century, their discovery had become "a
minor industry," with at least thirteen real tribes and five imaginary ones
identified as Madoc's descendants.[5]

My aim in this chapter is not to prove or disprove the authenticity of
the supposed twelfth-century Welsh migration to North America, a task
that has been undertaken by historians including Richard Deacon, Samuel
Eliot Morison, and Gwyn A. Williams, among others.[6] I agree with
Williams, whose book-length study of the Madoc myth is perhaps the most
even-handed, that "any story of Madoc *as a discoverer of America* was and is,
in itself, essentially *precarious*."[7] Given that this is the case, I will examine
why the Madoc myth might have flourished at the end of the eighteenth
century and what purposes it might have served for three groups of people
who shared claims to a British identity: the Welsh, the English, and the
Anglo-American inhabitants of the newly formed United States. Welsh,
English, and American writers incorporated the myth into genres ranging
from lyric poetry to the epic and the novel. These generic adaptations, along
with the new cultural contexts into which they introduced the myth, transformed its significance. In the lyric poetry of Iolo Morganwg, self-appointed
Welsh bard, the myth offered the Welsh the prospect of an American homeland during a period of economic depression and cultural revival in Wales.
Robert Southey's epic, *Madoc*, enlarged the claims of Iolo's bardic songs by
using the myth to claim the initial discovery of the Americas for Britain and
to suggest that the English held a continued interest in American settlement
even following the loss of their colonies. For Americans, the myth legitimated westward expansion and the forced migration of native populations
that this expansion caused by providing British racial origins for American
republicanism. Its incidental appearance in English and American novels
perhaps indicates the normalization of this myth, as it ceases to require

the commentary that typically surrounds it in periodical essays and topographical surveys.

The British identity to which the Madoc myth allowed Welsh, English, and
Anglo-Americans to lay claim was itself a mythical one. Wales had long been
regarded as the bastion of an original British identity because it was to the
mountainous regions of Wales that the ancient Britons—the original settlers
of the British Isles—had fled for refuge during the first-century Roman conquest of England.[8] These Britons were believed to have remained a pure and
distinct people over the centuries, preserving ancient British liberties and
virtues along with their British blood, while those who had stayed in England
were debased by mixing first with their Roman, and later their Anglo-Saxon
and Norman conquerors. The Welsh Britons not only resisted racial inter-
mixture, but also the impositions of the Roman church, practicing a primitive but supposedly indigenous form of Christianity. Myth meets history with
the death of the Welsh king Owen Gwynned around 1170, resulting in a civil
war that eventually left Wales vulnerable to English conquest under Edward
I in 1282.

Whereas Nicholas Canny has described Ireland as England's earliest colony, R. R. Davies and Richard Wyn Jones have made a strong case for Wales.[9]
Between the Edwardian conquest and the Anglo-Welsh Union of 1536, Wales
exhibited "the most well recognized features of a colonial society" including
"the settlement of colonists . . . on land which had been subject to what is now
known as ethnic cleansing . . . the imposition of a legal system . . . that dis-
criminated systematically in favor of the settler population; [and] the attempt
to 'civilize the Welsh' by bringing them 'into the mainstream of the moral practices of Western Christendom on such issues as marriage and legitimacy.'"[10]
The Anglo-Welsh Union brokered by Henry VIII did not entirely overturn
these practices, but it did allow the Welsh to play a greater role in their own
government and to assert a shared identity with their colonizers. The Tudor
monarchs' Welsh blood permitted Henry VIII to represent the Union as a
reunification of a single race that had been separated over time, an affirmation
of the English and Welsh peoples' shared origins as ancient Britons.[11] Peter
Roberts explains that Tudor "invocations of the British identity of the Welsh
worked towards cementing Anglo-Welsh bonds" so that "Wales and Welsh
identity emerged from the imperial programme of the Tudors strengthened
rather than undermined."[12] It was perhaps because Tudor imperialism was
less oppressive in Wales than Ireland that, by the eighteenth century, Wales
figured, in Philip Schwyzer's words as "the good child" of the British state
in contrast to the "rebellious prodigals, Ireland and Scotland."[13] The relative
longevity and stability of Anglo-Welsh union explains why the Madoc myth
was vulnerable to English appropriation in a way that Scottish and Irish legends of Ossian would not have been. Moreover, the fact that Wales had been
absorbed into the institutional framework of England since the thirteenth

century meant that its history as an autonomous entity was, by comparison with Ireland and Scotland, relatively obscure and open to fabrication not just by the English but by the Welsh themselves.

Madoc at Home

Despite the relative harmony of Anglo-Welsh relations, late eighteenth-century Welsh literature registered anxieties about the encroachments of both industrial capitalism and metropolitan English manners and mores on traditional Welsh agricultural communities. During the latter half of the century, the export of copper, brass, tinplate, and iron to Britain's colonies contributed to increasing land enclosure, rackrenting, and emigration. These transformations inspired new forms of nationalism as Welshmen of the middle and upper classes sought to preserve the language, literature, history, and traditions that seemed in danger of disappearing. London-Welsh societies including the Cymmrodorion and the Gwyneddigion revived traditions associated with bards and Druids such as the *eisteddfod*, a festival of music and poetry.[14] Poetry, the medium through which traditional lore had been passed down by the bards, and antiquarian histories were among the primary genres of cultural nationalism in Wales.

As demonstrated by the writings of the antiquarian, poet, and stonemason Edward Williams, better known by his bardic name, Iolo Morganwg, late eighteenth-century Welsh versions of the Madoc myth tended to be reactionary. Iolo and other Welsh nationalists responded to the demise of traditional ways of life in Wales by envisioning an already existing Welsh community in North America in which ancient British virtues and post-Revolutionary American liberties might be united. Iolo's own sense of Welsh identity was informed by his Unitarianism, his involvement with the Gwyneddigion society, his friendships with radical thinkers like Richard Price and William Godwin, and his exclusion from the inner circles of London's Anglocentric literary establishment.[15] Scathingly critical both of William Pitt's repressive government and of metropolitan English culture, Iolo looked to the relatively unsettled American Midwest as a place where he might establish a traditional Welsh society free from these pernicious influences. Iolo participated in the Gwyneddigion society's efforts to recruit funds and volunteers to find the Welsh Indians, and hoped to accompany his countryman John Evans in his explorations up the Missouri River.

In 1792, as part of these efforts, Iolo drafted a paper for the Royal and Antiquarian Societies titled "Some account of an Ancient Welsh colony in America." It argued that seeking out the Welsh Indians and possibly sending out a "hundred well-disposed *Welshmen*" to join them "would open a resource of considerable wealth to the nation, would be the means of greatly extending the inland trade of *America* and take off our hands very great quantities of *British Manufactures*. It would enable us to establish very strong posts in the heart of that Continent which, being done with caution and with a view to National Good rather than the enriching of individuals, would soon be a blessing to the Natives and be a means of protecting them against their savage neighbours."[16] Iolo was writing here primarily for an English audience, so it makes sense that he would emphasize a Welsh colony's potential economic benefits for Great Britain. However, he also hoped to restore to the small but steady stream of artisans, farmers, and industrial workers who migrated from Wales into upstate New York, Pennsylvania, and the Ohio Valley during the 1790s "a congenial nation" of their own in the United States.[17]

Iolo pursued this vision of a Welsh homeland on the western frontier in his two-volume collection of *Poems, Lyric and Pastoral* (1794). The *Poems'* extensive subscription list suggests that it was intended for English and Welsh readerships, a breadth that might explain what Mary-Ann Constantine describes as the collection's "conflict of voices."[18] Iolo in some verses adopts the voice of "a Shenstonian poet of nature" and in others the pose of "a full-blown British bard."[19] In the former pastoral guise, he associates Wales with moral purity and autonomy, the rational pleasures of rural life, and the process of poetic creation. Thus the speaker in "Banks of the Daw" represents the "thickets romantic, irregular meads" and "order fantastic" of "nature's gay plan" as the inspiration for his verse. He compares himself to the "sweet *British Blackbird*" that sings outside his cottage, and contrasts this homely bird's simple song to the "*parrot* pedantic" and "learned *macaw*" that might be found in the London homes of the wealthy.[20] In his role as bard, by contrast, Iolo celebrated a heroic Welsh past "when Nature's rural reign / With Freedom bless'd the British swain" (2: 5) and when bards encouraged their listeners to use this freedom wisely by offering them "glorious deeds divinely sung" (2: 6). The speaker in "Ode to the British Muse" provides a heavily annotated account of some of the most famous of Wales's "Bards of high renown" (2: 3); and, in doing so, he participates in and perpetuates bardic tradition, fulfilling his own prophecy that the "British Muse" will "return again," and "Assume once more, [its] glorious strain" (2: 9). As these examples suggest, the Wales of *Poems, Lyric and Pastoral* is highly romanticized. It is inhabited in some verses by bucolic shepherds, sighing lovers, and industrious, contented farmers, and in others by venerable bards and ancient British heroes. It displays none of the ills—poverty, political oppression, Anglicization—that Iolo mentions in his correspondence and that spurred his hopes of emigrating to United States in search of Madoc's descendants.[21]

In his "Address to the Inhabitants of Wales, Exhorting them to Emigrate with William Penn, to Pennsylvania," Iolo encourages his countrymen to leave Wales for the western frontier by suggesting that there, "amid the desert wild," a community of "long-lost brethren," a "free-born race, of manners mild," awaits Welsh emigrants (2: 67). By situating the increased Welsh migration of the mid-1790s in a tradition reaching back to Madoc's twelfth-century voyage, this poem figures late eighteenth-century emigration as kind of a return to a homeland and a means of recovering the ancient liberties and traditions of which centuries of English rule have deprived the Welsh. The "Address" invokes Madoc's migration as a precedent for William Penn's: whereas Madoc sought to escape the tyrannical rule of his brother David, Penn aimed to escape religious persecution under the Stuart monarchs, who, as Iolo explains in a footnote, not only attempted to impose Anglican religious practices and doctrines on the Quakers, but also "to force the *English language* on the *Welsh*" (2: 55). Both Madoc and Penn "from the tumults of a Crown, / Sought shelter in a *world unknown*" (2: 65); and, by implication, both provide a precedent for the late eighteenth-century migration that Iolo sought to encourage. The headnote to the "Address" informs us that it was "Written at Sea by an Anonymous Emigrant" in Penn's company, and has been translated from Welsh into English. Yet, when the anonymous emigrant exhorts "Ye, sprung from BRITAIN'S ancient race" to heed the calls of conscience and to eschew the "Tyranny, [that] with shameless face, / Enslaves your native plains," he addresses Iolo's late eighteenth-century readers as much as his purported audience of seventeenth-century Quakers. The "tyranny" in question might refer to Pitt's government as much as Charles II's, and the "enslavement" of Wales to industrial capitalism as much as to the feudal power of an Anglicized gentry and aristocracy. Iolo suggests that although lacking a Madoc or a Penn to lead them forth, late eighteenth-century Welsh emigrants, like their predecessors, seek to escape "a guiltless land involv'd in grief" (2: 50).

The speaker of the "Address" looks forward to joining the "Old *British* tribes" of Madoc's descendents that he believes are still to be found in the American wilderness. He regards his emigration as a kind of homecoming, and takes pains to point out that the Quakers are not guilty of re-enacting England's colonial rule of Wales on American soil. The land in "these far-sequester'd climes" belongs to the Welsh by right of Madoc's prior exploration and settlement (2: 63). Accordingly, the speaker can argue that Penn "from no native of the land / By conquest wrench'd with murd'ring hand"; instead, the emigrants "fairly claim our own" (2: 63). Yet the speaker imagines mingling with his "long-lost brethren" not as an equal, but rather as a teacher before his students or a clergyman among his flock:

> I'll teach them all the truth I know,
> To them extol the lively glow
> Of soul-refining grace;
> And heedless there of worldly gains,
> Will glide through life with these remains

Of BRITAIN'S injured race. (2: 68)

In a footnote to an earlier poem, "Ode to the British Muse," Iolo explains that the Welsh word for poet, *Prydydd*, means "embellisher, regulator, reformer or polisher" and that the "original intention of the bardic institution was to promote civilization" (2: 5). The speaker's plans to impart religious truths to the Welsh Indians thus reflect his bardic aspirations. He hopes to refine and polish the Welsh Indians spiritually even he while adapts materially to their primitive ways.

Together the Quaker settlers and the Welsh Indians will re-create in America the traditional Welsh ways of life that in Iolo's own time were disappearing. The speaker describes "Pennsylvania's happy groves" (2: 60) in language that Iolo uses elsewhere in *Poems, Pastoral and Lyric* to describe rural Wales:

> Here far extends the lib'ral soil,
> That, grateful to the Planter's toil,
> Waves wide with golden wheat;
> In slav'ry doom'd no more to pine,
> Beneath his own luxuriant vine
> Each rears a peaceful seat.
>
> With flocks and herds in verdant meads,
> A Patriarch's life he calmly leads,
> Blest with primeval health;
> Feels Virtue's ardour in his breast,
> Talks with Content, that lovely guest,
> And craves no greater wealth. (2: 61)

In the American West, the settlers will enjoy the pastoral simplicity that Iolo ascribes to Wales but will be independent, republican landowners rather than the "slaves" of either feudal lords or an oppressive government. The "Address" urges its Welsh readers to end their "tranquil days" in the land where "*Madoc*'s offspring still abides" and "Penn presides" (2: 69), envisioning a centuries-old homeland that awaits these migrants.

Sarah Prescott has argued that the late eighteenth-century novel failed as a vehicle for the expression of a Welsh identity both because the novel was an English genre and because, in the age of sensibility, it tended to celebrate passive feeling rather than the heroic courage celebrated by Welsh nationalists as characteristic of their people.[22] Novels like Charlotte Smith's *Emmeline; The Orphan of the Castle* (1788) and Elizabeth Gunning's *Orphans of Snowdon* (1796) responded obliquely to the transformation or eradication of traditional Welsh ways of life by representing an idealized pastoral Wales where beleaguered virtue might find refuge from the vices of metropolitan England. However, as Frances Jacson's allusions to the Madoc myth in *Disobedience* (1797) illustrate, novelists did occasionally borrow the myths and legends informing the "bardic nationalism" of Welsh poets and antiquarians.[23] *Disobedience* begins in rural Wales, where William, the virtuous and hard-working son of a Welsh farmer, falls in love with and marries Mary, an aristocratic but equally virtuous English heiress who, owing to her parents' neglect, has been raised by Welsh peasants. England's rigid hierarchies and corrupt mores cannot accommodate the unconventional marriage of an heiress and a farmer; and the depredations of their Anglo-Welsh landlord impede the couple's prosperity in Wales.[24] So William and Mary emigrate to Kentucky, which the novel describes in purple prose as "a land where there are no overgrown estates, with rich and ambitious landlords, to have undue and pernicious influence over the actions of their fellow-creatures. . . . a land which is *every* body's country. . . . Where men possess the land they cultivate and where human nature has regained its ancient dignity."[25] *Disobedience* contrasts this egalitarian Welsh-American community to the artificial distinctions and fashionable vices of metropolitan England on one hand and to the poverty of a politically and economically disempowered Wales on the other. William and Mary name their Kentucky farm after William's native Welsh valley and enjoy there all of the "simplicity, frugality, order, industry, and virtue" that they associate with Wales.[26] Only after they have begun to prosper in their new home do they learn that Kentucky "had once been inhabited by people further advanced in the arts of civilized life than are any tribe of Indians yet known; and . . . that those people were Welch [*sic*]."[27] The remnants of an earlier Welsh civilization legitimate their decision to settle in Kentucky, suggesting that their virtuous and harmonious community is less an innovation than a restoration of traditional Welsh ways of life.

Welsh-identified uses of the Madoc myth did not always imply revolutionary or republican sympathies, nor were they entirely celebratory. In contrast to Iolo's optimistic account of Welsh emigration in *Poems, Lyric and Pastoral*, Felicia Hemans's representation of Madoc's voyage in *Welsh Melodies* (1821) is elegiac, eulogizing the martial valor and heroic chivalry of a distant national past. Hemans is best known for the English patriotism of poems such as "The Homes of England," "England and Spain, or Valour and Patriotism," and "England's Dead," but her *Welsh Melodies* helped to popularize a romanticized version of Welsh culture and history. The collection of poems won her acclaim as a "poet for Wales" and membership in the Cymmrodorion Society.[28] Fittingly, given Hemans's own adoption of Wales, *Welsh Melodies* imagines a Welsh identity that is "spiritual and aesthetic rather than ethnic" or geographic;[29] and in the volume's two poems of exile, "Prince Madoc's Farewell" and "The Cambrian in America," the speaker's physical separation from Wales only affirms his spiritual connection to it.

"Like Iolo's "Address," Hemans's "Prince Madoc's Farewell" and "The Cambrian in America" establish an implicit comparison between Madoc's voyage to North America and later Welsh migrations. But in contrast to Iolo's adventurous Quaker, and perhaps more like the stream of Welsh migrants that steadily trickled away to the United States during the nineteenth century, Hemans's Madoc remains fixated on the land he leaves behind. "Prince Madoc's Farewell" lauds Madoc's courage in setting out for unknown lands by emphasizing his desire to remain in Wales. As he sets sail, his gaze lingers on the Welsh mountains and he laments, "Too fair is the sight for a wand'rer, whose way / Lies far o'er the measureless worlds of the deep!"[30] It his love of Wales, "Where the harp's lofty soul on each wild wind is borne," and his fidelity to his ancestors' virtues, that inspires his journey to seek out new worlds.[31] Madoc becomes a worthy successor to his ancestors' heroism by leaving his homeland:

> 'Tis not for the land of my sires, to give birth
> Unto bosoms that shrink when their trial is nigh;
> Away! we will bear over ocean and earth
> A name and a spirit that never shall die.
> My course to the winds, to the stars,
> I resign; But my soul's quenchless fire,
> O my country! is thine.[32]

Madoc's expansionist injunction rests uneasily beside his sentimental attachment to Wales, an attachment that is echoed by the speaker of "The Cambrian in America." Even while the nameless Cambrian wanders across the "green savannas," through the "eternal forests," and along the "boundless lakes" of North America, his mind dwells on "wild Cambria!"[33] Unlike Iolo's robust Quaker emigrant, who confidently predicts ending his days in a prosperous and tranquil community in America, Hemans's Cambrian seems to be an isolated wanderer in the wilderness, exiled geographically and spiritually from his home. Whereas Iolo displaces Welsh patriotism in space, imagining an American homeland for Welsh emigrants in which they can recreate traditional ways of life, *Welsh Melodies* displaces it across time, rendering nostalgia for a spiritually and culturally integral Welsh past compatible with allegiance to a British present. A heroic and independent Wales is, in Hemans's poems, always in the past, and never a future possibility. If, as Nanora Sweet has argued, Hemans often represented early nineteenth-century "Britain's empire less as glorious military expansion than as a dispersion of exiles into a new world with its abundance of watery graves," the valiant but doomed deeds of Madoc and other ancient Welsh heroes celebrated in the *Welsh Melodies* prefigure the sorrows of this later empire.[34]

For Hemans, the Madoc myth gave voice to a sentimental Welsh patriotism that was compatible with political allegiance to the British state. For Iolo, it permitted the imagining of Welsh resistance to, or at least escape from, eighteenth-century England's political and cultural hegemony. It offered an instance of historic Welsh heroism that set a precedent for late eighteenth- and early nineteenth-century Welsh emigration; and its poetic retellings preserved, in modified form, the Welsh traditions that both Iolo and Hemans feared were disappearing. Ironically, the Madoc myth simultaneously allowed the English to assert their political and cultural authority over Wales and to declare their imperial right to the contested regions west of the Mississippi in a context where the notion of "right" depended upon claims to first discovery.

Even after the United States had achieved political independence, Britain remained invested in westward expansion, competing with the United States, Spain, France, and native tribes for land and goods. As Robert Southey's *Madoc* demonstrates, by declaring their shared British ancestry with, and their long-standing governance of, the Welsh, the English could use the Madoc myth to lay claim to the settlement of the New World 300 years before Columbus's voyage, and thus could assert their "original" right to the American West. In employing the Madoc myth to claim Britain's continuing stake in the settlement of the Ohio Valley, Southey establishes a geographic and ideological equivalence between Wales and the western frontier as primitive regions offering an escape from political oppression, but, somewhat paradoxically, only if they could first be brought under civilized colonial rule.

Imperial Madoc

Whereas Iolo Morganwg used the Madoc myth to protest against English government of Wales and to imagine a Welsh homeland in North America where traditional ways of life could be rescued from the pressures of industrialization and land enclosure, Southey's epic poem, *Madoc*, shows how the Madoc myth just as easily could serve the ideological interests of Anglo-British imperial expansion. Critics have only recently begun to examine the importance of Welsh literature and culture to English Romanticism, and *Madoc* is one of the clearest illustrations of the racial and religious implications that Wales carried for English Romantic writers.[35] *Madoc*'s account of the twelfth-century British discovery of North America illustrates Gerard Carruthers and Alan Rawes's claims that in "English writing of the Romantic period, the Celtic is simultaneously reinvented for, reappropriated by, and yet excluded from, the historical and political British present."[36] Southey began composing *Madoc* in 1795 when he was trying to raise money for his own emigration scheme.[37] Similar to Iolo, whom he consulted on questions concerning Welsh history and traditions, Southey hoped to escape Pitt's efforts to contain political radicalism in Britain by emigrating to the United States.[38] He planned to settle with Samuel Taylor Coleridge and about a dozen of their friends and family members on the banks of the Susquehanna River near the Alleghenies, which were at that time the main gateway to the Ohio Valley. There, the group would establish a Pantisocracy, an agrarian cooperative in which property, manual labor, and the responsibilities of government would be shared equally, leaving the settlers plenty of time for intellectual pursuits.[39] However, after contemplating the difficulties of clearing the American wilderness with the far from hardy Coleridge, Southey became skeptical of the scheme and suggested that they instead establish the Pantisocracy in Caernarfonshire or Merionethshire. Southey had been favorably impressed with these regions during a Welsh walking tour in 1794 and, as Lynda Pratt has argued, seems to have considered them beyond "the reactionary politics of a benighted England."[40] Wales, in Southey's mind, was a more civilized and less distant version of the American West. Although plans for the Pantisocracy eventually deteriorated, the project informed Southey's representation of Madoc's American settlement in the poem that he finally published in 1805. Nigel Leask observes that "Pantisocracy was a *colonial* as well as a radical-democratic enterprise";[41] and similarly, *Madoc*'s harmonious Welsh-Indian agrarian community is also a colony built upon military and ideological coercion.

An epic poem conventionally recounts the founding of a nation, but it might be more accurate to say that Southey's *Madoc* relates the origins of British colonial exploration.[42] Like other versions of the myth, it recounts Madoc's voyage to the Gulf of Mexico to escape civil strife in Wales and his founding of a settlement in the Mississippi basin. There, Madoc and his men free the gentle Hoamen Indians—an imaginary tribe based partially on Southey's reading of Hernando Cortes's description of the Totonacs—from the coercive rule of the Aztecs, who demand Hoamen children for ritual sacrifice.[43] A few of the Hoamen resent the interference of the Welsh newcomers, and during Madoc's return to Wales to recruit additional settlers they form an alliance with some of the Aztec leaders, who seek to re-establish their rule over the Hoamen. Upon his return with the new Welsh recruits, Madoc re-defeats the Aztecs and exerts a firmer rule over the Hoamen by requiring them to convert to Christianity.

While Iolo's "Address" finds similarities among historically distinct Welsh migrations, *Madoc* establishes differences among various forms of colonial rule—England's conquest of Wales, the Aztecs' subjection of the Hoamen, and, finally, the Welsh governance of the Hoamen. But *Madoc* rests on a temporal split that complicates these comparisons. At the time that the action of its story occurs, around 1170, Wales had not yet been conquered by England; yet the poem continually reminds readers of events subsequent to Madoc's voyage, including the English conquest of Wales in 1282 and the Anglo-Welsh Union of 1536. Southey's allusions to these events allow him to claim Madoc's deeds for England twice—first, through the shared British origins of the Welsh and the English (notably, Southey consistently refers to Madoc as British rather than as Welsh), and second, through England's thirteenth-century conquest of Wales. Where Lynda Pratt finds Southey using Welsh heroism to criticize England's aggressive colonial expansion,[44] I see him claiming Welsh heroism on behalf of Anglo-British colonialism.

Madoc differentiates between the Hoamen, as noble savages, and the Aztecs, as unmitigatedly cruel savages, while also establishing analogies between the Welsh and the Hoamen, both of whom internal dissension renders vulnerable to conquest. In contrast to the bloodthirsty Aztecs, who engage in human sacrifice and cannibalism, the Hoamen are at once innocent and steadfastly courageous. Madoc relates that upon the Hoamen's first encounter with the Britons,

> fearless, sure, they were
> And while they eyed us, grasped their spears, as if,
> Like Britain's injured but unconquered sons,
> They, too, had known how perilous it was
> To see an armed stranger set his foot
> In their free country.[45]

The reference to "Britain's injured but unconquered sons" invites a comparison between the Hoamen and the ancient Britons who had fled into Wales during the Roman conquest, when armed strangers entered their own country. It also reminds readers of what Madoc, in the context of the poem, could not have known—that within a century these "unconquered sons" would be subdued by Anglo-Saxon soldiers.

The Aztecs' violent subjugation of the Hoamen resembles the tyranny Madoc finds upon his return home to Wales, where his brother David has assumed the throne. David has ended several years of civil strife by killing one of his brothers, imprisoning another, exiling a third, and cementing through marriage an alliance with the Anglo-Saxon Plantagenets. Lamenting that "From ourselves / The desolation and the ruin come," Madoc questions, "The House that is divided in itself, / How shall it stand?" (I.IX.79, 83). Although he is speaking of the Welsh, Madoc's words might apply to the Hoamen, whom he finds divided amongst themselves over questions of leadership upon his return to the colony. Both the Welsh and the Hoamen are internally divided peoples whose rifts render them vulnerable to conquest from without—whether by Anglo-Saxons or Aztecs.

At the same time that the poem emphasizes similarities between the Welsh and the Hoamen as conquered peoples, it strongly distinguishes Aztec from Welsh government of the Hoamen. The Welsh resemble the Aztecs to the extent that they establish authority over the Hoamen, but the similarities end there. Upon his arrival in the New World, Madoc declares his hopes that the Welsh might coexist peacefully with the region's indigenous tribes:

> I come not from my native isle
> To wage the war of conquest, to cast out
> Your people from the land which time and toil
> Have rightly made their own. The World is wide:
> There is enough for all. (I.VIII.51–55)

Madoc acknowledges that the natives' right to the land is based in their prior occupation and cultivation of the soil. He subsequently compares the Aztec's tyranny over the Hoamen with the Welsh conquest of the Aztecs, which restores the peaceable Hoamen to "The land of their forefathers" (II.XXII.30–31). He explains that the Aztecs came "Strangers as we, but not like us, in peace" (II.XXIV.103):

> They conquered and destroyed. A tyrant race
> Bloody and faithless, to the hills they drove
> The unoffending children of the vale,
> And, day by day, in cruel sacrifice
> Consumed them. God hath sent the Avengers here!
> Powerful to save we come, and to destroy,
> When Mercy on Destruction calls for aid. (II.XXIV.104–110)

In distinguishing violent Aztec conquest from merciful Welsh restitution, *Madoc* also implies a parallel between Aztec rule over the Hoamen and Anglo-Saxon subjugation of the Welsh.

The similarities between the Aztecs and Anglo-Saxons suggest that the latter are less civilized and less fit to rule than the Welsh people whom they conquered. Both Aztecs and Anglo-Saxons sacrifice the weaker members of society in order to cement their power, and both lack fitting reverence for the dead. Hoamen children are routinely sacrificed in the Aztecs' religious rituals. Emma, the Plantagenet princess, is metaphorically sacrificed when she is forced to become the wife of the brutal David in order to consolidate Anglo-Saxon rule in Wales. She is

> a sacrifice
> To that sad king-craft, which, in marriage vows
> Linking two hearts, unknowing each of each,
> Perverts the ordinance of God,
> And makes the holiest tie a mockery and a curse. (I. IX.54–58)

The Aztecs' lack of respect for the dead also recalls the irreverence of David and his Anglo-Saxon allies. The Aztecs insult Erillyab, Queen of the Hoamen, by leaving her husband unburied, his body "by devilish art / Preserved," after they kill him (I.VI.250–251). Similarly, David's men plan to desecrate the grave of the former Welsh king, Owen Gwynned. Madoc, catching word of the plan, disinters his "father's bones" and carries them to the New World so that they might find a "resting place" where Madoc's own "one day / May moulder by their side" (I.XV.252–254). The Aztecs and Anglo-Saxons are marked as savage by their shared lack of respect for the dead and of consideration for the disempowered—whether Hoamen or women.

Elisa E. Beshero-Bondar has argued that *Madoc*'s contrast between Aztec cruelty and Welsh mercy towards the conquered Hoamen invites a comparison between Spain's exploitative and violent colonial practices and early nineteenth-century Britain's self-proclaimed imperial benevolence.[46] But if this is so, then Southey traces British benevolence to the ancient Britons, or the Welsh, rather than to the cruel Anglo-Saxons. Indeed, he perhaps offers Madoc's conquest through conversion and assimilation as a model for nineteenth-century Anglo-British imperial practice. Before Madoc first assails the Aztecs, the blind bard Cadwallon advises him to win their respect and loyalty with a combination of courage and kindness:

> Be in the battle terrible, but spare
> The fallen, and follow not the flying foe;
> Then may ye win a nobler victory,
> So dealing with the captives as to fill
> Their hearts with wonder, gratitude, and awe,
> That love shall mingle with their fear, and fear
> Stablish the love, else wavering: let them see,
> That as more pure and gentle is your faith,
> Yourselves are gentler, purer. (I.VII.60–67)

As it turns out, love is not enough to win over the Aztecs. When the Aztecs foment rebellion among the Hoamen, Madoc realizes that he must exert his authority more strongly and appeals to Christianity to legitimate Welsh rule. It's unclear whether military might or the convenient eruption of a nearby volcano accounts for the Welsh defeat of the Aztecs. Madoc attributes their victory to "a trust / In more than mortal strength . . . a faith in God" (I.VI.185–186). After re-establishing Welsh rule over the Aztecs and Hoamen through force, Madoc justifies it with faith, urging Queen Erillyab,

> here let us hold united reign,
> O'er our united people; by one faith,
> One interest bound, and closer to be linked
> By laws and language, and domestic ties,
> Till both become one race, for ever more
> Indissolubly knit. (II.XXIV 29–34)

Madoc suggests that a shared Christian faith will enable other forms of integration—political, linguistic, cultural, and racial. Southey represents the conversion of the Hoamen and Aztecs as a benevolent conquest, or even a political union of sorts, suggesting that colonialism is justified when it includes a missionary component. Madoc and Erillyab will hold "united reign," although it is clear that Erillyab's rule will be largely symbolic when she replies to Madoc:

> Dear friend, and brother dear! Enough for me
> Beneath the shadow of thy shield to dwell,
> And see my people, by thy fostering care,
> Made worthy of their fortune. (II.XXIV.38–41)

The integration of the Welsh with the native tribes is furthered by the betrothal of Madoc's sister Goervyl to Malinal, one of the Aztecs who remained loyal to Madoc. In contrast to the sacrificial marriage of Emma to David, the union between Goervyl and Malinal is founded in mutual affection. We are invited to assume that the descendants of such intermarriages will become the Welsh Indians of the late eighteenth-century accounts with which Southey was familiar. While the Welsh and the Hoamen prepare to enjoy the fruits of their fertile and harmonious agrarian community, most of the defeated Aztecs choose to set forth into the wilderness rather than submit to Welsh rule. In their westward migration, they ultimately resemble Madoc and his compatriots who similarly chose to sail westward for unknown lands rather than endure colonial rule at home.

The colonial implications of Southey's *Madoc* are undeniably complicated.[47] But the most important of these implications for my purposes is that the poem allows Britain to lay claim, through Wales, to a pre-Columbian discovery of North America, and more particularly, to the Ohio Valley, at a time when this valuable land was at the center of a competition among imperial powers. By figuring England's conquest of Wales as the political formalization of ancient ties between the English and the Welsh, Southey effectively undercuts any independent Welsh claim to this land, like the one that Iolo made in his "Address." Thanks to their shared British blood, and to England's colonial authority, whatever belongs to Wales also belongs to England. If, in Iolo's "Address," the Welsh are simultaneously colonizers abroad and colonized at home, the divided temporality of Southey's poem negates this simultaneity. In place of the empty homogeneous time that Benedict Anderson ascribes to the nation as imagined community, Southey offers the temporal doubleness that, according to Homi Bhabha, emerges from "heterogeneous histories of contending peoples."[48] This doubleness reflects the difficulty of imagining a British identity predicated on internal colonialism, as well, perhaps, as the impossibility of settling in the New World without perpetuating English colonial endeavors there. Ironically, the central role that the opening of the Ohio Valley held in the resurgence of the Madoc myth meant that by 1805, when Southey finally published the epic he had been working on for ten years, the poem's moment had in some senses already passed.

Welsh Indians in America and American Indians in Wales

American versions of the Madoc myth were similar to Welsh and English ones insofar as they served a legitimating function. Because Anglo-Americans could trace their ancestry back through the English to the ancient Britons who supposedly had discovered their continent, the Madoc myth could be invoked to naturalize settlers' westward migration during the 1790s as a

form of return to lands already occupied by their ancestors. However, in
contrast to Welsh versions of the myth, which unsurprisingly emphasize the
Welshness of Madoc and his men, and to English versions, which emphasize their Britishness, American versions of the myth tend to emphasize
the Indianness of Madoc's supposed descendants. American retellings of
the Madoc myth reflect the early republic's ambivalence toward native peoples: their longstanding repudiation of Indians as irredeemable savages on
the one hand, and their identification with Native Americans' manly independence and stoic valor on the other. American writers were particularly
fascinated by the Welsh Indians' historical intermediacy, or their liminal
status as neither savage nor civilized, Indian nor European. Welsh Indians
perhaps represented the at once frightening and exhilarating possibility
that European settlers might adapt to the conditions of frontier life without
going entirely native and without renouncing all the cherished markers of
civilization.

In the newly formed United States, the flourishing of the Madoc myth coincided with increasing westward migration, particularly from Pennsylvania,
Virginia, and the Carolinas, into the region that would become Kentucky,
Tennessee, and Ohio. In contrast to English and Welsh versions of the Madoc
myth, in which Welsh Indians appear quite literally all over the map, American
writers consistently located the Welsh Indians in the Western Territory, the
regions north of Louisiana and west of the Mississippi. The story of Madoc's
migration is recounted in a number of discovery narratives and topographical surveys including John Filson's *Discovery, Settlement and Present State
of Kentucke* (1784), Amos Stoddard's *Sketches, Historical and Descriptive of
Louisiana* (1812), and Gilbert Imlay's *Topographical Survey of the Western
Territory of North America* (1792), which were intended to encourage westward
migration.

Imlay's *Topographical Survey* informed his novel *The Emigrants; or the
History of an Expatriated Family* (1793) not only in its representations of the
American West's "fertile and boundless Savannas" but also in its allusions
to Welsh Indians.[49] In the *Topographical Description*, Imlay recounts in full
the story of Madoc's migration even though he declares himself "sensible of
the ridicule which the vain and the petulant may attempt to throw on this
account."[50] Imlay's account follows Filson's closely, claiming that the remaining traces of "a nation farther advanced in the arts of life than the Indians"
can be found in the Ohio Valley in burial mounds, military entrenchments
and fortifications, iron tools, and earthen vessels.[51] Imlay refuses to definitively credit or invalidate the theory that the Ancient Britons were the first
settlers of the Ohio Valley, declaring evasively that "the day is not far distant,
when the farthest recesses of this continent will be explored, and the accounts
of the Welsh established beyond the possibility of a doubt, or consigned to
that oblivion which has already received so many suppositions founded on

arguments as plausible as these."[52] *The Emigrants* is similarly equivocal, but much more calculating, in its allusions to the myth of Welsh settlement. The novel conflates ancient Britons and Native Americans as models of primitive masculine virtue in order to justify the settlement of the Ohio Valley and to excuse the forced migration of native peoples that westward expansion caused.

Imlay's interest in westward migration and settlement grew out of his own experience, as he participated personally in the international competition for control of the Western Territory. Following his service in the American army during the Revolutionary War, Imlay became involved in land speculation in the Ohio Valley but left the United States for Europe in 1786 to escape prosecution for his corrupt land-jobbing deals. His publication of *A Topographical Description of the Western Territory* in 1792, the year that Kentucky joined the Union, brought Imlay to the attention of the French Girondists, who hoped to wrest the formerly French territory of Louisiana back from Spain, and eventually to forge a passage through the Western Territory to the Pacific Northwest. Imlay expressed his willingness to participate in a French military campaign against Spanish Louisiana, but when the Girondists were removed from power in 1793, the project was abandoned and Imlay is now remembered more for his romantic involvement with Mary Wollstonecraft than for his political imbrications.[53]

The Emigrants follows the T—n family's travels from London, where Mr. T—n, a merchant, has been ruined by the extravagance of his son George, across the United States. They arrive first in Philadelphia, which they find already spoiled by "the dissipation which . . . English and French manners had introduced" to the city, and subsequently remove to Pittsburgh and Kentucky, the latter of which they find as yet uncontaminated by "the unnatural customs of the European world" (55, 219). Imlay is represented in *The Emigrants* by his thinly disguised mouthpiece Mr. Il—ray, who reverses the T—ns' journey, traveling from Pennsylvania to England, before finally joining the T—ns in Kentucky. These two transatlantic journeys serve to contrast metropolitan England, where society has been corrupted by luxuries, "follies, and dissipation," with the Western Territory, a virgin region where natural rights and virtues flourish far removed from the Old World's moribund political institutions and social hierarchies.

The moral reformation of George T—n, one of the eponymous emigrants, develops the contrast between metropolitan England and the American West in distinctly gendered terms, associating England with a degenerate effeminacy and the Western Territory with a robust and republican masculinity. Upon arriving in the United States fresh from London, George embodies the self-interested effeminacy that, according to Imlay, characterizes many of the Englishmen who inhabit the metropolises of Britain. His idle squandering of his family's fortune has forced the T—ns to emigrate, and soon after they arrive in Pittsburgh, he flees back to London with what little remains of his father's money. Once in England, George quickly returns to his former "follies and dissipation," showing himself "forgetful of the ties of consanguinity and filial affection,—forgetful of the feelings of a man, and the principles of a gentleman" (165). George then endures several months in debtor's prison until his debts are paid by Mr. Il—ray, under whose guidance he experiences a rebirth of sorts. We learn in Il—ray's final letter that after a few months in Kentucky, George's "understanding has . . . been regenerated . . . his person has already become robust, and he now has more the appearance of an Ancient Briton, than one of those fine fellows, whose nerves require the assistance of hartshorn, to enable them to encounter the perils of a hackney coach, or even the fatigues of a masquerade" (256). George's reformation, which entails moral and physical discipline, transforms him from an effeminate, dissipated fop into the epitome of masculine republican virtue. He acquires the fortitude, generosity, and courage that, according to Imlay, characterized the ancient Britons.

In comparing George to "an Ancient Briton," Imlay suggests that he has recuperated the virtues and sentiments that characterized the original settlers of the British Isles and that "have decayed under the influence of the most capricious and violent despotism" (48) as successive peoples invaded Great Britain. *The Emigrants'* American Indians still inhabit the state of nature once enjoyed by the ancient Britons. They possess naturally the fortitude and generosity that dissolute Englishmen like George must work to recover. When George's sister Caroline is taken captive by a native tribe in Kentucky, we learn that "the Indians treated her the whole time with the most distant respect, and scrupulous delicacy" (203). The Indians' chivalry towards their female captive reveals that, despite their savage appearance, they are more virtuous than the novel's Englishmen. Indeed, Mr. Il—ray notes that some captive "women have been treated with such tenderness and attention by [the Indians], that they have from gratitude become their wives" (204). The single instance of Native American violence towards white settlers in the novel is attributed to English influence and takes place prior to the T—ns arrival in the United States. Mr. P—relates that shortly after the commencement of the War of Independence, he returned home to find his wife and children brutally murdered by some "ferocious savages" that English soldiers had "let loose to crimson their murderous weapons in the blood of the unoffending" (130). This incident suggests that native peoples' natural virtues have been debased by their contact with the supposedly more enlightened and more civilized English.

Imlay's representation of American Indians as naturally sharing the chivalrous courtesy and courage of the ancient Britons is not mere ethnocentrism, but instead illustrates his belief in the fundamental uniformity of human nature. Many Enlightenment thinkers shared this belief, positing that all peoples progress, albeit at very different rates, through discrete stages of development from the savagery to civilization. Accordingly, all primitive peoples should share similar traits, as should all civilized peoples. While some, like Adam Smith and William Robertson, held that people tend to become more refined and virtuous as they progress from savagery to civilization, Imlay clearly sides with those like Jean-Jacques Rousseau and Adam Ferguson who understood this trajectory as a process of gradual moral degeneration from a state of original virtue.[54]

The Emigrants imagines Kentucky as a place where the primitive masculine virtues common to ancient Britons and American Indians might be reconciled with enlightened Anglo-American political institutions. When Caroline's suitor and eventual husband Captain Arl—ton decides to establish a settlement in Kentucky, he designs it especially to cultivate these primitive virtues in its inhabitants. However, it is notable that the Indians themselves figure nowhere in the new settlement, having conveniently disappeared from the narrative after Arl—ton recovers Caroline, scratched by thorny branches but otherwise unharmed, from their clutches. While *The Emigrants'* Indians may share ancient British virtues, they evidently do not share the political rights and liberties to which these virtues entitle Anglo-American settlers. The moral equivalency or interchangeability of Indians and ancient Britons seems to justify for Imlay the exclusion, and perhaps the eradication, of the former. The convenient disappearance of the Indians from the narrative very likely reflects Imlay's desire to downplay the significant tensions between natives and white settlers in the Ohio Valley; however, their absence is also an accurate description of historical reality. Indian tribes removed from Kentucky rapidly as white settlers moved in, so that by the late eighteenth century, few natives remained in the area.[55]

While Arl—ton's settlement, Bellefont, is designed to reproduce among white settlers the characteristics of the native peoples it excludes, it also maintains continuity with an Anglo-American republican tradition. Although Bellefont does not incorporate Indians, it recalls eighteenth-century representations of both American Indians and ancient Britons as "virtuous, self-reliant rural dwellers" inhabiting simple, relatively egalitarian societies in which any hierarchies are defined by merit rather than birth.[56] Filson, Benjamin Franklin, and other writers represented Native American tribes as societies in which "all men are equal, personal qualities being most esteemed" and in which "no distinction of birth, no rank, renders any man capable of doing prejudice to the rights of private persons."[57] Similarly, William Godwin's *Imogen: A Pastoral Romance* (1784) depicts the ancient British inhabitants of the valley of Clwyd, "as strangers to riches, and to ambition, for they all lived in a happy equality."[58] At the same time, Arl—ton's settlement evokes the republican thought of Thomas Jefferson, and also of seventeenth-century writers like James Harrington and Andrew Fletcher, who advocated the wide and relatively equal distribution of property among men as a means of encouraging their political participation and their cultivation of civic virtue.[59]

To create an egalitarian and virtuous society, Arl—ton purchases a "tract of country lying upon the Ohio" and divides it into 256 plots, each of one square mile, which will be held in "fee-simple" rather than at a life-rent, as would be the case in most of Europe (233). Each male inhabitant of his community will be "eligible to [hold] a seat in a house of representatives consisting of twenty members, who are to assemble every Sunday in the year, to take into consideration the measures necessary to promote the encouragement of agriculture and all useful arts, as well to discuss upon the science of government and jurisprudence" (233). Arl—ton believes that this opportunity for civic participation will encourage each man to strive not for wealth or the ornaments of rank, but rather for "the thanks of his country" (234). In contrast to England, where political institutions reward servility and "aggrandize one citizen at the expence of another," in Kentucky "every expectation of aggrandizement will fall to the ground . . . and the respectability of every citizen be established upon that broad basis—the dignity of man" (3, 234). *The Emigrants* envisions the westward migration of Anglo-Americans into the Ohio Valley as a form of racial and moral regeneration. This rehabilitative process promises to unite new English emigrants with internal American migrants by restoring to both groups of settlers the virtues, liberty, and equality proper to the descendants of ancient Britons. Moreover, by eliding the primitive virtues of American Indians and ancient Britons, Imlay at once justifies the expulsion of native tribes from their land in the Ohio Valley and suggests that settlers can adapt to the conditions of frontier life while remaining essentially British.

Imlay's conflation of the virtues of ancient Britons and American Indians situates Bellefont in what Laura Doyle has described as "Atlantic modernity," a condition in which liberty was understood as "an interior, racial inheritance" that belonged to some peoples—for Doyle, Anglo-Saxons and their descendants—but was denied to others.[60] Doyle explores the emergence of racially inflected discourses of freedom during the English Civil War and their migration with settlers across the Atlantic to Britain's seventeenth-century American colonies, where they continued to flourish even after the political ties between Britain and the United States had been severed. Figuring liberty as a racial inheritance allowed Anglo-Americans to deny it to peoples including Africans and, as *The Emigrants* demonstrates, Native Americans. Bellefont belongs to the Atlantic modernity that Doyle describes insofar as it aims to restore to its citizens the natural sentiments, virtues, rights, and liberties that are their birthright. Imlay's attribution of liberty and virtue to the ancient Britons rather than to the Anglo-Saxons that figure centrally in Doyle's argument may simply reflect the tendency of eighteenth-century British and American writers to "mix up Saxons, Goths and Celts in one eclectic national muddle" in their representations of British antiquity.[61]

However, I would suggest that Imlay's attribution of innate rights and liberties to the ancient Britons, the first inhabitants of Britain, rather than to the Anglo-Saxons of Doyle's account, is deliberate given the novel's repudiation of England's history of conquest, tyranny, and corruption. Imlay's allusion to the virtues and liberties of the ancient Britons also invokes a precedent for eighteenth-century westward expansion, representing the settlement of the Ohio Valley as the fulfillment or extension of an earlier colonial project and as a restoration or regeneration of Anglo-American settlers' racial inheritance.

Although popular interest in the Welsh Indians supposed to be living in the American West peaked in 1790s, the Madoc myth became absorbed into what Tim Fulford has described as Romanticism's "cumulative cycle of literary import/export in which ancient Celts and contemporary Native Americans were imaged in terms of each other over and over again."[62] In this particular instance, not just Celts and Native Americans, but also Wales and the American West were rendered interchangeable. Mary Shelley's *Lodore* (1835) inverts the Madoc myth through its comparisons between the American West and Wales as places simultaneously of refuge and exile, where conditions of poverty and isolation demand primitive simplicity and fortitude from inhabitants. *Lodore* also recalls *The Emigrants* through the contrast that it draws between the simple virtues of the American West and the degenerate artifice of English metropolitan society. Shelley suggests that London, despite its entertaining bustle, can be more solitary than the plains of Illinois or the mountains of Wales. Fiona Stafford explains that *Lodore*, originally subtitled, "A Tale of the Present Time," represents Shelley's effort "to capitalize on the prevailing popularity of novels describing fashionable London life," the silver-fork fiction for which her publisher, Henry Colburn, was known.[63] Yet its exploration of various forms of alienation and exile and of the contrasts between primitive and civilized ways of life is unmistakably Romantic.

Lodore describes Lord Lodore's unwise marriage to the flirtatious and frivolous Cornelia, his subsequent emigration to Illinois with his daughter Ethel to escape his unhappy domestic life, Ethel's return to England after her father's death, and her eventual reunion with her repentant mother. When Lodore first encounters Cornelia in Rhyaider Gowy, Wales, she seems to unite primitive innocence with polished refinement: she appears to be "the nursling, so he fancied, of mountains, waterfalls, and solitude; yet endowed with all the softness and refinement of civilized society."[64] The sublime scenery misleads Lodore's fancy, however. Cornelia is not a "child of nature" (42), but rather the "willing disciple" of her "selfish and artful" mother, who has taught Cornelia "to view society as the glass by which she was to set her feelings" (44) and to seek the attention of the wealthy and fashionable elite above all else. Cornelia and her mother's residence in Wales was not inspired by their appreciation of its sublime scenery or the simple virtues of its inhabitants, but rather by the hope that "by living with stricter economy" in the summer (41), they might better afford "the engagements and amusements" of a winter in London (47). After her marriage to Lodore, such engagements leave Cornelia no time for domestic duties or the company of her husband and daughter; and when Lodore forces her to choose between emigrating with him and Ethel or remaining alone in London, her mother convinces her to choose the latter. Rejected by his wife, Lodore laments "Home! A Tartar beneath his tent—a wild Indian in his hut, may speak of home—I have none" (49). Given his belief that even primitive peoples must enjoy greater domestic comforts than he does in London, it is fitting that Lodore determines to emigrate to the American West, where he hopes to find among the "wild Indians" the tranquility he longs for.

Lodore's settlement in "the Illinois" roughly coincides in the novel's chronology with Morris Birkbeck's establishment of the colony described in his *Notes on the Illinois* (1817) and *Letters from Illinois* (1818), both of which Shelley seems to have read.[65] While Lodore seeks isolation rather than the collective living promoted by Birkbeck, George Flower, Robert Owen, and other founders of Midwestern communities, he embraces the "republican plainness and simplicity" embraced by these settlements. In Illinois, Lodore cultivates a "garden . . . in the wilderness" where he instills in Ethel the primitive virtues that he thought to have found in Cornelia. Yet he perceives his migration as a form of "banishment" and misses the pleasures of sociability, finding that tranquility brings "sameness" and "loneliness" (12). Ethel grows up among "the grandest objects of nature," albeit without "the thousand delights of civilization," and shares the unaffected sensibility and simple virtues that Shelley ascribes to the Indian natives of Illinois (17). We learn that "Ethel's visionary ideas were all full of peace, seclusion, and her father. America, or rather the little village of the Illinois which she inhabited, was all the world to her; and she had no idea that nearly everything that connected her to society existed beyond the far Atlantic in that tiny isle which made so small a show upon her maps" (20). While the plains of Illinois might have seemed to Shelley's British readers like the middle of nowhere, Shelley reduces Britain in its turn from the center of civilization and empire to an insignificant smudge on Ethel's map.

Ethel's insulation from English artifices and corruption, as well as her habit of relying on her father "as a prop that could not fail," leaves her unprepared after Lodore's death to return to England. To Ethel, the denizens of London seem like "so many automata" (101), and she and her maiden aunt feel amidst the bustle of genteel society as lonely as Lodore did in the American wilderness, like "solitary wanderers on earth, cut off from human intercourse" (155). Whether "in England or America," the narrator notes, Ethel "lived in a desart, as far as society was concerned" (144). She soon marries her only male acquaintance, Edward Villiers, an impetuous young man who had befriended Lodore shortly before his death, and to whom Ethel is as exclusively devoted as her mother was careless of Lodore. Villiers, whose name associates him with the metropolis, exposes the tendency of the "delights of civilization" to create an insatiable appetite for pleasure and luxury, and to undermine self-control and self-sufficiency; he refuses to accommodate his habits to the limited income that his profligate father is able to offer him. Their poverty is exacerbated by Cornelia's selfishness. Lodore, who feared that Cornelia's vices would contaminate Ethel, stipulated in his will that Cornelia would receive £600 per year in addition to her jointure on the condition that she has no contact with Ethel. If the two meet, then Ethel—who is unacquainted with the conditions of her father's will—inherits the money that would otherwise go to her mother, and Cornelia initially is anxious to keep it for herself.

Ethel's primitive American virtues—her stoicism, frankness, and love of simplicity and retirement—alienate her from London society, but they also enable her to endure the economic privations of marriage to Villiers. Her childhood among "settlers in a new country," and particularly her observations of the "privations and hardships suffered by the Red Indian and his squaw," have taught her a "practical philosophy" of "fortitude and patience" that is foreign to her husband (257). She urges Villiers to adopt a more "primitive" way of living, to imagine "that we are cottagers, the children of mechanics, or wanderers in a barbarous country, where money is not" (230). Villiers acknowledges that people "who truly make the earth, its woods and fells, and inclement sky, their unadorned dwelling place" possess a self-discipline and endurance that he lacks, but he also points out that such people are regarded in England as "barbarians and savages—untaught, uncivilized, miserable beings—and we the wiser and more refined, hunt and exterminate them" (186). Accordingly, Villiers is unwilling either to exchange indulgence for simplicity in England or to escape temptation by emigrating to "the wilds of the Illinois" (186): "To give up the world, the English world, formed no portion of his picture of bliss; and to occupy a subordinate, degraded, permitted, place in it, was, to one initiated in its supercilious and insolent assumptions, not to be endured" (145). Although Villiers recognizes the wisdom of Ethel's restraint, he cannot rid himself of his ingrained desire for the eminence conferred by wealth any more than Ethel can overcome her habitual preference for simplicity and seclusion.

Through Ethel's reverse migration, *Lodore* envisions a kind of reverse colonialism—an American transformation of English manners and mores. The novel's ending reclaims the primitive virtues supposedly proper to the American West and Wales for England. When Cornelia learns that Villiers has been imprisoned for debt and at last visits Ethel in jail, she is overcome with remorse for her self-interest. She determines to emulate her daughter's admirable restraint by giving up both her jointure and the extra £600 per year to Ethel and Villiers, and to "spend the residue of her days among the uncouth and lonely mountains of Wales, in poverty and seclusion" (261). Indeed, this poverty ensures that "her state of banishment would be far more complete than if mountains and seas only constituted its barriers" (266). Wales is to Cornelia what Illinois was to Lodore—a place of isolation and renunciation, so it is fitting that at this moment, "when about to imitate [Lodore's] abrupt and miserable act of self-banishment, [her] heart yearned for some communication with him" (269), and a "wish to cross the Atlantic, and to visit the scenes where he had dwelt so long, arose within her" (268). In *Lodore*, Wales becomes an American West within Great Britain, a place at once of refuge and exile, the primitiveness of which fosters virtues and habits that are incompatible with metropolitan ostentation. Yet the sacrifice that Cornelia makes for Ethel ultimately precludes her banishment, as Ethel, filled with gratitude, discovers her mother's plan and recalls her even before she gets to Wales. Cornelia's newfound ability to exercise the stoic self-control of Welsh peasants and American Indians renders her self-imposed exile unnecessary. Instead, she removes to Lodore's family estate in Essex, where she "learn[s] from Ethel to be happy, and to love" (252), and where they enjoy sociability in seclusion, and comfort without excess. Even as Shelley suggests that a morally corrupt imperial center might be regenerated by appropriating the virtues of the peripheries, the novel repudiates colonial exploration and expansion in favor of an insular domesticity—the cultivation of shared sympathies and simple pleasures at home. Although Ethel may share Madoc's fortitude, she exhibits none of his adventurous courage, instead bringing his republican virtues from the American West back to England.

The resurgence of the Madoc myth in the late eighteenth-century British Atlantic world initially may have been inspired by competition for control of the American West; however, it soon became implicated in the construction of multiple national identities—Welsh, American, English, and British. Moreover, the story also participated in generating a set of national and racial associations that came to operate quite independently of the myth and of reality. Thus the ancient Britons came to symbolize liberty and resistance to tyranny despite Wales's status as an internal colony; Wales came to connote the primitive and pastoral despite its rapid industrialization; and the American West became the bastion of an ancient British republicanism despite the fact that no Welsh-speaking Indians were definitively ascertained to exist there. As *Lodore* illustrates, by the early decades of the nineteenth century, writers could invoke comparisons between Wales and the American West, and between ancient Britons and American Indians, without relating the Madoc myth itself.

Welsh, English, and American retellings of the Madoc myth all share in common a concept of British identity defined by masculine virtues that differ somewhat from one version of the story to another but that include qualities such as fortitude, self-discipline, independence, love of liberty, and generosity. In the various manifestations of the myth, this identity legitimates and creates continuity among various westward migrations—from England into Wales at the time of the Roman conquest, from Wales to North America in the twelfth century, and from the eastern United States into the Ohio Valley at the end of the eighteenth century. Yet although British identity is defined by similar qualities in all versions of the Madoc myth, it does not always include and exclude the same peoples. While Iolo Morganwg's Britons are Welsh Jacobins who resist tyranny, Southey's are Anglo-British colonizers who exert a benevolent but unbending rule over their subjects. Perhaps strangest of all, Imlay's use of the Madoc myth unites these two seemingly incompatible positions, as his liberty-loving, republican Britons are also proponents of westward expansion and Indian removal.

The circulation of the Madoc myth throughout the Atlantic world demonstrates how those situated in what are perhaps misleadingly referred to as the peripheries of that world—in this case Wales and the newly formed United States—selectively allied themselves with each other and differentiated themselves from metropolitan England. Welsh writers looked to the United States as a refuge from English governance and American writers looked to Wales to justify westward expansion. Yet the myth also shows how the English borrowed from the cultures that they colonized to justify their colonial power, even as those cultures in turn reimagined metropolitan England. In fact, the various tellings and retellings of the Madoc myth reveal the inadequacy of the center/periphery opposition, as they position Wales as at once an internal English colony and the origin of British imperial power, and the Ohio Valley as at once the western outskirts and the future core of an American empire.

The Literary Sketch
and British Atlantic Regionalism

In 1842, William Carleton—author of *Traits and Stories of the Irish Peasantry* (1830), *Tales and Sketches, Illustrating the Character, Usages, Traditions, Sports and Pastimes of the Irish Peasantry* (1845), and a number of novels—celebrated the emergence of an indigenous Irish literary market that "rose above the narrow distinctions of creed and party."[1] Just two decades earlier, Ireland was "utterly destitute of a national literature": "our men and women of genius uniformly carried their talents to the English market, whilst we laboured at home under all the dark privations of a literary famine."[2] Much as Ireland continued to export grain and beef to England during the famines that plagued the eighteenth and nineteenth centuries, so the migration of Irish authors and their works to England contributed to a "literary famine" at home. Carleton explains that until 1830 or so "our literary men followed the example of our great landlords; they became absentees, and drained the country of its intellectual wealth precisely as the others exhausted it of its rents."[3] He locates the origin of an indigenous Irish literary market in the publication of his first series of *Traits and Stories* on an Irish press, with "no expectation that they would be read, or excite any interest whatever in either England or Scotland."[4] The "immediate popularity" of *Traits and Stories* in Ireland showed "that our native country, if without a literature at the time, was at least capable of appreciating, and willing to foster the humble exertions of such as endeavoured to create one."[5]

Traits and Stories belongs to the literary genre of "tales and sketches," collections of anecdotes or vignettes that usually focused on a specific location or population—in Carleton's case the Irish peasantry of County Tyrone. This chapter reads the flourishing of the literary sketch simultaneously in Scotland, Ireland, and the United States as a challenge to early nineteenth-century metropolitan England's cultural and literary centrality in the British Atlantic world.[6] Not only did the publication of collections of tales and sketches like Carleton's mark the development of regional literary markets in

Ireland, Scotland, and the United States; it also, I will argue, revealed literary and cultural connections among the non-English regions of the British Atlantic world.

The creation of a British Atlantic literature was facilitated not only by the migration of peoples and the circulation of narratives of origin, but also by the adaptation of literary genres to suit particular sites within the Atlantic world. The previous three chapters have already touched on versions of this phenomenon: Chapter 2 examines how Irish and American novelists turned to the Gothic to explore the anxieties surrounding Irish revolutionaries; Chapter 3 shows how James Fenimore Cooper racialized the myth of the ambitious Scottish migrant by adapting the conventions of Walter Scott's historical novels to the American frontier; and Chapter 4 traces the Madoc myth's imperial amplification as it passed from lyric to epic poetry, and then into the novel.

The numerous collections of tales and sketches that appeared in the non-English regions of the British Atlantic world during the 1820s and '30s illustrate the growing resistance of regional literary cultures to "metrocentric" English standards of literary and cultural value.[7] As a genre, the collection of tales and sketches is decentralized in two senses. First, it lacks a plot that would unify its parts in an organic whole; instead, it consists of a series of vignettes and anecdotes united only by their metonymic relationship to a particular population or location. Second, it privileges the local over the metropolitan and assumes that the delineation of local landscapes, customs, and characters holds inherent interest and value for readers.[8] Although a London-based English literary culture continued to exert its influence over the British Atlantic world in the early nineteenth century, the popularity of tales and sketches in Scotland, Ireland, and the United States makes visible literary traditions that circumvented the metropolitan center.

This chapter traces collections of tales and sketches from their initial late eighteenth-century emergence as a "metrocentric" English genre, produced by cosmopolitan writers for urbane readers, to their early nineteenth-century adaptation by Scottish, Irish, and American writers. Scottish and Irish writers used collections of tales and sketches to preserve in writing ways of life that Anglicization and emigration threatened to erase. American writers adopted the literary sketch to delineate the regional identities that developed as immigration, westward expansion, and forced Indian removal transformed an already racially and culturally complex American landscape. Both in form and content, collections of tales and sketches indicated the emergence of new patterns of affiliation in and among the non-English regions of the British Atlantic world.

The history of regional writing is somewhat different in Ireland, Scotland, and Wales than in the United States. The antiquarian movement in eighteenth-century Britain fostered a nascent regionalism as the recovery of local customs, artifacts, and oral traditions became a popular practice.

During the Romantic era, Scottish, Irish, and Welsh antiquarianism informed what Katie Trumpener has called "bardic nationalism," the literary assertion of the Celtic peripheries' cultural distinctiveness in response to English political and cultural hegemony.[9] The bardic nationalism expressed in works such as James Macpherson's Ossian poems or Walter Scott's Waverley novels also informed the emergence of collection of tales and sketches. Scottish and Irish collections of tales and sketches share the antiquarian impulse to collect and display local customs and curiosities; and like more canonical examples of bardic nationalism, they position the local in metonymic relation to the national. However, tales and sketches are arguably more concerned with synchronic than with diachronic forms of difference. That is, they aim to describe what makes one particular place or people unique and distinct rather than to provide a history for a nation or people.

In the United States, literary engagement with bardic nationalism was vexed because a nation that was only a few decades old had little to offer antiquarians unless they were willing to turn to a Native American past or to spurious narratives of origin. Studies of American regional writing thus tend to begin in the mid- rather than the early nineteenth century and to identify regionalism with literary realism, requiring that regional writing depict "authentic regional detail, including authentic dialect, authentic local characters, real geographical settings, authentic local customs and dress."[10] While it makes sense to equate regionalism with authentic detail, imposing such anachronistic standards of realism on early nineteenth-century writing by default excludes it from the category of regional writing. It does not follow that, as Josephine Donovan has argued, regionalism constituted a reaction to the sentimental conventions that dominated early nineteenth-century fiction.[11]

The collections of tales and sketches I discuss in this chapter suggest that sentimentalism was compatible with, possibly even integral to, a nascent American regionalism. These collections contain what we might consider authenticating details in their descriptions of landscape, historical events, and characters, but such details often are counterbalanced or even overshadowed by the stock conventions of sentimental fiction. For instance, the anonymously authored *Tales of an American Landlord, containing sketches of life south of the Potomac* (1824) incorporates regionally particular characters, such as a wealthy and corrupt plantation owner and an itinerant Methodist preacher, and regionally specific events and settings, including a hurricane that wreaks havoc within the first fifty pages. But these are painted with the bold, broad strokes of sentimental fiction rather than with the nuance that we often expect from regional writing. The corrupt plantation owner is the conventional villain of sentimental fiction, out to exploit feminine beauty and innocence; in this case, he just happens to live on a Virginia plantation. Nonetheless, the text asks us to recognize that the southeastern United

States is not the same as the northeastern United States. Thanks to its inclusion of regional details, the story could not have been set simply anywhere in the indeterminate countryside against which much late eighteenth- and early nineteenth-century sentimental fiction is staged. Collections of tales and sketches employed the didacticism proper to much sentimental fiction to educate readers about the customs, values, and characteristics of locales in and about which they were written.

Early nineteenth-century collections of tales and sketches may not have attained the standards of realism that we now expect from regional writing, but they did represent the region in question—whether the Ohio Valley, New England, the Scottish Highlands, or County Connaught—as the source of its own meaning and identity. For Ian Duncan and Franco Moretti, this integrity differentiates regional from provincial writing. A province is defined, in Moretti's words, by "*what is not there,*" or by its difference from the metropolis, much as a periphery is defined by what it lacks in comparison to the imperial core.[12] By contrast, a region asserts its own value based on what *is* there, and regional writing "specifies its setting by invoking a combination of geographic, natural-historical, antiquarian, ethnographic, and/or sociological features that differentiate it from any other region."[13] Accordingly, the term "regional," which I will use throughout this chapter to refer to the collections of tales and sketches written in various locales in Scotland, Ireland, England, and the United States, "implies a neutral or even positive set of multiple local differences," whereas "provincial" and "peripheral" constitute the inferior term in a binary opposition.[14] Indeed, I contend that early nineteenth-century collections of tales and sketches participated in transforming the peripheries or provinces into regions by assigning them positive and desirable characteristics. In doing so, regional writing did not, as critics have argued, seek to capture "what has never been debased by industry, capital, and above all, immigration," or to preserve an idealized ethnically and morally homogeneous community.[15] On the contrary, they often described the changes that occurred in particular locations within the writer's memory, demonstrating that, as Duncan has suggested, "Historical change—modernization—is the condition through which the . . . region becomes narratable."[16]

When the literary sketch emerged in the late eighteenth century, it was a "metrocentric" rather than a regional genre. Although, as Richard Sha has shown, the sketch was a very diverse genre, used to discuss politics, history, and philosophy, a substantial subset of literary sketches was written by travelers, and provided descriptions of the places and peoples they encountered on their domestic or overseas journeys—for instance William Bray's *Sketch of a Tour into Darbyshire and Yorkshire* (1778), Rowley Lascelle's *Sketch of a Descriptive Journey through Switzerland* (1796), or Helena Maria Williams' *Sketches of the State of Manners and Opinions in the French Republic* (1801).[17] These literary sketches complemented the collections of visual travel sketches that were popularized by William Gilpin during the last decades of the eighteenth century, and they often included at least a few illustrations. Whether literary or pictorial, travelers' sketches offered subjective and spontaneous impressions gleaned in passing. In asserting their subjectivity and spontaneity, these sketches artfully claimed to lack artifice. Their claims to authority and authenticity as representations of foreign lands and peoples lay in their writers' status as outsiders and thus in their supposedly disinterested distance from the subjects they depicted.

By the first decade of the nineteenth century, writers situated in the Celtic peripheries had begun to respond to collections of sketches written by metropolitan writers for metropolitan readers by producing their own collections. Sha explains that as sketching became a particularly middle-class activity, it allowed artists to claim symbolic ownership of land that they could never hope to purchase: by sketching the landscape, they could "convert someone else's property into aesthetic property."[18] Similarly, producing their own collections of tales and sketches allowed writers situated in the peripheries to reassert ownership of their respective regions by challenging the representations offered by English visitors—a scenario dramatized in novelistic representations of the encounter between English tourist and Celtic native.[19] Regional writers could claim for their works a deeper authenticity than sketches produced by an outsider. Like nations, regions are not natural geographic entities; rather, they are constructed discursively, and their construction reveals unequal power relations between provinces and metropolis, or peripheries and center. Frank Davey has observed that twentieth-century regional writers developed strategies "for resisting meanings generated by others in a nation-state, particularly those generated in geographical areas which can be constructed . . . as central or powerful."[20] The same holds true of their nineteenth-century predecessors.

Sidney Owenson's *Patriotic Sketches of Ireland, Written in Connaught* (1807), one of the earliest collections of literary sketches by a writer from the Celtic peripheries, demonstrates some of these strategies of resistance. In her preface to the work, Owenson explains that although she had lived in Ireland all her life, only by leaving Ireland did she learn of the "turpitude, degradation, ferocity and inconsequence" of the Irish. "This ungracious information," she remarks dryly, "I acquired during a short tour through a sister Isle."[21] Without explicitly calling English representations of Ireland bigoted and erroneous, Owenson implies that her sketches offer more accurate and informed views of the country. At the same time, however, Owenson exploits the aesthetic connotations of the literary sketch to downplay the force of her challenge. She suggests the desultoriness and subjectivity of her sketches when she notes that "they were drawn in the moment of passing observation, as the heart was touched by objects of moral interest, or the fancy awakened by scenes of natural beauty."[22]

Owenson's *Patriotic Sketches* offers evidence of the transatlantic circulation of regional collections of sketches, and suggests the appeal they may have had to readers in other, far distant regions. When independence freed American publishers from compliance with British copyright law, reprinting British books became cheaper than importing them, and buying American reprints rather than British imports became a way of expressing patriotism.[23] Thus an 1809 edition of *Patriotic Sketches* published in Baltimore informs "local readers" that "the type was cast expressly for this volume at the Baltimore Foundry" and "the paper manufactured by Conrad, Lucas & Co.," another Baltimore company. The publisher's advertisement represents the purchase of this reprint as a form of patriotism comparable to Owenson's own "ardent attachment to the 'Emerald Isle,'" which "elicits patriotic fire in every page of her writings when 'the green fields of Erin' are the subject."[24] By linking readers' purchase of a local edition of the *Patriotic Sketches* to Owenson's localized depictions of Ireland, the publisher imagines a kind of trans-regional literary affiliation that circumvents London, the literary center of the Atlantic world.

Irving, Mitford, and the Development of the Literary Sketch

Despite the significant contributions of Irish and Scottish writers, it was an American and an English writer who did most to inspire the spate of regional collections of tales and sketches published during the 1820s and '30s. The former was Washington Irving, who, with *The Sketch Book of Geoffrey Crayon* (1819–1820), became one of the first American authors to be published by a major British bookseller and to achieve widespread, albeit short-lived, popularity in Britain. The latter was Mary Russell Mitford, who acknowledged Irving's influence when she explained to a correspondent that the work that would eventually become *Our Village: Sketches of Rural Character and Scenery* (1824–1832) "will consist of essays and characters and stories, chiefly about country life, in the manner of the 'Sketch Book.'"[25] American travelers to Britain and Europe had previously used the sketch "as a way of commemorating, or giving permanence to, the responses that the beauties and wonders of the Old World had elicited from them"; but it was Irving, according to Jeffrey Rubin-Dorsky, who first transformed these sketches into fiction.[26]

The Sketch Book developed two conventions in particular that would inform the many regional collections of tales and sketches published during the 1820s and '30s. First, it addressed a bifurcated audience through the narrative perspective of the participant-observer. Irving wrote the majority of *The Sketch Book* while residing in England, and his narrator, Geoffrey Crayon, offers American readers an informed outsider's view into English customs, manners, and peculiarities. Crayon represents himself as a traveler since childhood. Rather than seeking perpetual novelty, however, he always sought to become intimately familiar with the places to which he wandered. When, as a child, he visited neighboring villages, he increased his "stock of knowledge, by noting their habits and customs, and conversing with their sages and great men."[27] Crayon's perspective is not that of a traveler passing through on his way to the next site and sight; it is closer to that of an ethnographer intently familiarizing himself with a foreign society. Although clearly mocking his younger self in this description of his childhood journeys, Crayon brings the same desire for an insider's perspective to his travels in England, wandering through obscure alleyways in London, and learning about "the quaint customs of antiquity" during his time at Bracebridge Hall.[28] The participant-observer stance allows Irving to reverse the often demeaning "imperial gaze of the European traveler" toward the United States.[29]

Whereas Irving used a split subjectivity to address American and British audiences, later writers adapted the perspective of the participant-observer to address metropolitan and regional readers. For instance, James Lawson's *Tales and Sketches, by a Cosmopolite* (1830) is narrated primarily by a self-proclaimed "wanderer" through "strange and varied scenes" from the northeastern United States to the west of Scotland.[30] While traveling through the latter region, he encounters an old man who is a native of western Scotland and who acquaints the cosmopolite with local legends. By using two narrators, Lawson's *Tales and Sketches* combines an outsider's distanced and worldly perspective with an insider's familiar knowledge of western Scotland.

Irving initially intended Crayon's participant-observer perspective to cater to American readers who might share Crayon's curiosity about English culture. "It was not my intention to publish them in England," he explained of his sketches, "being conscious that much of their contents could be interesting only to American readers." When they "began to find their way across the Atlantic" to England, Irving decided to bring out his own English edition of *The Sketch Book* before a "spurious" one was produced.[31] The republication of *The Sketch Book* in England required Irving to provide an insider's view of American customs and history for an English audience to complement the insights into English culture that Crayon offered an American readership. He added two sketches about American subjects for his new audience, "Traits of Indian Character" and "Philip of Pokanoket," which joined the two tales included in the American edition—"Rip Van Winkle" and "The Legend of Sleepy Hollow"—in offering British readers an insider's view of the United States. Together, these tales and sketches represented the United States as a nation with a history and culture quite distinct from Britain's, a nation that incorporated indigenous peoples and European settlers of diverse origins.

The Sketch Book's two tales constitute Irving's second innovation upon previous collections of literary sketches, and it was imitated by many regional writers. Admittedly, the distinctions between tales and sketches are hazy, but to late eighteenth- and early nineteenth-century readers, the term "tale," as

Gary Kelly explains, "would have suggested a short narrative, probably deal-ing with rustic or provincial life and with daily and domestic reality, celebrat-ing values of simplicity, naturalness and candour, and perhaps featuring an eccentric storyteller as mediator of the simple matter."[32] Sketches, a form in which description dominates over plot, laid claim to a truth value or empiri-cal realism from which tales departed. While Irving's tales and sketches each blend elements of truth and fiction, history and fantasy, he marked superficial generic distinctions by assigning his tales a different narrator from that of his sketches. Rather than Geoffrey Crayon, the American participant-observer narrator of the sketches, the *Sketch Book*'s tales are attributed to Diedrich Knickerbocker, the crotchety Dutch historian whom Irving had invented as the narrator of his *History of New-York* (1815). As "Rip Van Winkle" and "The Legend of Sleepy Hollow" illustrate, tales were associated with oral traditions and local lore, and—like the sketch—with popular rather than high culture. The *Sketch Book*'s tales thus showed British readers that although the United States was a comparatively new nation, it already had its own legends and histories derived from its indigenous peoples and early settlers.

If *The Sketch Book*, according to Lawrence Buell, was "the single most impor-tant American prose work in teaching native writers to exploit regional mate-rial for literary purposes," Mitford's *Our Village*, albeit not an American work, came a close second, lending itself to American writers' "township-oriented sense of place."[33] Mitford began publishing her sketches of rural life in the Berkshire village of Three Mile Cross in the *Lady's Magazine* in 1822. The first collection of these sketches appeared as *Our Village* in 1824, and a new volume was published every other year after that until 1832. While she was work-ing on *Our Village*, Mitford also assembled for British readers two antholo-gies of American short fiction—*Stories of American Life* (1830) and *Lights and Shadows of American Life* (1832). Judith Fetterly and Marjorie Pryse bring *Our Village* into dialogue with these anthologies to suggest that Mitford may have viewed "both the United States and England as regions of some larger Anglo-American entity and as themselves composed of regions."[34] Both the collection of sketches and the anthology of stories work through a process of accretion, as each individual sketch and or story gestures towards a social whole only part of which it depicts.

Like *The Sketch-Book*, *Our Village* epitomizes two tendencies that were appropriated and modified by Scottish, Irish, and American writers of tales and sketches. The first of these is its synecdochic construction of local and national identities. As virtually all of Mitford's recent critics have noted, *Our Village* makes its "rural scenes represent England in part by foreclosing ques-tions of *how* rural locality and nations are connected."[35] *Our Village* situates Three Mile Cross in a synecdochic relationship to England when its narrator remarks on the "peculiar charm of the English scenery" or describes features of the landscape as "thoroughly English."[36] Elizabeth Helsinger describes this technique as "metaphoric substitution";[37] yet Three Mile Cross is never simply equivalent to England. Instead, England is an ambiguous, shadowy entity that individual sketches gesture toward but never attempt to clarify or define. *Our Village*'s synecdochic construction of regional and national identities is more common in Scottish, Irish, and American collections of tales and sketches than in English ones, perhaps because, as Tim Killick has argued, "English regions lacked the collective enemy and history of occupation that bound together the people and districts of Ireland and Scotland."[38] English collections like Mary Linwood's *Leicestershire Tales* (1808) and John Roby's *Traditions of Lancashire* (1829–1831) simply aimed to record the manners, customs, and histories of a particular county or shire. In contrast, William Carleton's *Tales and Sketches, Illustrating the Character, Usages, Traditions, Sports and Pastimes of the Irish Peasantry* took County Tyrone, where Carleton had grown up, as the basis of "a broader picture of Irish life."[39]

The second characteristic that *Our Village* shares with regional collections of tales and sketches is its tendency to call into question the value of the urban and cosmopolitan, a strategy common to pastoral writing. *Our Village* represents Three Mile Cross as a refuge from "the heat, the glare, the noise, and the fever of London," offering those passing through it the opportunity to "regain the repose of mind, the calmness of heart, which has been lost in that great Babel."[40] Such seemingly simplistic oppositions between city and country appear to enshrine an idealized image of rural Englishness that rests upon "a barely concealed fiction of isolation."[41] Yet *Our Village* acknowledges the interdependency between the city and the country, even while asserting the latter's moral primacy, when—for instance—it describes the economic rehabilitation of Farmer Allen, one of the last remaining representatives of "an order of cultivators now passing rapidly away, but in which most of the best part of the English character, its industry, its frugality, its sound sense, and its kindness might be found." Allen and his family "have had a hard struggle to . . . keep their property undivided," the narrator relates, "but good management and good principles, and the assistance afforded them by an admirable son, who left our village a poor 'prentice boy, and is now a partner in a great house in London have enabled them to overcome all the difficulties of these trying times."[42] If the countryside provides a much-needed moral and aesthetic refuge for city-dwellers, the city offers economic support for "the best part of English character," thus contributing to the preservation of the rural virtues on which the nation's identity historically has been founded.

Regional collections of tales and sketches tend to complicate *Our Village*'s opposition between the city and the country by exploring further the interdependencies and tensions between them. Andrew Picken's *Tales and Sketches of the West of Scotland* (1824) points out that "we are more readily reminded of some of the great changes of modern times, in such cities as Manchester or Glasgow, than even in London" because provincial cities

more clearly demonstrate "the amazing effects of a new species of mechanical power" in their "enormous manufactories."[43] The volume's "Sketch of
Changes in Society and Manners, in the West of Scotland, During the Last
Half-Century" laments the pernicious effects of Glasgow's commercial and
industrial growth on "genuine Scotch character," even while acknowledging the significance of the city's location for trade and communication with
North America.[44] Whereas Picken fears that industrialization will undermine the distinctive manners and mores of western Scotland, Benjamin
Drake's *Tales and Sketches from the Queen City* (1838) celebrates Cincinnati's
importance to the development of the Ohio Valley. The first sketch, simply titled "The Queen City," lays out the temporal parameters within
which the subsequent sketches take place. It describes the encounter of a
"solitary hunter" with three Indians on a "virgin plane" one autumn eve-
ning, and then jumps forward fifty-five years as "this same pioneer, revis-
iting the spot of this perilous adventure, stands with blanched locks and
tottering limbs," viewing the landscape.[45] The "hills and the streams" are
the same, "but in all else, nature has yielded to art—savage to civilized
life": "the pebbly beach, once richly fringed by weeds and willows, is con-
verted into extensive quays, on which a fleet of steam boats are unlading
the varied products of foreign climes, and receiving in return the staples of
the surrounding region, brought hither by canals and turnpike roads; the
very atmosphere of the valley is darkened by the smoke of a thousand factories; stately mansions, tastefully embellished—extensive ware-houses filled
with merchandize—school-houses—college-halls, and magnificent temples
dedicated to public worship, rise upon the plain."[46] Cincinnati registers
dramatically the transformation of the Ohio Valley from a series of small,
embattled settlements into a prosperous agricultural and industrial region
that no longer need cede dominance to the eastern seaboard in the arenas of
culture, art, and education. The ensuing sketches explore the causes of this
transformation as they take readers through the villages of Yellow Springs,
Springfield, Xenia, and Dayton and further afield into Illinois and Kentucky.

While Picken and Drake represent cities as key in the development of
regional identities, other writers claimed that cities by their very nature could
not foster the kinds of individuating characteristics that might distinguish
one region from another. Sarah Hale suggests that urbanization leads to cultural homogenization in her *Sketches of American Character* (1828), the aim of
which is "To exhibit some of those traits, originated by our free institutions,
in their manifold and minute effects on the minds, manners, and habits of
the citizens of our republic."[47] This project leads Hale "into the remote villages, and among the scattered settlements of the interior of New-England"
rather than to New York, Boston, or Philadelphia because "it is not in cities, or among the educated and fashionable of a community, that national
peculiarities can be well, or truly, discovered."[48] Arguably, the inhabitants of

late eighteenth-century London and Philadelphia may have shared more in common culturally than did the inhabitants of London and rural Yorkshire. Although the title *Sketches of American Character* signifies Hale's intent to sketch the rudiments of a *national* identity, she locates the foundation of that identity specifically in New England, and, like Mitford, makes a part stand for the whole. In "A Winter in the Country," the Boston-born and -bred protagonist, Owen Ashley, stands in for Hale's metropolitan readers, becoming a lens through which they perceive rural New England's manners and mores. When Ashley is sent by his father to work in the Green Mountains, in Vermont, he initially expects that "the farther I receded from the sea shore, the more rude and uncultivated the land and the people would be."[49] But after experiencing the hospitality and refinement of his new friends and neighbors he concludes that "the country is the strength of our Republic. Luxury may enervate our cities, but through our wide spread country, the healthful tide of liberty will still flow uncorrupted. There is no other land where the people are so free, so virtuous, so intelligent, so happy. I no longer connect the idea of American greatness, with the greatness of our cities."[50] This sketch, which concludes Hale's collection, does more than simply affirm Jeffersonian ideals of agrarian virtue; by locating these ideals in a specific region of the country, *Sketches of American Character* transforms New England into the bastion of national identity.

Owenson's *Patriotic Sketches of Ireland* resembles *Our Village* and *Sketches of American Character* in designating a single region—in this case, Connaught—as the source of national identity, and in contrasting urban cosmopolitanism to rural peculiarities. However, for Owenson, writing in an Ireland scarred by conflicts between Anglo-Irish Protestants and Gaelic-speaking Irish Catholics, urban cosmopolitanism connotes enlightened tolerance rather than cultural conformity. Owenson hypothesizes that because "small remote places" foster "proportionably contracted" sentiments, "the lesser towns of every country must still be as centres to which the radii of illiberality and cabal point with the greatest force."[51] While the "destructive spirit of intolerance in religion and of faction in politics . . . is now happily fading away in its leading cities," it "may still be found flourishing in all its pristine vigour, in the hearts of those little towns and great villages," where "the respective prejudices of each party, tear away in their vortex every unbiased sentiment of public good, every generous principle of patriotic feeling, and sacrifice at the shrine of religious and political intolerance, the peace, the welfare, and the prosperity, of a nation."[52] *Patriotic Sketches* offers in its depictions of battle sites and ruined buildings repeated instances of the destruction caused by religious and political prejudice in Connaught. If rural Connaught's character stands in for Ireland's, then Owenson suggests that urban growth and the cosmopolitanism it brings might increase national harmony and stability.

American Exceptionalism and American Regionalism

Patriotic Sketches, published over a decade before *The Sketch Book* and almost two decades before *Our Village*, is a reminder that Irving and Mitford did not create the genre that was appropriated by so many regional writers during the 1820s and '30s. They did, however, give it definition and bring it to prominence. The collection of tales and sketches became a genre particularly appealing to writers in Scotland, Ireland, and the United States in part because it asserted the value of the local over the cosmopolitan, the provincial over the metropolitan, the peripheries over the center. Yet these collections functioned rather differently in the Celtic peripheries than in the United States simply because, in the early nineteenth century, the former remained politically dependent upon England, while the latter had gained independence. Scottish and Irish collections of tales and sketches thus tend to downplay intra-national differences and conflicts—for instance between Highlands and Lowlands, or Belfast and Dublin—in order to emphasize Scotland's and Ireland's differences from England. This conflation of region with nation is characteristic of "bardic nationalism," the literary resuscitation or creation of indigenous traditions in opposition to metropolitan England's efforts to Anglicize and homogenize its Celtic peripheries.[53]

In contrast, early nineteenth-century American collections of tales and sketches emphasize the United States' internal cultural and geographical differences. Their explorations of intra-national differences reflect the relatively decentralized state of the printing trade in the United States, where, as Robert Gross explains, "the production and distribution of books took place at multiple sites" compared to the United Kingdom, where it was concentrated primarily in London, and secondarily in Edinburgh and Dublin.[54] In contrast to the London-dominated trade in Britain, print culture in the early republic "was at once local and cosmopolitan"—local in that there were printers and booksellers scattered throughout the United States' territory and cosmopolitan in that much of their stock was reprints of European, and particularly British, books.[55] Not until the 1840s, when it became possible to produce and distribute printed goods throughout the entire United States, did a national, as opposed to regional, print culture begin to emerge. It is unsurprising then, that the inhabitants of the early republic "saw themselves as New Englanders or Virginians more than they identified as Americans."[56] Collections of tales and sketches helped to create these regional identifications even as they also participated in imagining a broader American identity by examining the changes that increased immigration, westward expansion, and forced Indian removal wrought on hitherto-insular communities.

Scottish and Irish collections of tales and sketches existed in dialectical relation to their American counterparts. The former sought to preserve in writing traditional ways of life threatened by Anglicization, emigration, and urbanization, while the latter aimed to trace the influences of large-scale mobility on the creation of new communities and customs. As Hsuan L. Hsu has noted of later nineteenth-century American writing, scenes of "migration often, and paradoxically, contribute to the formation of regional identifications on the part of narrators, characters, and presumed readers."[57] As the remainder of this chapter will demonstrate, early nineteenth-century American collections of tales and sketches corroborate Hsu's theory that regional identification requires the depiction of mobility as much as stasis. These collections move beyond Irving's and Mitford's peripatetic narrators through their representations of the intra- and international movements of peoples. The forms of mobility explored in collections of tales and sketches exceed the transatlantic migrations discussed in the preceding chapters, and reflect the United States' consolidation as a nation and growth as a formative colonial power.

"The Springs," one of the pieces in Sarah Hale's *Sketches of American Character*, explores the effects of travel, a recreational and volitional form of mobility, on creation of an American identity that encompasses differences between northern and southern states. The sketch is set in Saratoga Springs, where people from all over the United States converge to enjoy the healing benefits of the water. Mr. Chapman, a Connecticut man who owns a mill and several cotton factories owner, suggests that while the medicinal qualities of the springs might be overrated, the area is nonetheless "of importance in promoting an intercourse, and thus strengthening the harmony between the different sections of our country. People from every quarter, will here meet and mingle, and become acquainted; prejudices will be, in part, overcome, and attachments formed, till we shall feel we have friends, and therefore a personal interest, in every state in our Union."[58] After talking to some women from the south, Mr. Chapman's ward, Emily, agrees that "I certainly feel much more interested for these southern ladies, more as if we are indeed of one country, than I should have done had we never met."[59] Her conversation with the "southern ladies" allows Emily both to recognize the traits that make her a New Englander and to feel herself part of a national community that includes a variety of regional characters. During their stay in Saratoga Springs, Mr. Chapman meets a cotton grower from Virginia with whom he forms a business partnership, and whom Emily eventually marries. In "The Springs," the mid-Atlantic state of New York offers a middle ground where New Englanders and southerners can meet each other quite literally halfway, discovering the shared economic interests and social sympathies that unite them as Americans.

While Hale's *Sketches of American Character* represents the travels of relatively affluent men and women, Lydia Sigourney's *Sketch of Connecticut, forty years since* (1824) depicts the movements of the socially marginal inhabitants of the village of N—, from Mrs. Rawson, the poor widow who walks three miles in the snow to carry newly spun yarn to a customer, to the middle passage of Primus, a former slave. The village depicted in *A Sketch of Connecticut* is, according to Sandra Zagarell, perhaps "the most heterogeneous in antebellum village-sketch literature" because it embraces religious, political, and ethnic forms of difference, including Catholics and Protestants, Loyalists and Patriots, Mohegan Indians and white settlers of various European origins.[60] Sigourney represents the Mohegans as a nomadic people whose habits are unsuited to settlement: "To roam freely over the forests, and drink the pure breath of the mountains; to earn with their arrow's point, the food of the passing day, and wrap themselves in a blanket from the chill of midnight, seemed all the riches they coveted—all the happiness they desired."[61] When the growth of the village of N—and its surrounding farm lands impede their roaming, the Mohegans, under the guidance of the Reverend Sansom Occom, embrace a different form of mobility—removal to a settlement provided by the Oneidas in upstate New York.

Sigourney contrasts the figures of Occom and the Mohegan chief Robert Ashbow, both Indians who have interacted extensively with white Americans, to present arguments for and against the removal. Occom, who has chosen to accompany the tribe on its journey, hopes that associating "their broken spirits with others less degraded" will help to regenerate the Mohegans, who "are but shadows of their ancestors" (158). Ashbow refuses to participate in the removal himself, but has consented to let his tribe go because he has seen "written, the dispersion of all our race" and is sure that Indians are destined to be eradicated by white settlers. He questions the motives underlying the removal and the assertions of white Christians when he asks, "Why are those . . . who profess an inheritance in the skies so ready to quarrel about the earth, their mother? Why are Christians so eager to wrest from others lands when they profess that it is gain for them to leave all, and die?" (160). Occom, by contrast, believes that so long as the Mohegans' "roving and degraded character" is improved through exposure to "civilization and Christianity . . . then it will be but a small matter to have yielded . . . perishable possessions" (160). To persuade the Mohegans that the removal is in fact God's will, and that they are exchanging an earthly kingdom for a heavenly one, Occom preaches a sermon on "the division of land among the people of Egypt, and the departure of half the tribe of Manasseh, to a distant inheritance with the Reubenites, and Gadites" (171). Despite this Biblical precedent, the sketch's narrator seems to side with Ashbow rather than Occom, lingering in her description over the "sorrowful countenances" of the two hundred "emigrants" as they sing "a parting hymn . . . expressive of their sympathies and devout hopes" (172, 177). Nonetheless, the Indians' departure from the region "forty years since" arguably enables the prosperity of the "agriculturalists" whose virtues the *Sketch* celebrates as the foundation of N—'s "strength and peace" (149).

Although neither Hale nor Sigourney represents the frontier settlements found in Cooper's *Prairie* or Imlay's *Emigrants*, their collections share
American writers' growing interest in the effects of the internal, as opposed
to transatlantic, movements of peoples on the formation of regional and
national identities. To some extent, this inward turn reflects global changes in
transnational migration. Although the years leading up to the Great Famine
of 1845–1850 saw a substantial spike in Irish migration to the United States,
far greater numbers of British and Irish migrants in the 1830s and '40s headed
to Canada and Australia than to the United States. Beginning in the 1850s,
fears about the disruptive potential of migrants would find a new focus in
the Chinese who arrived on the west coast hoping to profit from California's
Gold Rush. While British, and particularly Irish, immigrants, do not disap-
pear from mid-nineteenth-century American literature, representations of
newcomers tend to be more formulaic than they had been just a few decades
earlier.

Catharine Maria Sedgwick's second series of *Tales and Sketches* (1844) is a
useful example with which to close this discussion of American regional collections because it illustrates the impact of an increasingly xenophobic environment on literary representations of migrants and migration. Sedgwick's
second series of *Tales and Sketches* is also remarkable for the sophisticated
connections it establishes between transatlantic and westward migration,
which situate its delineation of New England life in an Atlantic rather than
a national context. Sedgwick published her first series of *Tales and Sketches*,
which brought together a number of short pieces previously published in
magazines and journals, in 1835. Her growing preference for shorter forms
than the novels with which she had established her literary reputation perhaps
reflected her desire to explore more fully the peculiarities of New England
identity—a task she had begun in 1822 with the publication of *A New-England
Tale*. The task of compiling collections of tales and sketches from pieces that,
as Sedgwick reminded her readers, had been previously published in "various magazines and annuals," allowed her to represent New England society
from a range of angles.[62] In pieces including "The Railroad Car," "Our Burial-
Place," "The Postoffice," and "The Irish Girl," the second series of *Tales and
Sketches* explores the effects of westward migration and Irish immigration on
rural New England's character and landscape. By representing New England
as both a destination and a point of origin for migrants, and thus as both the
foreign and the familiar, Sedgwick fragments the perspective of the participant-observer and represents through bricolage the dramatic socioeconomic
changes that rural New England experienced during the early nineteenth
century.

"The Railroad Car," first published in *Godey's Lady's Book* in 1842 and
reprinted in the second series of *Tales and Sketches*, compares New England
sociability to English indifference by describing the interactions of passengers

on a train traveling through the northeastern United States. The narrator observes that New Englanders have not yet attained "that philosophical indifference to individual character and history which characterizes an older civilization. They are as yet but an extended family. Even our huge railroad cars, which very nearly reduce humanity to floating particles, have not yet divested our travellers of their customary social charities and interests" (169). Describing the "trifling intercommunication" between passengers in the New England railroad carriage, the narrator predicts that "In a similar situation in Europe, the individuals, each comprising in his own existence a world of interests, purposes, and hopes, would make their entrances and exits without exciting more sensation or inquiry than the luggage thrown into the baggage car" (170). The narrator herself exhibits a sociability in which readers perforce share as she strikes up conversations with various passengers. The train, which initially seems like a vehicle of deracination and even dehumanization, turning people into "floating particles," instead offers a space in which national and regional differences can be articulated and explored. The narrator is troubled by a solitary, quiet young woman who is dressed in mourning and who refuses to divulge any information about herself other than that she has come from "Far West." This information immediately transforms the unassuming young woman into an exotic object of attention, and New England, which in comparison to England, is a newly established society, comes instead to occupy the position of "an older civilization." Despite her seeming foreignness, the nameless young woman embodies the truth of the narrator's claim that New Englanders are still "members of an extended family" when she turns out to be the long-lost grand-niece of an aging and equally solitary old woman who resides in the narrator's town. While the discovery of the stranger's identity emphasizes New England's insularity, her mobility reveals the formative connections between New England and regions "Far West" as well as the growing differences between New and Old England.

Although geographic mobility in "The Railroad Car" reinforces the social bonds defining New England's identity, migration in "Our Burial-Place" threatens to undermine republican virtue by severing those bonds. The sketch describes the narrator's wanderings through the cemetery near Lowell, Massachusetts, where she explores "the interesting associations of a country burial-place" (389) by describing the headstones. Her meanderings inspire a cultural comparison between Native Americans' and white New Englanders' attitudes towards death. Lauding American Indians' "filial fondness at the graves of their fathers" (385), she opines that "the most touching passages in their eloquent remonstrances against their forced removals are those that allude to their being driven far away from their native burial-places" (385). In contrast, New Englanders' eagerness to migrate westward has already begun to undermine their sense of connection to their ancestors, and hence also their respect for the republican virtues their ancestors embodied. In a nation where a house is "rarely tenanted by the same family for two successive generations," the narrator asks, what will happen to the "ashes of the fathers who have died in Massachusetts, when their children move to the Valley of the Mississippi, and their grandchildren, perchance, to Oregon?" (387). As is so often the case, Sedgwick's sketch has an unmistakably practical agenda—here, to encourage the building of cemeteries in newly settled territory, to which people "may hereafter resort to indulge in affectionate memories and holy contemplations" (396). While the children of the first settlers on the frontier may move further westward, these cemeteries will await subsequent generations of settlers, creating for them a connection to a shared national past. A triumphant endnote to "Our Burial-Place" explains that since the first publication of the sketch in *Knickerbocker* in 1835, "many beautiful cemeteries have been laid out in different parts of the country. . . . Many of our inland towns have selected lovely spots, adorned them, and consecrated them to this holy use" (396).

Sedgwick's second series of *Tales and Sketches* sets internal migration in the context of transatlantic migration through two other tales, "The Postoffice" and "The Irish Girl," both of which take recent Irish immigrants as their protagonists. As Sedgwick relates in her autobiography, the state of Massachusetts became home to a "swarm" of Irish immigrants during the 1830s. Between 800,000 and one million people left Ireland for the United States between the end of the Napoleonic Wars in 1815 and the beginning of the Great Famine in 1845, and the majority of them settled along the eastern seaboard.[63] While these migrants, who were primarily either textile workers or tenant farmers, may have been less wealthy and less well educated than the Irish radicals who emigrated in the 1790s and early 1800s, they were better prepared to assimilate into American society than the Gaelic speakers who would emigrate during the Great Famine, between 1845 and 1850.[64] Nonetheless, their numbers frightened and angered the nativist fraternities of American-born white Protestants that formed during the 1830s and '40s. These fraternities attributed a slowing economy, scarcity of jobs, and urban crime to an influx of Irish Catholic immigrants. In the hopes of discouraging immigrants from settling in their regions, nativists published anti-Catholic newspapers, organized riots in urban areas, and endorsed legislation that would make naturalization more difficult.[65] Although Sedgwick shared the nativist assumption that the Irish were governed by passion rather than reason, her representations of Irish immigrants nonetheless aimed to counter nativism and to champion their potential contributions to New England's character.[66]

"The Postoffice," originally published in *Graham's Magazine* in 1843, is one of the few pieces in the second series of *Tales and Sketches* that is not set in New England. It reflects on the manners and mores of northeastern city dwellers by depicting the settlement of Clifton, Illinois, where migrants from the eastern United States mingle with recent arrivals from the Old World. The narrator represents Clifton as the vortex of multiple diasporas: in "our

Western settlements . . . there are members of families newly sent out from their birthplaces, their fibres still trembling with the disruption from the parent stock; there are exiles from the Old World, too, their pulses still answering to every beat of the old heart at home" (308). Because everyone in Clifton is displaced, "the arrival of the mail," with its promise of news from home, "is the great event of the day" (308). Rosy O'Moore, who has recently arrived from Ireland with her parents, is anxiously awaiting letters from her brother Thomas and her suitor Dennis Rooney that will inform her of when each will be able to leave Ireland and join the family in Clifton. Due to the family's poverty, Rosy must use her last shilling—the equivalent, according to the narrator, of 25 cents—which Dennis had given her as a love token, to pay for the mail. Yet the shilling is only enough for one letter, and when she arrives at the post office, Rosy finds that there are two letters waiting for her. When the postmaster taunts Rosy for her inability to pay, a bystander complains on her behalf about the injustices of the postal system: "It is too bad. . . . Here comes this cavern of a mail-bag, filled with all manner of trash—speeches not worth a groat, and letters worth less—brought all the way from Washington with the frank of some poor devil of a Congressman, who had better be planting potatoes at home: why should his letters be free, and these poor emigrants pay a quarter of a dollar for a single sheet? who are thirsting for a work of news from their old home—who, in their hard toil and hard fare, look forward to a letter to cheer and sustain them—who think of it by day and dream of it by night, and when it comes—their manna in the wilderness—it is loaded with postage they cannot pay: an unrighteous, infamous tax it is" (315).

With her usual concern for practical reform, Sedgwick explains in a note appended to the story that "The Postoffice" was originally written "to illustrate the evils of our post-office department, its abuses, and occasional mal-administration" (318). Clearly, however, it was also written to protest against the prejudices faced by Irish immigrants. On her way to the post office, Rosy stops at "the comfortable farmhouse of an Eastern settler," where Mrs. Johnson, "a city-bred lady, from one of the Atlantic States" gives Rosy two 25-cent pieces to redeem the two letters that Mrs. Johnson expects. When Rosy asks Mrs. Johnson to lend her another 25 cents so that she might redeem the two letters that she too expects, Mrs. Johnson refuses on the grounds that a poor Irish girl couldn't possibly get *two* letters. The narrator remarks that Mrs. Johnson is "quite unconscious of the wrong she had done [to Rosy], for the Irish were out of the pale of her sympathies" (308). Mrs. Johnson may be a "city-bred lady," but she lacks the compassion that would mark true refinement. Economic disparity and cultural difference prevent her from recognizing that she and Rosy share in common feelings of displacement and homesickness. Thanks to Sedgwick's didacticism, Mrs. Johnson is punished for her ignorance: a legacy left to Rosy's suitor Dennis enables the O'Moores to settle in New York, where they prosper, while Mrs. Johnson must remain in the backwaters of Clifton.

"The Irish Girl," first published in the *United States Magazine and Democratic Review* in 1842 and reprinted in Sedgwick's second series of *Tales and Sketches*, addresses more explicitly than "The Postoffice" the prejudices confronting Irish immigrants through its characters' repeated uses of the phrases "your people" and "our people." In the Midwestern town of Clifton, everyone is a migrant, and divisions between "your people" and "our people" are somewhat less marked and meaningful. But in Becket, Massachusetts, where "The Irish Girl" is set, the long-established New Englanders do not take kindly to the Irish immigrants that the building of the railroad has brought to their town. Margaret O'Brien, the eponymous Irish Girl, is described as one of those "people, who driven forth from their own land by misery and multiplied oppressions, come here to do our roughest work and share our bread and freedom" (190). She is employed as a servant by the kindly but misguided Mrs. Ray, who, enamored of Margaret's "tidy ways" and "sweet manners" (191, 199), attempts to nurture a nascent romance between the Catholic Margaret and Mrs. Ray's Protestant nephew, William Maxwell. Knowing that "there is nothing William Maxwell's parents have such a horror of as a Romanist, and there is nothing his father despises like an Irish person," Mrs. Ray assures Margaret that if she would only cut ties with her Irish friends and convert to Protestantism, she would seem "no more an Irish girl than Belinda Anne Tracy" (197), the Protestant girl whom William's parents hope he will marry. Margaret's tearful but adamant rejection of this advice, suggests that her Irishness runs deeper than Mrs. Ray realizes. Margaret acknowledges to Mrs. Ray that "your people" express their feelings in a "quiet, regular way"; but, as for the Irish, "our feelings come in a storm, and you may as easy keep the winds that come howling over your Becket hills quiet, as keep them still" (195). Sedgwick's representation of the Irish as deeply emotive is not dissimilar to the nativist caricature of the feckless, childlike Irishman. The difference is that while nativists saw the supposedly passionate nature of the Irish as unfitting them for employment, Sedgwick regards their feelings as a valuable complement to the cold, calculating reason on which New Englanders pride themselves. Mr. Maxwell, William's father, embodies the worst of this shrewdness in his habits as a shopkeeper: "His industry [ran] into anxious toil, his enterprise into avarice, his economy into miserliness, his sagacity into cunning, his self-preserving instincts into selfishness" (201). Although it is his "principle to keep clear of the Paddies," he is not averse to selling his goods to Irish immigrants at "exorbitant prices" (200).

"The Irish Girl" envisions assimilation as a two-way process that would entail the "Irishization" of New Englanders as much as the Americanization of Irish immigrants. Praising the industry, domestic affections, and generosity of Irish newcomers, the narrator questions: "Would it not be well for our people to consider more maturely than they have yet done, the designs of Providence in sending these swarms of Irish people among us? Is it not possible that their vehement feelings, ardent affections, and illimitable generosity might mingle with our colder, and (we say it regretfully) more selfish natures, to the advantage of both? And at any rate, by losing the opportunity of promoting their happiness, of binding them to us by the blessed links of humanity, are we not doing a wrong to our own souls? Can good be effected to them or to ourselves by contemning their nation and deriding their religion?" (198–199). Sedgwick invokes the Puritan ideal of America as God's chosen land to argue against its isolation and impermeability, suggesting instead that Irish immigration might be divinely ordained because it promises to morally improve New England's character. While Irish generosity and affection might counteract New Englanders' self-interestedness, New Englanders' self-control might in turn teach the Irish to moderate their excessive emotions. In excluding and excoriating the Irish, then, New Englanders only indulge their coldness and selfishness to their own detriment.

While Margaret and William's marriage might have participated in the process of cultural hybridization that Sedgwick advocates, it is instead Margaret's death that increases sympathies between the Irish and Anglo-American inhabitants of Becket. Mr. Maxwell and William each demonstrate their self-interestedness when the father persuades the son to break off his engagement with Margaret, threatening, "I'll cast you off forever if you marry one of the Paddy folks!" (207). When Margaret drowns, shortly after her final parting with William, it is unclear whether her death is accidental or intentional. Regardless of its cause, her death incites precisely the moral integration that Sedgwick advocates. Margaret's brother James, the epitome of Irish vehemence and ardor, finds solace for "the howling tempest in [his] breast" after his sister's death in Margaret's last words to him: "Mrs. Ray is every way mother-like to me" (214). As Mrs. Ray and James cry "hot tears" over Margaret's body, James imagines a society in which "there would be an end to cruelty and hate, and love would bind all hearts together—even your people's and mine!" (214). Margaret's death elicits in Mrs. Ray the tenderness that, according to Sedgwick, New Englanders lack. Witnessing Mrs. Ray's grief in turn helps James to control his initially overwhelming feelings of outrage and hatred towards the New England prejudices on which he blames the unhappy Margaret's death. Margaret's death thus accomplishes the reciprocal moral transformation that her marriage to William similarly might have encouraged while conveniently allowing Sedgwick to avoid the potentially offensive move of marrying an Irish Catholic to an Anglo-American Protestant. While the tale clearly implies that the assimilation of Irish immigrants might benefit New Englanders economically and culturally, it also acknowledges that it will take time to establish mutual toleration and sympathy between Irish Catholics and Anglo-American Protestants.

The exploration of how immigration, westward migration, and other forms of geographic mobility affected regional identity was central to early nineteenth-century American collections of tales and sketches from Irving's *Sketch Book* onwards. For the most part, however, Scottish and Irish collections did not directly represent emigration or examine its effects on regional or national identities. Yet migration, along with the Anglicization wrought by industrialization and the transformation of farming practices, nonetheless informs the very existence of Irish and Scottish collections of tales and sketches, which sought to preserve, in writing if not in lived experience, what was in the process of being lost or altered. For instance, William Carleton explained that his *Tales and Sketches, Illustrating the Character, Usages, Traditions, Sports and Pastimes of the Irish Peasantry* was valuable because "several of the originals, who sat for their portraits here presented, were the last of their class which the country will ever again produce."[67] Like Sedgwick's patchwork of New England people and places, Carleton's collection brought together sketches that had appeared in various periodicals over the preceding years to create a composite picture of Irishness. His collection of what he termed "Irish Social Antiquities" included "Mickey M'rory, the Irish Fiddler"; "Buckrum-Back, the Country Dancing-Master"; "Mary Murray, the Irish Match-Maker"; and "Barney M'Haigney, the Irish Prophecy Man," among others (ix). Carleton represents himself as a historian or collector of "antiquities" rather than an observer of current events. The Great Famine, which began the year that *Tales and Sketches of the Irish Peasantry* was published, would render the survival of these traditional figures even more dubious, as emigration reached new highs.

One of the few instances of a collection of tales and sketches from the Celtic peripheries that does mention emigration is Alexander Bethune's *Tales and Sketches of the Scottish Peasantry* (1838). Bethune, a manual laborer from Fife, was injured while blasting rock and began writing his *Tales and Sketches* during his recovery. While most of its pieces describe "the humble abodes of hardy industry" in early nineteenth-century Scotland (131), "The Covenanter's Grave" is set in the mid-seventeenth century, and addresses the Scottish Covenanters' resistance to Charles II's efforts to impose Anglican religious forms on the Scottish Presbyterian church.[68] The story is at once intensely local and transatlantic in scope. It opens with a sweeping view across the landscape of the parish of Abdie in Fife, from the "ruined walls of what was once a shepherd's cot" on the southern bank of "the little loch of Lindores" to the top of a hill called "The Black Cairn" where "at some forgotten peak of the country's history, a small tumulus had been formed" (194). The ensuing tale traces the origins of the isolated grave to the double courtship of Jane Turner by the poor but upstanding Covenanter Alan and the wealthy apostate Black Ritchie, who joins the Royal troops under Claverhouse at the Battle of Bothwell Brig. The Coventanters' resistance to Charles II becomes in this story a historical precedent for the American Patriots' resistance to Parliament's efforts to impose taxes on the colonies, and Jane's heart is won by Alan's courage, when he explains, "There is a secret satisfaction in believing that the sacrifice of property, liberty, and even life itself, is made for the general weal, and that posterity may reap a harvest of happiness from the blood that is shed on a battle field, which inspires fortitude, and makes endurance its own reward" (216). When Alan and Jane are killed by Black Ritchie during a skirmish between Covenanters and Cavaliers, their friends bury the two lovers atop the Black Cairn because "the common burial-place of the parish was in the hands of their enemies" (261). To escape further persecution, the Covenanters of Abdie determine to emigrate to America, obtaining secret passage in a trading vessel. As a result of their emigration, the story behind the little tumulus of earth had almost been forgotten until Bethune's narrator, by writing it down, managed to "rescue it from oblivion" (262). Emigration has also changed the landscape of the parish, transforming it from a village into farmland, so that "the plough has passed over" the remains of the "dwellings of our forefathers" and "the crops of many years have been reaped from the place where their hearthstones once were lying" (195). "The Covenanter's Grave" not only describes the effects of migration on the landscape of Abdie, but also on the character of the newly formed United States. "In their adopted country," the narrator relates, the new settlers "became prosperous and happy; and it was remarked, that from among their offspring arose some of the most zealous contenders for the freedom of the United States" (263).

Like Sedgwick's *Tales and Sketches*, Bethune's collection situates a regional identity in the context of transatlantic affiliations. Although many collections of tales and sketches do not share this transatlantic scope in terms of content, the genre itself was notable for its popularity on both sides of the Atlantic. Because the genre privileged description over plot, it offered writers in the Celtic peripheries and the United States something that the novel didn't: the opportunity to delineate in deep detail the manners and mores of a particular people and the landscape of a specific locale. If the nineteenth-century novel, according to Franco Moretti, "*is the most centralized of all literary genres,*" working to homogenize the nation's manners and mores, the collection of tales and sketches is a distinctively regional form that resisted the novel's homogenizing tendencies in order to preserve cultural difference.[69] Charles Dickens's *Sketches by Boz*, which, as it subtitle explains, describes "Everyday Life and Every-day People," arguably renders London just one of the many regions represented by this genre. By 1836, when *Sketches by Boz* was published, the collection of tales and sketches was already a thriving genre beyond London. Dickens adopted a regional genre and made it metropolitan. Collections of tales and sketches thus participated in the literary decentering of the British Atlantic world, revealing that while London still held the lion's share of cultural and literary authority, it was no longer unchallenged.

American independence had done much to inspire cultural nationalism in Scotland and Ireland, and British migration had in turn done much to swell and diversify the population of the United States and to expand its boundaries. Both of these factors contributed importantly to the development of the regional identities explored in collections of tales and sketches. The term "peripheries" thus seems inappropriate to describe the position of Scotland, Ireland, and the United States in the British Atlantic literary culture of the 1830s and '40s. In literary, if not political, terms, the early to mid-nineteenth-century British Atlantic world consisted not of center and peripheries, but of interconnected and interdependent regions.

{ Epilogue }

British Atlantic Literatures

ANGLO-AMERICAN, COLONIAL, AND ARCHIPELAGIC

The primary aim of this book has been to decenter the Anglo-American focus of transatlantic literary studies by extending the reach of archipelagic criticism to include the literature of the early American republic. In the British context in which it originated, archipelagic criticism counters the Anglocentric tendencies that have long characterized the study of British literature by shifting our attention to sites of literary production and reception beyond metropolitan southern England, particularly London. This archipelagic or "devolved" approach reveals hitherto-overlooked genealogies connecting the literatures of the British Isles and enables the microgeographic exploration of local and regional literary cultures. Archipelagic criticism avoids taking the nation-state as a primary or natural unit of analysis while nonetheless acknowledging its long-standing role in organizing literary study. Extending the reach of archipelagic criticism to include the literature of the early American republic has enabled me to bring to light a British Atlantic literature including Irish, Scottish, and Welsh dimensions that have been obscured by the Anglo-American focus of most studies of transatlantic literature. I've tried to show that writing by and about each of these migrant groups contributed not only to the making of a British Atlantic literature, but also to the simultaneous but far from symmetrical processes of nation-state formation occurring in Britain and the United States during the late eighteenth and early nineteenth centuries.

The question that I was most frequently asked by interlocutors while I was writing this book concerned Canada's place—or lack thereof—in the project. I offered a short answer to this question in the book's introduction: namely that, during the period covered here, Canada remained a British imperial possession and thus was not an independent participant in the dialectical processes of nation-state formation in which the United States and Britain were involved. British Canadians sought to define themselves against French

Canadians on one hand and Americans on the other, while also attempting to balance their colonial affiliation with Britain with some degree of local autonomy. The early Canadian literature of migration and settlement deserves its own book-length study;[1] this epilogue can only briefly explore some of the implications of late eighteenth- and early nineteenth-century Canada's colonial status both for British migrants and for the study of the literature of the British Atlantic world.

To state the obvious, critical perspectives and methodologies to a large extent determine the version of the Atlantic world that any study of transatlantic literature brings into view. I've spent the preceding chapters describing an archipelagic counterpart to the Anglo-American Atlantic world made familiar by recent scholarship.[2] Here, I want to contrast this archipelagic Atlantic to what I'm going to call the colonial Atlantic world—namely, Britain, Canada, and the West Indies. The Anglo-American, archipelagic, and colonial constitute overlapping and interlocking parts of the British Atlantic world. By comparing the literature of the archipelagic Atlantic with that of the colonial Atlantic, I hope to demonstrate how archipelagic criticism might serve as a complement to postcolonial criticism in delineating distinct but intersecting Atlantic worlds. To date, studies of the literary connections among Britain, Canada, and the West Indies, like studies of those between Britain and the United States, have been strongly Anglocentric in focus.[3] The most comprehensive survey of the connections among the literatures of the Celtic peripheries, Canada, and the West Indies during the late eighteenth and early nineteenth centuries remains Katie Trumpener's *Bardic Nationalism: The Romantic Novel and the British Empire* (1997). Trumpener's groundbreaking "prehistory of postcolonial perspectives" explores how the strategies adopted by Scottish, Irish, and Welsh writers to resist metropolitan England's cultural ascendancy both informed and were informed by literature written in and about the West Indies and Canada, among other regions of Britain's empire.[4] *Bardic Nationalism* excludes American literature from its survey of British colonial and anticolonial writing on the very sensible grounds that for most of the Romantic era (which for Trumpener runs from roughly 1760 to 1830), the United States was no longer a British colonial possession.

However, I have argued in this book that American writers continued to share a sense of cultural secondariness with their Irish, Scottish, and Welsh counterparts even after the United States became an independent nation-state. The archipelagic Atlantic, which is delimited by the connections among Irish, Scottish, Welsh, and American literatures, constitutes a counterpart to *Bardic Nationalism*'s colonial Atlantic, which is defined by the relations among British, Canadian, and West Indian literatures. These two Atlantic worlds are made visible, respectively, through archipelagic and postcolonial lenses. They are complementary rather than competing, but they do reflect different methodological assumptions. Trumpener regards England's so-called internal colonies—Ireland, Scotland, and Wales—as comparable to Britain's imperial possessions overseas, whereas I contend that each of the Celtic peripheries developed a historically unique relationship with the English metropolitan center. Moreover, Trumpener's postcolonial perspective re-inscribes the English imperial center as the standard of literary and cultural authority insofar as it understands Irish, Scottish, and Welsh writers (not to mention those in the farther-flung outskirts of empire) as either adopting a centrist position and participating in British imperialism or "writing back" to metropolitan England in opposition to its colonial agenda. Admittedly, archipelagic criticism does not entirely eschew the opposition between center and peripheries; after all, it aims to direct critical attention to sites of literary production and reception that have been overlooked in comparison to the English metropolitan literary center. But as a result of this aim, archipelagic criticism acknowledges (and sometimes actively seeks out) multiple literary centers. Instead of examining the dialectical relationships between peripheral and metropolitan literatures and cultures, archipelagic criticism traces the genealogical connections among various regional or local literatures.

To illustrate some of the differences between the archipelagic Atlantic literature that this book has examined and the colonial Atlantic literature that *Bardic Nationalism* discusses, I will turn to two novels by John Galt, a Scottish writer who was deeply involved in the settlement of Upper Canada, and who, according to Francis Russell Hart, "first gave fictive power to the provincial... as an imaginative territory."[5] Galt is best known for his "theoretical histories of society"—the term he gave to his novels about western Scotland, including *Annals of the Parish* (1821), *The Provost* (1822), and *The Entail* (1823), among others.[6] However, two of his late and lesser-known works, *Lawrie Todd; or, The Settlers in the Woods* (1830) and *Bogle Corbet; or, The Emigrants* (1831), which he described as "theoretic biographies," together offer a particularly useful example of the distinctions between the archipelagic and colonial Atlantic worlds. Galt intended *Lawrie Todd* and *Bogle Corbet*, which describe the Scottish settlement of, respectively, upstate New York and Ontario, to be read as companion texts by middle-class Britons considering emigration to North America. He wrote them while imprisoned in the King's Bench for debt that he had accumulated during his employment as superintendent for the Canada Company from 1826 to 1829.[7] Although Galt's earlier "theoretical histories" have figured importantly in recent studies of the Romantic novel, critical interest in *Bogle Corbet* has until quite lately been confined to Canada, where an abridged paperback version was published in 1977.[8] *Lawrie Todd* has suffered even greater critical neglect, and despite going through four British and sixteen American editions during the nineteenth century, it has not been reprinted since.[9] *Bogle Corbet* may be, as Elizabeth Waterston has claimed, "the first major work to define Canadianism by reference to an American alternative"; but Galt is not generally considered a Canadian author any more than he is an American one.[10] Rather, his works are migrant fictions, traversing the archipelagic and colonial Atlantic worlds, and, in doing so, revealing the intersections and divergences of their literatures. By examining *Bogle Corbet*'s and *Lawrie Todd*'s representations of North American settlement, I will argue that, in Galt's view, migration to the United States, unlike migration to Canada, offered Scots an opportunity to break free from the cycle of colonial victimization and oppression in which they were involved, and by which the colonial Atlantic world was defined.

In representing migration to the United States as less problematic for Scots than migration to Canada, Galt countered popular opinion. A large number of the guidebooks for emigrants published in Britain during the 1820s and '30s claimed to offer an unbiased discussion of the pros and cons of settling in the United States or in Canada; but many were in fact intended to deter migration to the United States and repeatedly emphasized the benefits of remaining under British dominion. *The Counsel for Emigrants* (1834) informs its readers, "So long a period has elapsed since [the United States] were peopled from the British Isles, that we have in a great degree lost the feeling that they are of common stock with ourselves; but in the Canadas we meet thousands of our countrymen located there, (comparatively within a few years) with all the feelings, habits, tastes, &c. of British subjects, living under the protection of British laws, and having all the privileges of commerce that are possessed by us."[11] *The Counsel*'s compilation of letters and periodical essays represent migration to Canada as less financially risky and emotionally upsetting than settlement in the United States because it allowed migrants to maintain close ties to their homeland. Whereas Canadians preserved British customs and manners, Americans supposedly despised them. *The Counsel for Emigrants* warns, "An American thinks no country so good as his own; none so wise or brave or powerful; and he is not content with believing all this himself, without endeavouring to make others acknowledge it also."[12] Accordingly, "An Englishman or Scotchman settled amongst [Americans] must learn to gulp down in silence, or at least with little observation or dispute, many severe reflections on his country and its institutions."[13] Even those writers who conceded that settlement in the United States might be economically advantageous warned that migrants who settled there should expect to renounce or conceal their affection for their native country.

Similar to *The Counsel for Emigrants* and other guidebooks, *Lawrie Todd* and *Bogle Corbet* allowed readers to evaluate the advantages and drawbacks of settlement in Canada and the United States. A comparison of the two narratives not only illustrates the differences between Canada and the United States as destination for migrants but also distinguishes the contours of the British colonial and British archipelagic Atlantic worlds. Bogle Corbet's migration to Upper Canada comes at the end of the painfully protracted downward spiral that marks his absorption into Britain's imperial system. Trumpener and Kenneth McNeil have described *Bogle Corbet* and its eponymous protagonist as "profoundly melancholic," and attribute this melancholy to the "long chain of substitutions and displacements" that characterize Corbet's narrative of his experiences in "an Atlantic world marked by impermanency and migration."[14] Born on a plantation in Jamaica, Corbet is sent to live in Scotland after his parents' deaths, where, at his guardian's behest, he enters the cloth trade as a weaver, later becoming partner of a company. Corbet abjures Scotland early in his career, setting his sights on London, the center of the British colonial world. Despite his marked lack of business acumen, he returns temporarily to Jamaica to develop his company's ties to the West Indies. Financial woes in the wake of the Napoleonic Wars coupled with a growing family finally motivate him to emigrate to Upper Canada, where he is charged by his former and far more successful business partner with establishing a settlement peopled by a group of Scots from Paisley.

By this point, however, Corbet has become an inextricable part of the imperial system that he hopes, through migration, to escape. Thus Trumpener sees Upper Canada as offering "not so much a personal fresh start" for Corbet "as a last chance for the entire imperial system" to which he belongs. In the Canadian wilderness, Corbet manifests "the British compulsion to repeat, again and again, the fundamental injustices of colonization."[15] For instance, he establishes the settlement of Stockville "using a capitalist and feudal model derived from the plantation system," governing his neighbors so high-handedly that they eventually decamp for other more prosperous and welcoming settlements.[16] Corbet frequently criticizes British government of the Canadas even while he unthinkingly replicates its errors in his own person. He faults "the Provincial Governments for not having regular establishments to guide and aid those who, to the natural depression arising from their friendless condition, ever stand so much in want of counsel and assistance" (*BC* 2: 273); yet he offers little friendship or counsel to the settlers under his own care. Corbet lacks the self-awareness to notice his imbrication in Britain's imperial projects, let alone to change his behavior, and he is left at the novel's end isolated and depressed by the failure of his hopes. Galt presents Corbet as at once an unwitting victim of and a self-interested participant in the "economic exploitation, moral disconnection, and psychic dislocation" caused by British imperial expansion.[17]

Trumpener's and McNeil's analyses of *Bogle Corbet* offer persuasive alternatives to readings that, based on incomplete evidence—namely, the abridged version of the novel—have interpreted it as an "affirmative account of imperial growth."[18] Yet the extent of the disconnection and isolation underlying Corbet's re-enactment of colonial injustices in Stockville only becomes fully apparent in contrast to Lawrie Todd's prosperous and comparatively democratic settlement of Judiville. If *Bogle Corbet* is a tale of imperial disconnection

and displacement, *Lawrie Todd* depicts the formation of enduring transatlantic ties. It tells the rags-to-riches story of a young Scottish radical's flight to
the United States, where he exchanges his youthful idealism for strenuous
capitalism. After building his stock of capital as a storekeeper and merchant,
Todd founds the thriving settlement of Judiville, a "shadowy and subdued"
fictional version of Rochester, New York (*LT* 1: iv), the fame of which eventually spreads through New York state and back to Scotland. Todd wins the
respect of more recent Scottish migrants and rises to a position of power in
Judiville before returning home to Scotland at the novel's end. *Lawrie Todd* is
not simply a happier version of *Bogle Corbet*: its protagonist too experiences
the hardships and frustrations of settlement in a new country. But it is paradoxically the possibility of renouncing forever his affiliations with Britain and
its empire—a possibility that Corbet does not confront—that affirms Todd's
loyalty to Scotland.

P. H. Scott describes "the whole atmosphere" of *Lawrie Todd* as "distinctly
American: restless, ambitious, expansive, egalitarian and conducive to successful capitalist speculation."[19] Yet these qualities originate in Todd's Scottish
childhood, merely coming to fruition after his migration to the United States.
From the beginning of his story, Lawrie Todd is a little man with a big person-
ality. His growth is stunted by a childhood illness that leaves him a "lamiter
for life," yet he is as undaunted by this seeming impediment as by his humble
origins (*LT* 1: 4). Todd's resourceful self-confidence offers a welcome contrast to Corbet's melancholy, but sometimes leads him into scrapes. In 1792,
Todd, "with the brave confidence in myself which has been so often a staff
in my hand in the perils of tribulation" (*LT* 1: 22), joins the Scottish Friends
of the People along with some other "young lads of mechanical vocations"
(*LT* 1: 25) and is soon afterwards arrested for treason. At his anxious father's
request, Todd sails for New York before the trial takes place, but he never
completely renounces his radicalism, instead learning to promote his own
self-interest along with general liberty and equality. As he transforms himself from a nail-maker—his father's trade—to a shopkeeper, farmer, inves-
tor, and public official, Todd remains "desirous of renown, but anxious to
serve the community" (*LT* 3: 193). As an instance of the transatlantic myth of
the successful Scottish migrant, *Lawrie Todd* suggests that Scots' prosperity
in the New World depended on the conditions of possibility that the United
States opened to them as much as on any inherent predispositions towards
successful settlement.

In contrast to guidebooks like *The Counsel for Emigrants, Lawrie Todd*
and *Bogle Corbet* together suggest that, in Galt's opinion, migration to the
United States, or within the archipelagic Atlantic, allowed Scots to maintain
a purer attachment to the past and to their homeland than did migration to
Canada, or within the colonial Atlantic. Settlement in New York allows Todd
to develop an attachment to the United States while maintaining his ties to

Scotland, whereas Corbet, in Canada, continues to identify with the English imperial center from which he feels himself exiled. Lawrie Todd maintains an apparently uncompromised affection for his homeland during several decades of prosperous enterprise in New York. Although he revisits Scotland during this time, his dual loyalties to his native land and to the United States, which he terms "the country of my adoption" (*LT* 3: 199), do not seem to come into conflict until he is nominated to stand for election as Judiville's representative to the New York state legislature. While he is proud of the honor, Todd comes to realize that it would not be "consistent with the zeal and truth of a Scottish heart, to abet counsels that may be for the molestation of his native land" (*LT* 3: 198). Running for a seat in the state legislature would require him to decisively renounce Scotland and to declare allegiance to the United States. "America had been to me a land of refuge; verily, a land flowing with milk and honey" (*LT* 3: 199), Todd acknowledges. Yet he cannot bear "the thought of renouncing the right to claim paternity with Sir William Wallace and the brave old bald-headed worthies of the Covenant; my father's household gods, on whose altar our lowly hearth, the incense of a special thanksgiving was every sabbath-evening offered to Heaven" (*LT* 3: 198–199). The United States has provided scope for Todd's restless striving, but his "auld-lang-syne-feelings" bind him to the land of his birth, and he determines to return permanently with his wife and youngest child to Scotland. (*LT* 3: 198).

Lawrie Todd's relationship to his past and to Scotland is not less complex than Bogle Corbet's; it is simply differently complex. Wherever he is, Corbet never feels at home. In Canada, he feels himself to be an exile rather than an emigrant, separated from all the intellectual and material goods that he enjoyed in London. At the same time, however, Canada's status as a British possession, and Corbet's own identification with Britain's imperial mission, means that he is in a sense already at home there, even though the landscape and ways of life are largely unfamiliar. After all, the "the King's dominions," as one of Corbet's fellow settlers points out, "is the next thing to a native land" (*BC* 3: 210). Todd, by contrast, is at home on both sides of the Atlantic. Consequently, his attachments are irreparably divided; for whether he is in Judiville or in Bonnytown, New York or Scotland, he misses the other place. In returning to Scotland, he leaves the adult children of an earlier marriage behind him, a parting that moves him to "an agony of tears" (*LT* 3: 292–293). Yet, in a world where a transatlantic crossing takes only twenty-two days, New York and Scotland are closely connected, as the passage of people, goods, and ideas between the two sites in *Lawrie Todd* demonstrates.

While *Bogle Corbet* represents Jamaica, the Scottish Highlands, and Upper Canada as iterations of an imperial pattern emanating from London, *Lawrie Todd* figures New York state and Scotland as discrete but interconnected sites within the British Atlantic world, and represents its characters' movements between them as a matter of choice. My aim in juxtaposing these novels is not to suggest that, for Galt, settlement in the United States was preferable to settlement in Canada, although his falling out with the Canada Company's board may well have led him to feel that this was the case. Nor do I intend to imply that *Bogle Corbet* and *Lawrie Todd* are representative of the respective historical realities of the emigrant experience in Ontario and upstate New York. Rather, my aim has been to illuminate through these novels the similarities and differences between a British colonial Atlantic world that includes Canada and Jamaica, and a British archipelagic Atlantic world that includes the United States. These versions of the Atlantic world intersect and overlap, much as the Scottish migrants who initially people Bogle Corbet's settlement easily crisscross between Ontario and upstate New York. Many leave Stockville to ply their trades in the more populous and economically diversified United States, and some return to Canada to escape the "clish-maclavering" and "argolbargoling" of American democracy (*BC* 3: 210). The ease of these crossings should remind us that in terms of geography and climate, Ontario and upstate New York are virtually indistinguishable, and that during the eighteenth century they were a North American version of the "debatable ground" between Scotland and England. Yet by the 1830s, settlement in Canada and settlement in the United States entailed quite distinct cultural and political experiences for prospective migrants, and Canada had become the more popular destination of the two. Settlement in Canada entailed participation in Britain's imperial project, and thus an ongoing, perhaps intensified, allegiance to an Anglocentric version of Britishness, while settlement in the United States, as *Lawrie Todd* suggests, might entail a doubled, but comparatively fluid, allegiance to two countries—one native and one adopted—connected by the circulation of goods, people, and ideas. The diasporic literatures of a colonial British Atlantic world and an archipelagic British Atlantic world thus invite somewhat different questions and approaches of study.

The literature of British migration by no means disappeared after the 1830s, but it acquired different characteristics as settlers headed for new regions of the globe, each with a historically and geographically specific relation to the British archipelago. While we tend to think of our contemporary world as globalized in unprecedented ways, large-scale migration has a long history, as do its literary representations. These representations sometimes have fallen into obscurity because they do not fit comfortably into the national categories through which we tend to organize literary study, and particularly the study of literature written between 1700 and 1900, the era that saw the consolidation of the nation-state. In *Nation and Migration* I have attempted to formulate some new categories. I hope others will refine and develop them as they continue to explore the history of the diasporic literatures that are being written today.

{ NOTES }

Introduction

1. Kariann Akemi Yokota, *Unbecoming British: How Revolutionary America Became a Postcolonial Nation* (Oxford: Oxford University Press, 2011), 9. Britons perhaps began to regard Americans as a distinct people earlier than Americans began to assert their own distinctiveness. See Stephen Conway, "From Fellow-Nationals to Foreigners: British Perceptions of the Americans, circa 1739–1793," *William and Mary Quarterly*, 3rd ser., LIX.1 (2002), 65–99.

2. On eighteenth-century British nation formation, see Linda Colley, *Britons: Forging the Nation 1707–1837* (New Haven: Yale University Press, 1992); and Alexander Grant and Keith J. Stringer, eds. *Uniting the Kingdom? The Making of British History* (London: Routledge, 1995). As Grant and Stringer's collection demonstrates, the term "United Kingdom" is slippery and carries a lot of historical baggage. I use it in this book exclusively to refer to the entity created by the 1800 union of Great Britain and Ireland, which lasted from 1801 to 1922.

3. Nicholas Canny, "Introduction," in *Oxford History of the British Empire*, vol. 1, *The Origins of Empire*, ed. Nicholas Canny (Oxford: Oxford University Press, 1998), 24–25.

4. Eric Richards, *Britannia's Children: Emigration from England, Scotland, Wales and Ireland since 1600* (London: Hambledon, 2004), 16.

5. Bannet argues that migrant fictions "fell out of favor less for aesthetic reasons, than because they fit so poorly into later nationalist master-narratives." Eve Tavor Bannet, *Transatlantic Stories and the History of Reading: Migrant Fictions* (Cambridge, UK: Cambridge University Press, 2011), 1.

6. The phrase is from the title of Spender's *Love-Hate Relations: English and American Sensibilities* (New York: Random House 1974).

7. Elisa Tamarkin, *Anglophilia: Deference, Devotion, and Antebellum America* (Chicago: University of Chicago Press, 2008); Robert Weisbuch, *Atlantic Double-Cross: American Literature and British Influence in the Age of Emerson* (Chicago: University of Chicago Press, 1986), xviii.

8. Leonard Tennenhouse, *The Importance of Feeling English: American Literature and British Diaspora, 1750–1850* (Princeton: Princeton University Press, 2007), 8.

9. Thomas Paine, *Rights of Man, Common Sense, and Other Political Writings*, ed. Mark Philp (Oxford: Oxford University Press, 1998), 23, 22.

10. James Belich, *Replenishing the Earth: The Settler Revolution and the Rise of the Anglo-World, 1783–1939* (Oxford: Oxford University Press, 2009), 66.

11. In addition to Belich, *Replenishing the Earth*, see Bernard Bailyn, *Voyagers to the West: A Passage in the Peopling of North America on the Eve of Revolution* (New York: Vintage, 1988); Bernard Bailyn and Philip D. Morgan, eds., *Strangers within the Realm:*

Cultural Margins of the First British Empire (Chapel Hill: University of North Carolina Press, 1991); Barbara DeWolfe, ed. *Discoveries of America: Personal Accounts of British Emigrants to North America during the Revolutionary Era* (Cambridge, UK: Cambridge University Press, 1997); and David Hackett Fischer, *Albion's Seed: Four British Folkways in America* (New York: Oxford University Press, 1989).

12. James Horn, "British Diaspora: Emigration from Britain, 1680–1815," in *Oxford History of the British Empire*, vol. 2, *The Eighteenth Century*, ed. P. J. Marshall (Oxford: Oxford University Press, 1998), 30–31; see also Richards, *Britannia's Children*, 76.

13. Hugh Henry Brackenridge, *Modern Chivalry*, ed. Claude M. Newlin (New York: American Book Company, 1937), 577. "Colluvies" can refer either to foul discharge, as from an ulcer, or to the rabble. Brackenridge undoubtedly hoped to evoke both meanings.

14. J. G. A. Pocock, "The Limits and Divisions of British History: In Search of the Unknown Subject," *The American Historical Review* 87 (1982), 317.

15. John Kerrigan, *Archipelagic English: Literature, History, and Politics 1603–1707* (Oxford: Oxford University Press, 2008), 11.

16. Kerrigan, *Archipelagic English*, 12.

17. Claire Lamont, "Jane Austen and the Nation," in *A Companion to Jane Austen*, ed. Claudia L. Johnson and Clara Tuite (Oxford: Wiley-Blackwell, 2009), 312.

18. David Armitage, *The Ideological Origins of the British Empire* (Cambridge, UK: Cambridge University Press, 2000), 21.

19. Kerrigan, *Archipelagic English*, 58.

20. On the circulation of texts between Britain, Ireland, and the United States during the eighteenth and early nineteenth centuries, see Joseph Rezek, *London and the Making of Provincial Literature: Aesthetics and the Transatlantic Book Trade, 1800–1850* (Philadelphia: University of Pennsylvania Press, 2015).

21. On the high incidence of back-migration see David Cressy, *Coming Over: Migration and Communication between England and New England in the Seventeenth Century* (Cambridge, UK: Cambridge University Press, 1987), 191–212; and Stephen Fender, *Sea Changes: British Migration and American Literature* (Cambridge, UK: Cambridge University Press, 1992), 142–147, 205–233. Alan L. Karras distinguishes those who went abroad with the intention of returning to Britain as "sojourners" rather than "emigrants." See his *Sojourners in the Sun: Scottish Migrants in Jamaica and the Chesapeake, 1740–1800* (Ithaca: Cornell University Press, 1992) for the difficulties particular to studying this population.

22. Belich, *Replenishing the Earth*, 65. Eric Richards concurs that that emigration was "simply an extension to . . . widespread systems of internal mobility." *Britannia's Children*, 52.

23. See Belich, *Replenishing the Earth*, 65–68; and Horn, "British Diaspora," 29, 51.

24. These studies of Anglo-American literary relations include the following: Nancy Armstrong and Leonard Tennenhouse, "The American Origins of the English Novel," *ALH* 4 (1992), 386–410; Bannet, *Transatlantic Stories*; Eve Tavor Bannet and Susan Manning, eds., *Transatlantic Literary Studies, 1660–1830* (Cambridge, UK: Cambridge University Press, 2012); Lawrence Buell, "American Literary Emergence as a Postcolonial Phenomenon," *ALH* 4.3 (1992), 411–442; Amanda Claybaugh, *The Novel of Purpose: Literature and Social Reform in the Anglo-American World* (Ithaca: Cornell University Press, 2006);

Laura Doyle, *Freedom's Empire: Race and the Rise of the Novel in Atlantic Modernity, 1640–1940* (Durham: Duke University Press, 2008); Fender, *Sea Changes*; Paul Giles, *Transatlantic Insurrections: British Culture and the Formation of American Literature, 1730–1860* (Philadelphia: University of Pennsylvania Press, 2001); Paul Giles, *The Global Remapping of American Literature* (Princeton: Princeton University Press, 2011); Richard Gravil, *Romantic Dialogues: Anglo-American Continuities, 1776–1862* (New York: St. Martin's Press, 2000); Christopher Hanlon, *America's England: Antebellum Literature and Atlantic Sectionalism* (Oxford: Oxford University Press, 2013); David S. Shields, *Oracles of Empire: Poetry, Politics, and Commerce in British America, 1690–1750* (Chicago: University of Chicago Press, 1990); Stephen Spender, *Love-Hate Relations*; Tamarkin, *Anglophilia*; Tennenhouse, *The Importance of Feeling English*; Robert Weisbuch, *Atlantic Double-Cross*; W. M. Verhoeven, *Revolutionary Histories: Transatlantic Cultural Nationalism, 1775–1815* (London: Palgrave, 2002).

25. See Tamarkin, *Anglophilia*; and Rezek, *London and the Making of Provincial Literature*.

26. Carole Gerson, "Writers without Borders: The Global Framework of Canada's Early Literary History," *Canadian Literature* 201 (2009), 15–33. On the question of whether *The History of Emily Montague* is an English or a Canadian novel, see also Pam Perkins, "Imagining Eighteenth-Century Quebec: British Literature and Colonial Rhetoric," in *Is Canada Postcolonial? Unsettling Canadian Literature*, ed. Laura Moss (Waterloo, ON: Wilfred Laurier University Press, 2003), 151–161.

27. Peter J. Marshall, "British North America, 1760–1815," in *The Oxford History of the British Empire*, vol. 2, *The Eighteenth Century*, ed. Peter Marshall (Oxford: Oxford University Press, 1998), 372–393.

28. On the peculiar difficulties nineteenth-century Canadian writers faced in publishing their works, see Gwendolyn Davies, "Publishing Abroad," in *History of the Book in Canada*, vol. 2, ed. Patricia Lockhart Fleming, Yvan Lamonde, and Fiona Black (Toronto: University of Toronto Press, 2005), 139–146; Nicholas Mount, *When Canadian Literature Moved to New York* (Toronto: University of Toronto Press, 2005); and George Parker, *The Beginnings of the Book Trade in Canada* (Toronto: University of Toronto Press, 1985).

29. Trevor Burnard, "European Migration to Jamaica, 1655–1780," *William and Mary Quarterly* 53 (1996), 769–794.

30. Alison Games, "Migration," *The British Atlantic World, 1500–1800*, ed. David Armitage and Michael J. Braddick (New York: Palgrave, 2002), 49.

31. Bailyn, *Voyagers*, 52. See also Mildred Campbell, "'Of People Either too Few or too Many': The Conflict of Opinion on Population and its Relation to Emigration," in *Conflict in Stuart England: Essays in Honour of Wallace Notestein*, ed. William Appleton Aiken and Basil Duke Henning (London: Jonathan Cape, 1960), 169–202.

32. James Anderson, *The Interest of Great Britain, with Regard to her American Colonies, Considered* (London: Cadell, 1782), 24, italics in original.

33. Morgan J. Rhees, *The Good Samaritan. An Oration delivered . . . in behalf of the Philadelphia Society for the Information and Assistance of persons Emigrating from Foreign Countries* (Philadelphia: Lang & Ustick, 1796), 12.

34. Oliver Goldsmith, *The Poetical Works of Oliver Goldsmith*, ed. Austin Dobson (Oxford: Oxford University Press, 1949), 21–37, lines 57–62.

35. Goldsmith, *Deserted Village*, 275–276.

36. Goldsmith, *Deserted Village*, 273–274.

37. Goldsmith, *Deserted Village*, 267–268.

38. Austin Dobson traces the endeavor to identify Auburn with Goldsmith's native village of Lissoy to Thomas Macaulay, who claimed that *The Deserted Village* "is made up of incongruous parts. The village in its happy days is a true English village. The village in its decay is an Irish village. . . . The hamlet [Goldsmith] had probably seen in Kent; the ejectment he had probably seen in Munster." See *The Poetical Works of Oliver Goldsmith*, ed. Austin Dobson (Oxford: Oxford University Press, 1949), 178. Recent criticism that assumes an Irish location for Auburn includes C. C. Barfoot, "Deserting the Village," in *The Clash of Ireland: Literary Contrasts and Connections* (Amsterdam: Rodopi, 1989), 52–97; and Michael Griffin, "Delicate Allegories, Deceitful Mazes: Goldsmith's Landscapes," *Eighteenth-Century Ireland/Iris an dá chultúr* 16 (2001), 104–117. For a contrary argument, see Mavis Batey, "Oliver Goldsmith: An Indictment of Landscape Gardening," in *Furor Hortensis*, ed. Peter Willis (Edinburgh: Elysium Press, 1974), 57–71, which claims that Auburn is modeled on Nuneham Courtney in Oxfordshire, one of the counties badly affected by enclosure.

39. See P. J. Marshall, *Remaking the British Atlantic: The United States and the British Empire after American Independence* (Oxford: Oxford University Press, 2012), 226–231.

40. *Public Advertiser*, February 27, 1783.

41. On immigration policy in the early republic, see James H. Kettner, *The Development of American Citizenship, 1608–1870* (Chapel Hill: University of North Carolina Press, 1978), 213–247; Susan F. Martin, *A Nation of Immigrants* (Cambridge, UK: Cambridge University Press, 2011), 60–85; Robbie Totten, "National Security and U.S. Immigration Policy, 1776–1790," *Journal of Interdisciplinary History* 39 (2008), 37–64; and Aristide R. Zolberg, *A Nation by Design: Immigration Policy in the Fashioning of America* (Cambridge, MA: Harvard University Press, 2006), 79–95.

42. Thomas Jefferson, *Notes on the State of Virginia* (Philadelphia: Prichard and Hall, 1788), 93.

43. *Annals of Congress*, 1st Congress, 2nd session, February 1790.

44. Benjamin Franklin, *Writings*, ed. J. A. Leo Lemay (New York: Library of America, 1987), 975.

45. Franklin, *Writings*, 710.

46. Franklin, *Writings*, 1102.

47. Humphry Marshall, *The Aliens: A Patriotic Poem* (Philadelphia, 1798), 7, 10.

48. Marshall, *The Aliens*, 11, 13.

49. Marshall, *The Aliens*, 11.

50. J. Hector St. John de Crèvecoeur, *Letters from an American Farmer and Sketches of Eighteenth-Century America*, ed. Albert E. Stone (New York: Penguin, 1986), 85–86.

51. Crèvecoeur, *Letters*, 85.

52. Chandler Robbins Gilman, *Life on the Lakes: Being Tales and Sketches collected during A Trip to the Pictured Rocks of Lake Superior*, 2 vols. (New York: George Dearborn, 1836), vol. 1, 32.

53. Gilman, *Life on the Lakes*, vol. 1, 32.

54. On the shift in destinations for British migrants from the United States to Australia and Canada, see Belich, *Replenishing the Earth*, 261–305; and Fender, *Sea Changes*, 39–40.

55. On Scottish slaveholding see David Hancock, "Scots in the Slave Trade," in *Nation and Province in the First British Empire: Scotland and the Americas, 1600–1800*, ed. Ned C. Landsman (Lewisburg, PA: Bucknell University Press, 2001), 60–93.

56. See Noel Ignatiev, *How the Irish Became White* (New York: Routledge, 1995).

57. On Spanish settlement, see Ralph Bauer, *The Cultural Geography of Colonial American Literatures* (Cambridge, UK: Cambridge University Press, 2003); on German migration, see Aaron Spencer Fogleman, *Hopeful Journeys: German Immigration, Settlement, and Political Culture in Colonial America, 1717–1775* (Philadelphia: University of Pennsylvania Press, 1996); and on the Dutch, see Wim Klooster, *The Dutch in the Americas* (Providence: The John Carter Brown Library, 1997).

58. DeWolfe, *Discoveries of America*, 11.

59. See note 24 for a list of these studies.

60. Gilman, *Life on the Lakes*, vol. 1, 40.

61. Tilar J. Mazzeo, "The Impossibility of Being Anglo-American: The Rhetoric of Emigration and Transatlanticism in British Culture, 1791–1830," *European Romantic Review* 16 (2005), 60.

62. Christopher Flynn discusses these travelers' development of an ethnography of Americans in *Americans in British Literature, 1770–1832: A Breed Apart* (Aldershot: Ashgate, 2008), 113–138.

63. In his study of the migration of Anglophone peoples during the long nineteenth century, Belich explains that although England provided the most emigrants "in terms of absolute numbers," Scottish and Irish rates of emigration were proportionally much higher than England's. See *Replenishing the Earth*, 58.

64. Susan Kubica Howard, "Introduction," in *Euphemia*, by Charlotte Lennox, ed. Susan Kubica Howard (Peterborough, ON: Broadview, 2013), 11.

65. Others include Susanna Rowson's *Charlotte Temple* (1791) and Samuel Pratt's *Emma Corbett* (1780).

66. Charlotte Lennox, *Euphemia*, ed. Susan Kubica Howard (Peterborough, ON: Broadview, 2013), 203. Subsequent references will be made parenthetically by page number.

67. Tamarkin, *Anglophilia*, 150.

68. Tim Fulford, *Romantic Indians: Native Americans, British Literature, and Transatlantic Culture 1756–1830* (Oxford: Oxford University Press, 2006), 103–104.

Chapter 1

1. *A Vindication of the Rights of the Americans* (London: n.p., 1765), 10.

2. During the seventeenth century, the balance of power in England shifted from the king to Parliament. Especially after 1689, when the king's legitimacy rested upon a Parliamentary title, "sovereignty rested not in the king alone, but in the king-in-Parliament," and Parliament thus regulated the colonies' trade with Britain. See Jack P. Greene, *Peripheries and Center: Constitutional Development in the Extended Polities of the British Empire, and the United States, 1607–1788* (Athens: University of Georgia Press, 1986), 57. For an overview of the broader issues at stake in the conflicts between Britain and the American colonies, see, Bernard Bailyn, *The Ideological Origins of the American*

Revolution (Cambridge, MA: The Belknap Press, 1967); Gordon S. Wood, *The Creation of the American Republic, 1776–1787* (Chapel Hill: University of North Carolina Press, 1969); Stephen Conway, *The British Isles and the War of American Independence* (Oxford: Oxford University Press, 2000); and Eliga H. Gould, *The Persistence of Empire: British Political Culture in the Age of the American Revolution* (Chapel Hill: University of North Carolina Press, 2000).

3. Ireland's Parliament was made subordinate to and dependent upon the British Parliament through the Declaratory Act of 1719. The issue of the Declaratory Act of 1766, declaring the subordination of the American colonial assemblies to the British Parliament, led to the eventual loss of the American colonies and impelled Britain to reconsider its treatment of Ireland. The British Parliament repealed the Declaratory Act of 1719 and Ireland's Parliament enjoyed a brief period of independence from 1782 to 1800. For a discussion of eighteenth-century Ireland's political relations with the British Parliament, see S. J. Connolly, "Eighteenth-Century Ireland: Colony or *ancien régime?*" in *The Making of Modern Irish History: Revisionism and the Revisionist Controversy*, ed. D. George Boyce and Alan O'Day (London: Routledge, 1996), 15–33.

4. J. H. Elliott, "A Europe of Composite Monarchies," *Past and Present* 137 (1992), 60.

5. On this usage see Nicholas Canny, "The Origins of Empire: An Introduction," in *The Oxford History of the British Empire*, vol. 1, *The Origins of Empire*, ed. Nicholas Canny (Oxford: Oxford University Press, 1998), 28.

6. See Michael Hechter, *Internal Colonialism: The Celtic Fringe in British National Development 1536–1966* (Berkeley: University of California Press, 1975); and Nicholas Canny, *Kingdom and Colony: Ireland in the Atlantic World, 1560–1800* (Baltimore: Johns Hopkins University Press, 1988).

7. See David Armitage, *The Ideological Origins of the British Empire* (Cambridge, UK: Cambridge University Press, 2000); Mary Sarah Bilder, *The Transatlantic Constitution: Colonial Legal Culture and the Empire* (Cambridge, MA: Harvard University Press, 2008); Jack P. Greene, *Peripheries and Center*, and *Creating the British Atlantic: Essays on Transplantation, Adaptation, and Continuity* (Charlottesville: University of Virginia Press, 2013); and *The British Atlantic World, 1500–1800*, ed. David Armitage and Michael J. Braddick (New York: Palgrave, 2002).

8. For some of the other connotations of Englishness in the eighteenth century see Krishan Kumar, *The Making of English National Identity* (Cambridge, UK: Cambridge University Press 2003); Paul Langford, *Englishness Identified: Manners and Character, 1650–1850* (New York: Oxford University Press, 2000); and Gerald Newman, *The Rise of English Nationalism: A Cultural History, 1720–1830* (New York: St. Martin's Press, 1987).

9. Bailyn, *Ideological Origins*, 55–93; and Caroline Robbins, *The Eighteenth-Century Commonwealthman: studies in the transmission, development, and circumstance of English liberal thought from the Restoration of Charles II until the War with the thirteen colonies* (Cambridge, MA: Harvard University Press, 1961). On the colonial adaptation of commonwealth discourses of English liberty, see Wood, *The Creation*, 10–17. J. C. D. Clark argues that religious sectarianism played an important part in modifying commonwealth thought in the American colonies. See *The Language of Liberty, 1660–1832: Political Discourse and Social Dynamics in the Anglo-American World* (New York: Cambridge University Press, 1994).

10. Bailyn, *Ideological Origins*, 68.

11. Laura Doyle, *Freedom's Empire: Race and the Rise of the Novel in Atlantic Modernity, 1640–1940* (Durham: Duke University Press, 2008), 2.

12. Robert Folkenflik, "Johnson's Politics," in *The Cambridge Companion to Samuel Johnson*, ed. Greg Clingham (Cambridge, UK: Cambridge University Press, 1997), 105.

13. Nicholas Hudson, *Samuel Johnson and the Making of Modern England* (Cambridge, UK: Cambridge University Press, 2003), 190.

14. On the hairy question of how Burke's Irishness may have influenced his political views, see Conor Cruise O'Brien, *The Great Melody: The Thematic Biography and Commented Anthology of Edmund Burke* (London: Sinclair-Stevenson, 1992); Luke Gibbons, *Edmund Burke and Ireland: Aesthetics, Politics, and the Colonial Sublime* (Cambridge, UK: Cambridge University Press, 2003); and Ian McBride, "Burke and Ireland," in *The Cambridge Companion to Edmund Burke*, ed. David Dwan and Christopher J. Insole (Cambridge, UK: Cambridge University Press, 2012), 181–194.

15. Isaac Kramnick offers this hypothesis in *The Rage of Edmund Burke: Portrait of an Ambivalent Conservative* (New York: Basic, 1977), 120–121.

16. See Donald J. Greene's introduction to *Taxation No Tyranny* in Samuel Johnson, *The Political Writings*, ed. Donald J. Greene (New Haven: Yale University Press, 1977), 401–402.

17. Hudson, *Samuel Johnson*, 197.

18. Thomas M. Curley, "Johnson and Burke: Constitutional Evolution versus Political Revolution," *Studies on Voltaire and the Eighteenth Century* 263 (1989), 265.

19. Samuel Johnson, "Taxation No Tyranny; an Answer to the Resolutions and Address of the American Congress," in *Political Writings*, ed. Donald J. Greene (New Haven: Yale University Press, 1977), 419. Subsequent references to this edition will be made parenthetically.

20. *A Summary View of the Rights of British America* (London: G. Kearsley, 1774), 7.

21. Edmund Burke, *Reflections on the Revolution in France*, ed. L. G. Mitchell (Oxford: Oxford University Press, 1993), 33.

22. Richard Bland, "The Colonel Dismounted: Or, the Rector Vindicated," in *Pamphlets of the American Revolution, 1750–1776*, ed. Bernard Bailyn and Jane N. Garrett, vol. 1 (Cambridge, MA: The Belknap Press, 1965), 319.

23. For Johnson's views on empire, see Donald Greene, *The Politics of Samuel Johnson*, 2nd ed. (Athens: University of Georgia Press, 1990), 218–239.

24. On Johnson's opposition to slavery, see James G. Basker, "Johnson and Slavery," *Harvard Library Bulletin* 20 (2009), 29–50.

25. Ironically, given the colonies' complaints, Poyning's Law restricted the Irish Parliament's jurisdiction almost exclusively to internal taxation.

26. Cornwall had been an English county since the ninth century, and by the end of the eighteenth century the Cornish language had virtually disappeared, along with traditional forms of dress and entertainment. See Mark Stoyle, *West Britons: Cornish Identities and the Early Modern British State* (Exeter: University of Exeter Press, 2002).

27. "Speech on Conciliation with America, 22 March 1775," in *Writings and Speeches of Edmund Burke*, vol. 3, ed. Warren M. Elofson (Oxford: Oxford University Press, 1996), 120. Subsequent references will be made parenthetically by page number.

28. *The Declaration by the Representatives of the United Colonies of North America, now met in General Congress at Philadelphia, Setting forth the Causes and Necessity of taking up Arms. The Letter of the Twelve United Colonies by their Delegates in Congress to the*

Inhabitants of Great Britain, Their Humble Petition to this Majesty, and Their Address to the People of Ireland. Collected together for the Use of Serious Thinking *Men. By Lovers of Peace* (London, 1775), 13.

29. *Declaration*, 13.

30. Edmund Burke, "Speech on American Taxation, 19 April 1774," in *The Writings and Speeches of Edmund Burke*, vol. 2, ed. Paul Langford (Oxford: Oxford University Press, 1981), 460.

31. Burke, "Speech on American Taxation," 460.

32. On the consistency of this understanding of empire throughout Burke's political writings, see Jennifer Pitts, "Burke and the Ends of Empire," in *The Cambridge Companion to Edmund Burke*, ed. David Dwan and Christopher J. Insole (Cambridge, UK: Cambridge University Press, 2012), 145–155.

33. James Macpherson, in his *Rights of Great Britain Asserted against the Claims of America* (London: Cadell, 1776), turned Burke's argument on its head by asserting that the colonies ought to have followed the examples of Chester and Durham by petitioning "for the privilege of sending Members to Parliament." Had they done so in a "peaceable and dutiful manner," Macpherson declares condescendingly, "I can perceive no reason why their request should be refused" (8).

34. Carl B. Cone, *Burke and the Nature of Politics: The Age of the American Revolution* (Louisville: University of Kentucky Press, 1957), 281. On Burke's self-representation as a "man who felt for empire" and who used the language of sensibility to imagine the reformation of British imperial government, see Robert W. Jones, *Literature, Gender, and Politics in Britain, 1770–1785* (Cambridge, UK: Cambridge University Press, 2011), 44–53.

35. A number of contributors to the debates over these rights and liberties brought up the fact that many Englishmen were not directly represented in Parliament because they could not vote. Daniel Dulany, for instance, argued in *Considerations on the Propriety of Imposing Taxes in the British Colonies* (London: J. Almon, 1776) that the colonies are comparable to other groups that are "virtually" represented in Parliament, or that do not elect their own representatives. These groups include "monied" rather than "landed" property holders: "The merchants of London, the proprietors of the Public Funds, the Inhabitants of Leeds, Halifax, Birmingham and Manchester, and that great corporation of the East India Company" (3). According to Dulany, these nonvoters are virtually represented through their shared interests with voters. For colonists, this virtual representation offered little comfort or security when Britain's economic interests were directly at odds with those of the colonies. On the emerging concept of virtual representation, see Gould, *Persistence of Empire*, 119–142.

36. Jack P. Greene, *Peripheries and Center*, 198.

37. *The Federalist: A Commentary on the Constitution of the United States, Being a Collection of Essays written in Support of the Constitution agreed upon September 17, 1787 by the Federal Convention*, ed. Edward Mead Earle (New York: The Modern Library, 1937), 57. Subsequent references to this edition will be made parenthetically by page number.

38. For a fuller discussion of the differences between Federalists and anti-Federalists, see Isaac Kramnick, "The 'Great National Discussion': The Discourse of Politics in 1787," *William and Mary Quarterly*, 3rd ser. 45.1 (1988), 3–32.

39. Under the Treaty of Union, Scottish peers and commoners held 61 of 764 seats in the newly formed British Parliament. While the British Parliament determined matters

of taxation and defense for all of Britain, Scots retained limited control over local government. On the differences between incorporating and federal union, see John Robertson, "An Elusive Sovereignty: The Course of the Union Debate in Scotland 1698–1707," in *A Union for Empire: Political Thought and the British Union of 1707*, ed. John Robertson (Cambridge, UK: Cambridge University Press, 1995), 198–227.

40. The nickname originated with Gary Wills in *Explaining America: The Federalist* (Garden City, NJ: Doubleday, 1981), 248. Wills surmises that Jay was assigned the early series of papers, which ran under the title "Concerning Dangers from Foreign Force and Influence," because of his extensive diplomatic experience (252). While the authorship of some of *The Federalist* essays is disputed, manuscripts of numbers 2 through 5 exist in Jay's hand. See Richard Bucci, "John Jay and 'The Federalist No. V': A Bibliographic Discussion," *The Papers of the Bibliographical Society of America* 105.3 (2011), 377–406.

41. Todd Estes, "The Voices of Publius and the Strategies of Persuasion in *The Federalist*," *Journal of the Early Republic* 28 (2008), 536.

42. Robert A. Ferguson, "The Forgotten Publius: John Jay and the Aesthetics of Ratification," *Early American Literature* 34 (1999), 227.

43. Ferguson, "The Forgotten Publius," 232.

44. See Cecilia M. Kenyon, *The Antifederalists* (Indianapolis: Bobbs-Merrill, 1966), xxi–cxvi; and Kramnick, "Great National Discussion," 3–32. Christopher M. Duncan argues that the anti-Federalists were a more ideologically coherent group than Kenyon and Kramnick allow. See *The Anti-Federalists and Early American Political Thought* (DeKalb: Northern Illinois University Press, 1995), 123–172.

45. Kenyon, *The Antifederalists*, xlvi.

46. Quoted in Kenyon, *The Antifederalists*, 157.

47. "Scotland and England—A Case in Point" was reprinted in a Boston newspaper, *The American Herald*. All quotations are from the version of the essay included in *The Antifederalist Papers*, ed. Morton Borden (Lansing: Michigan State University Press, 1965), 11–15.

48. Elisa Tamarkin, *Anglophilia: Deference, Devotion, and Antebellum America* (Chicago: University of Chicago Press, 2008), xxiv–xxviii.

Chapter 2

1. Hugh Henry Brackenridge, *Modern Chivalry*, ed. Claude M. Newlin (New York: American Book Company, 1937), 6. On the British and American tradition of the "stage-Irish," and particularly its manifestations on the Philadelphia stage, see Herb Smith, "Hugh Henry Brackenridge's Debt to the Stage Irish Convention," *Ball State University Forum* 30 (1989), 14–19. The *OED* dates "bog-trotter" as a nickname for Irishmen to the late seventeenth century. Captain Farrago uses the term as a synonym for servant, also referring to Teague's Scottish replacement, Duncan Ferguson, as a bog-trotter.

2. Brackenridge, *Modern Chivalry*, 405.

3. For an overview of post-Revolutionary Irish migration to the United States, see Kerby A. Miller, *Emigrants and Exiles: Ireland and the Irish Exodus to North America* (New York: Oxford University Press, 1985), 169–192; and David A. Wilson, *United*

Irishmen, United States: Immigrant Radicals in the Early American Republic (Ithaca: Cornell University Press, 1998).

4. Brackenridge, *Modern Chivalry*, 24, 58.

5. Brackenridge, *Modern Chivalry*, 17. On Brackenridge's critique of American democracy, see Grantland S. Rice, *The Transformation of Authorship in America* (Chicago: University of Chicago Press, 1997), 125–143; and Emory Elliott, *Revolutionary Writers: Literature and Authority in the New Republic* (New York: Oxford University Press, 1986), 184–217.

6. Smith, "Brackenridge's Debt," 18. Lynn Haims makes a similar argument in "Of Indians and Irishmen: A Note on Brackenridge's Use of Sources for Satire in 'Modern Chivalry'," *Early American Literature* 10.1 (1975), 88–92.

7. William Cobbett, "Detection of a Conspiracy, Formed by the United Irishmen, with the Evident Intention of Aiding the Tyrants of France in Subverting the Government of the United States of America," in *Peter Porcupine in America: Pamphlets on Republicanism and Revolution*, ed. David A. Wilson (Ithaca: Cornell University Press, 1994), 242.

8. Quoted in R. B. McDowell, *Ireland in the Age of Imperialism and Revolution, 1760–1801* (Oxford: Clarendon, 1979), 244. Jim Smyth demonstrates strong support in Ulster for the American Revolution in *The Men of No Property: Irish Radicals and Popular Politics in the Late Eighteenth Century* (Houndmills, Basingstoke: Macmillan, 1992), 84–85, but Irish public opinion concerning the American Revolution was complicated by religious and ethnic factors. For a comprehensive overview, see Vincent Morley, *Irish Opinion and the American Revolution, 1760–1783* (Cambridge, UK: Cambridge University Press, 2002).

9. The United Irishmen's Rebellion, which aimed to undermine British colonial rule of Ireland, had practical and ideological roots in the American Revolution. In practical terms, the War of Independence brought together Anglo-Irish Protestants and Irish Catholics in nonsectarian volunteer corps, armed bodies of citizens that operated independently of government control. These volunteer corps were formed to protect Ireland from invasion by France or Spain, but they also enabled the dissemination of republican ideas. Ideologically, the American Revolution encouraged the Irish to reflect on Britain's colonial rule of Ireland. Although the Irish Parliament voted in support of Britain's war against the colonies, many among the Protestant Ascendancy, Ireland's ruling class, feared that the British Parliament might extend the economic restrictions it had placed on the American colonies to Ireland. On the American Revolution's influence on the United Irishmen, see Michael Durey, *Transatlantic Radicals and the Early American Republic* (Lawrence: University of Kansas Press, 1997); R. B. McDowell, *Ireland in the Age of Imperialism and Revolution;* and Vincent Morley, *Irish Opinion and the American Revolution.*

10. *Life of Theobald Wolfe Tone: Memoirs, journals and political writings, compiled and arranged by William T. W. Tone, 1826,* ed. Thomas Bartlett (Dublin: The Lilliput Press, 1998), 450.

11. Wilson, *United Irishmen*, 8. From 1700 to 1770, most Irish emigrants were fairly affluent farmers and artisans from the predominantly Protestant Ulster region—a population we now refer to as "Scotch-Irish." This designation only came into wide use in the mid-nineteenth century, when Irish Protestants in the United States sought to avoid nativist hostility by distinguishing themselves from the masses of Catholic, Gaelic-speaking Irish peasants that migrated during the famine. See Maldwyn A. Jones, "The Scotch-Irish in British America," in *Strangers within the Realm: Cultural Margins of*

the First British Empire, ed. Bernard Bailyn and Philip D. Morgan (Chapel Hill: University of North Carolina Press, 1991), 284–287. In keeping with the practices of the writers I am discussing in this chapter, I refer to all migrants from Ireland, regardless of their religion or region of origin, as "Irish."

12. Quoted in Durey, *Transatlantic Radicals*, 272–273.

13. Durey, *Transatlantic Radicals*, 248. Irish settlers demonstrated their newfound political consciousness by participating in riots against the Neutrality Proclamation of 1793 and in the Whiskey Rebellion in 1794. Many of them opposed Jay's Treaty of 1794 on the grounds that it effectively allied the American government with Britain against France, and thus against Ireland, which sought French aid in gaining independence from British rule.

14. Quoted in Edward C. Carter II, "A 'Wild Irishman' Under Every Federalist's Bed: Naturalization in Philadelphia, 1789–1806," *Proceedings of the American Philosophical Society* 133 (1989), 180.

15. *United States Statutes at Large*, Vol. 1, Public Acts of the Fifth Congress, Second Session, Chapter LVIII.

16. Cobbett, "Detection," 248.

17. Nigel Leask, "Irish Republicans and Gothic Eleutherarchs: Pacific Utopias in the Writing of Theobald Wolfe Tone and Charles Brockden Brown," *Huntington Library Quarterly* 63 (2000), 353. The American Society of United Irishmen was established in Philadelphia in 1797 and quickly formed branches from New York to South Carolina. Similar to its Irish counterpart, the American society's stated aim was "to promote the emancipation of Ireland from the tyranny of British government," but its detractors feared that the United Irishmen were more concerned with fomenting revolution in the United States. On the United Irishmen's practices of secrecy, see Durey, *Transatlantic Radicals*, 116–117. On the formation of the American Society of United Irishmen, see Wilson, *United Irishmen*, 45.

18. Cobbett, "Detection," 253.

19. In "The Uncanny" (1919) Freud explains that the uncanny is marked by the return of the repressed, as the familiar but concealed manifests itself in unfamiliar and frightening ways. See *The Standard Edition of the Complete Psychological Works of Sigmund Freud*, trans. and ed. James Strachey et al., vol. 17 (London: The Hogarth Press, 1964), 219–256.

20. Cannon Schmitt, *Alien Nation: Nineteenth-Century Gothic Fictions and English Nationality* (Philadelphia: University of Pennsylvania Press, 1997), 2.

21. For a more comprehensive discussion of Gothic conventions than I provide in this chapter, see Eve Kosofsky Sedgwick, *The Coherence of Gothic Conventions* (New York: Arno Press, 1980).

22. Peter Kafer has noted additional Irish connections elsewhere in Brown's writing. "The Story of Cooke," one of Brown's unpublished early pieces, features a drunken, abusive Irishman; the eponymous protagonist of *Ormond* (1799) has an Irish name; and in *Arthur Mervyn* (1799) Welbeck is modeled on the Irish-American politician John Swanick. See *Charles Brockden Brown's Revolution and the Birth of the American Gothic* (Philadelphia: University of Pennsylvania Press, 2004), 181.

23. Pamela Clemit, *The Godwinian Novel: The Rational Fictions of Godwin, Brockden Brown, and Mary Shelley* (Oxford: Clarendon, 1993), 5, 6. On the influence of radical novels on Brown's fiction, see also Cathy N. Davidson, *Revolution and the Word: The*

Rise of the Novel in America, expanded ed. (Oxford: Oxford University Press, 2004), 328.

24. Clemit, *Godwinian Novel*, 105. Cooper received his appellation in W. H. Gardiner's review of *The Spy, A Tale of Neutral Ground*, in the *North American Review* 15 (1822), 275. Brown was labeled by American critic John Neal in an 1824 essay in *Blackwood's Magazine*.

25. Christopher Looby, *Voicing America: Language, Literary Form, and the Origins of the United States* (Chicago: University of Chicago Press, 1996), 146. On Brown and the Gothic, see also Bill Christophersen, *The Apparition in the Glass: Charles Brockden Brown's American Gothic* (Athens: GA: University of Georgia Press, 1993); Leslie Fiedler, *Love and Death in the American Novel*, 3rd ed. (New York: Stein and Day, 1982), 157–161; and Kafer, *Brown's Revolution*.

26. W. M. Verhoeven, "'This blissful period of intellectual liberty': Transatlantic Radicalism and Enlightened Conservatism in Brown's Early Writings," in *Revising Charles Brockden Brown: Culture, Politics, and Sexuality in the Early Republic*, ed. Philip Barnard, Mark L. Kamrath, and Stephen Shapiro (Knoxville: University of Tennessee Press, 2004), 30.

27. On the national tale see Ina Ferris, *The Romantic National Tale and the Question of Ireland* (Cambridge, UK: Cambridge University Press, 2002); Juliet Shields, *Sentimental Literature and Anglo-Scottish Identity, 1745–1820* (Cambridge, UK: Cambridge University Press, 2010), 110–138; and Katie Trumpener, *Bardic Nationalism: The Romantic Novel and the British Empire* (Princeton: Princeton University Press, 1997), 128–157.

28. Leonard Tennenhouse, *The Importance of Feeling English: American Literature and the British Diaspora, 1750–1850* (Princeton: Princeton University Press, 2007), 110.

29. Charles Brockden Brown, *Edgar Huntly, or Memoirs of a Sleepwalker*, ed. Norman S. Grabo (New York: Penguin, 1988), 14. Subsequent references to this edition will be made parenthetically.

30. Looby, *Voicing America*, 10.

31. Bryan Waterman, "The Bavarian Illuminati, the Early American Novel, and Histories of the Public Sphere," *William and Mary Quarterly* 3rd ser. 62.1 (2005), 16.

32. William Godwin, *An Enquiry Concerning Political Justice*, ed. Isaac Kramnick (Harmondsworth: Penguin, 1976), 313. On Brown's admiration of Godwin's writing, see Clemit, *The Godwinian Novel*, 105–136. What Clemit reads in *Wieland* as Brown's conservative critique of Godwin's ideas I see as a cautious endorsement of them.

33. Charles Brockden Brown, *Wieland; or, the Transformation: An American Tale and Memoirs of Carwin the Biloquist*, ed. Jay Fliegelman (New York: Penguin, 1991), 6, 7. Subsequent references to this edition will be cited parenthetically.

34. Looby, *Voicing America*, 157, 155.

35. Aaron Spencer Fogleman, *Hopeful Journeys: German Immigration, Settlement, and Political Culture in Colonial America, 1717–1775* (Philadelphia: University of Pennsylvania Press, 1996), 82. On German migration and settlement, see also Marianne S. Wokeck, "German and Irish Immigration to Colonial Philadelphia," *Proceedings of the American Philosophical Society* 133.2 (1989), 128–143.

36. Ed White, "Carwin the Peasant Rebel," *Revising Charles Brockden Brown: Culture, Politics, and Sexuality in the Early Republic* (Knoxville: University of Tennessee Press, 2004), 45–48.

37. Benjamin Franklin, "Observations Concerning the Increase of Mankind, Peopling of Countries, &c," *Writings*, ed. J. A. Leo Lemay (New York: Library of America, 1987), 374.

38. *A Memorial of the Case of the German Emigrants Settled in the British Colonies of Pensilvania, and the back Parts of Maryland, Virginia, etc.* (London: 1754), 12, 13.

39. Shirley Samuels, "Wieland': Alien and Infidel," *Early American Literature* 25.1 (1990), 60.

40. Bill Christophersen offers an alternative reading, arguing that the real transformation in the novel occurs in Clara, as she confronts her brother's madness and changes from a model of rational virtue to a fearful and conflicted protagonist and an unreliable narrator. See *The Apparition in the Glass*, 34–38.

41. Brown's writings on the Louisiana Purchase mock the xenophobia that French proximity inspired in Americans. See Robert S. Levine, "Race and Nation in Brown's Louisiana Writings of 1803," *Revising Charles Brockden Brown*, ed. Philip Barnard, Mark Kamrath, and Stephen Shapiro (Knoxville: University of Tennessee Press, 2004), 332–353.

42. Kafer, *Brown's Revolution*, 129. Christophersen similarly dismisses Carwin as "more red herring than protagonist." See *The Apparition in the Glass*, 34.

43. Godwin, *Enquiry*, 314.

44. Steven Watts points out that Brown had himself indulged in such schemes. His journal included "a long explication of a utopian commonwealth"; and Brown's friend and biographer William Dunlap reported finding among Brown's paper several plans for utopias that aimed "to improve and secure human happiness." See *The Romance of Real Life: Charles Brockden Brown and the Origins of American Culture* (Baltimore: The Johns Hopkins University Press, 1994), 30, 65.

45. Theobald Wolfe Tone, "Memoirs," *Life of Theobald Wolfe Tone: Memoirs, journals and political writings, compiled and arranged by William T.W. Tone, 1826,* ed. Thomas Bartlett (Dublin: The Lilliput Press, 1998), 25. Leask explores allusions to Tone and the United Irishmen in Carwin's *Memoirs*, though without reference to *Wieland*, in "Irish Republicans and Gothic Eleutherarchs." It is possible that Brown might have encountered or heard of Tone, who fled to Philadelphia in 1795 to avoid prosecution for treason after his name was implicated in a plot against the English government.

46. Tone, "Memoirs," 25, 34, 35. When Tone claims to have imagined "the Bucaniers, who were my heroes . . . as the archetypes of the future colonists" (25), he may have been alluding to the Buccaneers' democratic methods of government and egalitarian distribution of property as much as to their semi-legal privateering. As Leask explains, in the eighteenth century, the term "utopia," which Tone uses, although Carwin does not, "often carried a technical meaning of communal or strictly egalitarian property-holding opposed to commerce and the accumulation of private wealth." See Leask, "Irish Republicans and Gothic Eleutherarchs," 349.

47. Godwin explains, "Did every man impose this law upon himself, did he regard himself as not authorized to conceal any part of his character and conduct, this circumstance alone would prevent millions of actions from being perpetrated in which we are now induced to engage by the prospect of secrecy and impunity." *Enquiry*, 311.

48. Eve Tavor Bannet, "Charles Brockden Brown and England: Of Genres, the Minerva Press, and the Early Republican Reprint Trade," *Transatlantic Literary Exchanges 1790–1870: Gender, Race, and Nation,* ed. Kevin Hutchings and Julia M. Wright (Farnham, Surrey: Ashgate, 2011), 133–152.

49. Bannet, "Brown and England," 138.

50. Bannet, "Brown and England," 151.

51. Roche was born in Waterford, Ireland, and grew up in Dublin. She moved to London upon her marriage in 1794 and published her best-known novel, *The Children of the Abbey*, in 1796. Roche has been overlooked in recent studies of Irish fiction including Ina Ferris's *The Romantic National Tale and the Question of Ireland* and Clare Connolly's *A Cultural History of the Irish Novel, 1790–1829* (Cambridge, UK: Cambridge University Press, 2012), perhaps because only a handful of her novels are about Ireland. For critical discussions of her work, see: Jarlath Killen, *Gothic Ireland: Horror and the Irish Anglican Imagination in the Long Eighteenth Century* (Dublin: Four Courts, 2005), 182–190; and Natalia Schroeder, "Maria Regina Roche and the Early Nineteenth-Century Irish Novel," *Eire-Ireland* 19.2 (1984), 116–130.

52. Leonard Cassuto explores the psychology of Edgar's responses to and representations of Indians in light of this childhood trauma in "'[Un]consciousness Itself is the Malady': *Edgar Huntly* and the Discourse of the Other," *Modern Language Studies* 23.4 (1993), 118–30.

53. Jared Gardner reads the doubling of Edgar, Clithero, and the nameless Indians as a critique of the Alien and Sedition Acts, as a it blurs the boundaries between native and alien. See *Master Plots: Race and the Founding of an American Literature, 1787–1845* (Baltimore: The Johns Hopkins University Press, 1998), 53–80.

54. Luke Gibbons, "Ireland, America, and Gothic Memory: Transatlantic Terror in the Early Republic," *boundary 2* 31.1 (2004), 31.

55. Gardner, *Master Plots*, 69–77; Gibbons, "Gothic Memory," 37–38.

56. Regina Maria Roche, *The Munster Cottage Boy: A Tale*, 4 vols. (London: A. K. Newman, 1820), 2: 318. Subsequent references will be made parenthetically by volume and page number.

57. Miller, *Emigrants and Exiles*, 193.

58. *The Exile of Erin!* (Dublin: Wholesale and Retail Book Warehouse, n.d.).

59. Schroeder, "Maria Regina Roche," 116. Roche certainly could have used a "resounding success" when she published *The Munster Cottage Boy*, as she had just declared bankruptcy, and, as a result, became involved in a decade-long Chancery suit that left her deeply in debt.

60. Connolly, *Cultural History*, 164.

61. Connolly, *Cultural History*, 164.

62. Connolly, *Cultural History*, 179.

63. Roche's indictment of British rule and an oppressive Anglo-Irish landowning class was hardly original. Earlier anti-emigration writing had made the same claim. See, for instance, *A View of the Present State of Ireland* (Dublin: L. Fay, 1780); and *The Strong-Box Opened; or, a Fund found at Home for the Immediate Employment of our People and for Preventing Emigration* (Dublin: T. T. Faulkner, 1780).

64. Charles Brockden Brown, "A Sketch of American Literature, for 1806–7," *The American Register; or, General Repository of History, Politics, and Science*, vol. 1 of 2 (1807), 174.

65. Baucom asserts that Irish emigrants to the United States did not "exchang[e] the place of the nation for the placelessness of the extranational," but instead entered "into an Irish place of belonging unbounded by the borders of the nation, a place of belonging that was less insular than circular, less rooted than routed, less national than Atlantic," implying that "routes" are better than "roots" and that to be Atlantic is preferable to being merely "national." See "Found Drowned: The Irish Atlantic," *Nineteenth-Century Contexts* 22 (2000), 120.

Chapter 3

1. Daniel Defoe, *A Tour through the Whole Island of Great Britain*, 7th ed., 4 vols. (London: J. and F. Rivington, 1769), vol. 4, 144–145.

2. Eric Richards, "Scotland and the Uses of the Atlantic Empire," in *Strangers within the Realm: Cultural Margins of the First British Empire*, ed. Bernard Bailyn and Philip D. Morgan (Chapel Hill: University of North Carolina Press, 1991), 77. See also Linda Colley, *Britons: Forging a Nation 1707–1832* (New Haven: Yale University Press, 1992), 120.

3. Bernard Bailyn, *Voyagers to the West: A Passage in the Peopling of America on the Eve of Revolution* (New York: Vintage, 1988), 44–49.

4. Richards, "Scotland and the Uses of the Atlantic Empire," 87. On the figure of the "enterprising Scot," see also Alan L. Karras, *Sojourners in the Sun: Scottish Migrants in Jamaica and the Chesapeake, 1740–1800* (Ithaca: Cornell University Press, 1992), 15–16. Karras argues that the Scots who were most successful abroad tended to enjoy a relatively comfortable socioeconomic position at home in Scotland.

5. Andrew Mackillop, "'*More Fruitful than the Soil*': Army, Empire, and the Scottish Highlands, 1715–1815* (East Linton, Scotland: Tuckwell Press, 2000), 198–221.

6. Barbara DeWolfe, ed., *Discoveries of America: Personal Accounts of British Emigrants to North America during the Revolutionary Era* (Cambridge, UK: Cambridge University Press, 1997), 194, 193.

7. DeWolfe, *Discoveries of America*, 156.

8. David A. Gerber, "Epistolary Ethics: Personal Correspondence and the Culture of Emigration in the Nineteenth Century," *Journal of American Ethnic History* 19 (2000), 10.

9. Stephen Fender, *Sea Changes: British Emigration and American Literature* (Cambridge, UK: Cambridge University Press, 1992), 127.

10. On this point, see Eve Tavor Bannet, *An Empire of Letters: Letter Manuals and Transatlantic Correspondence, 1688–1820* (Cambridge, UK: Cambridge University Press, 2005).

11. Linda Colley asserts that "Wilkite complaints that Scots were invading the British polity to an unprecedented extent . . . were true," but her argument is based on the virulence of anti-Scottish propaganda rather than on migration statistics, which are extremely difficult to ascertain. See *Britons*, 113–121. On English prejudices against Scots during the eighteenth century, see also Vincent Carretta, *George III and the Satirists from Hogarth to Byron* (Athens, GA: University of Georgia Press, 1990), 59–64 and 199–206; and Pat Rogers, *Johnson and Boswell: The Transit of Caledonia* (Oxford: Oxford University Press, 1996), 193–201.

12. Roxann Wheeler, *The Complexion of Race: Categories of Difference in Eighteenth-Century British Culture* (Philadelphia: University of Pennsylvania Press, 2000), 21.

13. For an introduction to stadial theory, see Christopher J. Berry, *Social Theory of the Scottish Enlightenment* (Edinburgh: Edinburgh University Press, 1997), 91–115. Silvia Sebastiani explores stadial theory's implications for eighteenth-century understandings of racial diversity in *The Scottish Enlightenment: Race, Gender, and the Limits of Progress*, trans. Jeremy Carden (New York: Palgrave Macmillan, 2013), 45–72. On climatic theory see Sebastiani, *The Scottish Enlightenment*, 23–44, and Wheeler, *The Complexion of Race*, 21–28, 183–188.

14. On this transition, see Nancy Stepan, *The Idea of Race in Science: Great Britain 1800–1960* (London: Macmillan, 1982), 1–46.

15. See Nicholas Hudson, "From 'Nation' to 'Race': The Origins of Racial Classification in Eighteenth-Century Thought," *Eighteenth-Century Studies* 29 (1996), 247–264.

16. *A Candid Enquiry into the Causes of the Late and the Intended Migrations from Scotland, in a letter to J--- R--- Esq; Lanark-shire* (Glasgow: P. Tait, 1771), 55.

17. *A Candid Enquiry*, 55.

18. *A Candid Enquiry*, 48.

19. *A Candid Enquiry*, 53.

20. J. M. Bumsted makes the case that much late eighteenth-century Highland migration was voluntary in *The People's Clearance: Highland Emigration to North America 1770–1815* (Edinburgh: Edinburgh University Press, 1982). Eric Richards contests Bumsted's argument in *The Highland Clearances: People, Landlords and Rural Turmoil* (Edinburgh: Birlinn, 2000), pointing out the extent to which the clearances resulted from colonial practices imposed upon the Highlands.

21. By comparing the published account of Johnson's journey with the letters that Johnson wrote during his time in Scotland, Rogers argues in *Johnson and Boswell* that Johnson retrospectively chose to foreground the issue of Highland depopulation (125). For a detailed discussion of the anti-Scottish prejudices that Johnson's contemporary readers found in the *Journey* see Rogers, *Johnson and Boswell*, 202–215.

22. Samuel Johnson, "A Journey to the Western Islands of Scotland," in *A Journey to the Western Islands of Scotland and The Journal of a Tour to the Hebrides*, ed. Peter Levi (London: Penguin, 1984), 58. Subsequent references to this edition will be made parenthetically.

23. Karen O' Brien, "Johnson's View of the Scottish Enlightenment in *A Journey to the Western Islands of Scotland*," *The Age of Johnson* 4 (1991), 59–82.

24. Charlotte Sussman, "The Colonial Afterlife of Political Arithmetic: Swift, Demography, and Mobile Populations," *Cultural Critique* 56 (2004), 104.

25. Oliver Goldsmith, *The Poetical Works of Oliver Goldsmith*, ed. Austin Dobson (Oxford: Oxford University Press, 1949), 21–37, lines 275–276.

26. Sussman, "Colonial Afterlife," 109.

27. Samuel Ayscough, *Remarks on the Letters from an American Farmer; or a detection of the errors of Mr. J. Hector St. John; Pointing out the pernicious Tendency of these Letters to Great Britain* (London: John Fielding, 1783), 5.

28. Ayscough, *Remarks*, 4, 20.

29. Albert E. Stone, "Introduction," *Letters from an American Farmer and Sketches of Eighteenth-Century America* (New York: Penguin, 1981), 8.

30. On the impact of Crèvecoeur's life experiences on his *Letters*, see Norman S. Grabo, "Crèvecoeur's American: Beginning the World Anew," *William and Mary Quarterly*, 3rd series, 48.2 (1991), 159–172.

31. J. Hector St. John de Crèvecoeur, *Letters from an American Farmer and Sketches of Eighteenth-Century America*, ed. Albert Stone (New York: Penguin, 1981), 41, 43. Subsequent references to this edition will be made parenthetically.

32. See Ralph Bauer, *The Cultural Geography of Colonial American Literatures* (Cambridge, UK: Cambridge University Press, 2003), 209–215; and Grantland S. Rice, *The Transformation of Authorship in America* (Chicago: University of Chicago Press, 1997), 102–105.

33. Rice argues that Crèvecoeur "challenges James's acclamatory epistemology with empirical and historical realities" that call into question the farmer's "utopian panegyrics." See *The Transformation of Authorship*, 101–102. On the contradictions embedded in James's account of the colonies, see also Larzer Ziff, *Writing in the New Nation: Prose, Print, and Politics in the Early United States* (New Haven: Yale University Press, 1991), 18–33.

34. Sussman, "Colonial Afterlife," 103.

35. Sussman, "Colonial Afterlife," 120.

36. Robert J. C. Young, *Colonial Desire: Hybridity in Theory, Culture and Race* (London: Routledge, 1995), 9–16.

37. Emily B. Todd, "Walter Scott and the Nineteenth-Century American Literary Marketplace," *Papers of the Bibliographical Society of America* 93.4 (1999), 496. William B. Todd and Anne Bowden's *Walter Scott: A Bibliographic History, 1796–1832* (Newcastle, DE: Oak Knoll Press, 1998) includes a list of American reprints of Scott's novels.

38. See [W. H. Gardiner], rev. of *The Spy, A Tale of Neutral Ground*, by James Fenimore Cooper, *North American Review* 15 (1822), 275.

39. See George Dekker, *James Fenimore Cooper: The American Scott* (New York: Barnes and Noble, 1967).

40. Ian Dennis, "The Worthlessness of Duncan Heyward: A Waverley Hero in America," *Studies in the Novel* 29 (1997), 1. For additional comparisons of Scott's and Cooper's historical fiction, see Paul Frank Armin, "Writing Literary Independence: The Case of Cooper—the 'American Scott' and the un-Scottish American," *Comparative Literature Studies* 34 (1997), 41–70; Alide Cagidemetrio, "A Plea for Fictional Histories and Old-Time Jewesses," in *The Invention of Ethnicity*, ed. Werner Sollors (New York: Oxford Univ. Press, 1989), 14–43; Donald Davie, *The Heyday of Sir Walter Scott* (London: Routledge and Kegan Paul, 1961), 101–116; and Leslie Fiedler, *Love and Death in the American Novel*, 3rd ed. (New York: Stein and Day, 1982), 162–182.

41. Nina Baym refers to Munro, Heyward, and Alice as English in *Feminism and American Literary History: Essays* (New Brunswick, NJ: Rutgers University Press, 1992), 28. Forrest G. Robinson even more problematically describes "the marriage of Alice and Duncan as a union of racially pure Anglo-Saxons" even though Scots' racial origins were extensively debated in the late eighteenth and early nineteenth centuries. See "Uncertain Borders: Race, Sex, and Civilization in *The Last of the Mohicans*," *Arizona Quarterly* 47 (1991), 16. While Lowland Scots claimed Anglo-Saxon descent, and Highlanders claimed Celtic origins, it is far from clear that either Duncan or Alice is from the Lowlands; indeed, their families' Jacobitism suggests otherwise.

42. On Norton's Scottish and Cherokee family, see Carl F. Klinck, "Biographical Introduction," in *The Journal of Major John Norton, 1816*, ed. Carl F. Klinck and James J. Talman (Toronto: The Champlain Society, 1970), xiii–xcvii. On Alexander McGillivray's integration with the Creeks of Alabama, see Michael D. Green, "Alexander McGillivray," in *American Indian Leaders: Studies in Diversity*, ed. R. David Edmunds (Lincoln: University of Nebraska Press, 1980), 41–63. On John Ross's leadership of the Cherokees, see Gary E. Moulton, "John Ross," in *American Indian Leaders: Studies in Diversity*, 88–106.

43. Tim Fulford, *Romantic Indians: Native Americans, British Literature, and Transatlantic Culture, 1756–1830* (New York: Oxford University Press, 2006), 196.

44. James Fenimore Cooper, *The Last of the Mohicans; A Narrative of 1757*, ed. James A. Sappenfield and E. N. Feltskog (Albany: State University of New York Press, 1983), 151. Subsequent references are to this edition and appear parenthetically in the text.

45. See, for example, Michael Hechter, *Internal Colonialism: The Celtic Fringe in British National Development*, 2nd ed. (New Brunswick, NJ: Transaction Publishers, 1999), 7–39; and Katie Trumpener, *Bardic Nationalism: The Romantic Novel and the British Empire* (Princeton: Princeton University Press, 1997), 19–34.

46. On the role of the Jacobite rebellions in Scottish migration patterns, see David Dobson, *Scottish Emigration to Colonial America, 1607–1785* (Athens: University of Georgia Press, 1994); and Richards, "Scotland and the Uses of the Atlantic Empire," 67–114.

47. Berkhofer, *The White Man's Indian: Images of the American Indian from Columbus to the Present* (New York: Alfred A. Knopf, 1978), 71. On early nineteenth-century racial theory and Indian removal, see Reginald Horsman, *Race and Manifest Destiny: The Origins of American Racial Anglo-Saxonism* (Cambridge, MA: Harvard University Press, 1981), 189–207.

48. Adam Smith, *The Theory of Moral Sentiments*, ed. D. D. Raphael and A. L. Macfie (Oxford: Clarendon Press, 1976), 205. George Dekker discusses the influence of stadial theory on American historical fiction in *The American Historical Romance* (Cambridge, UK: Cambridge University Press, 1987), 73–78.

49. Smith, *Theory of Moral Sentiments*, 207.

50. John Millar, *The Origin of the Distinction of Ranks*, 3rd ed. (London: J. Murray, 1779), 55.

51. Millar, *Origin*, 87.

52. Millar, *Origin*, 96.

53. Dyer, "Irresolute Ravishers and the Sexual Economy of Chivalry in the Romantic Novel," *Nineteenth-Century Literature* 55 (2000), 350.

54. See Robinson, "Uncertain Borders," 16; and Dennis, "Worthlessness of Duncan Heyward," 2. The classic account of Scott's protagonists' passivity is Alexander Welsh's *The Hero of the Waverley Novels* (New Haven: Yale University Press, 1963).

55. James Fenimore Cooper, *The Deerslayer; or, The First War-Path*, ed. James Franklin Beard, et al. (Albany: State University of New York Press, 1987), 159.

56. On Leatherstocking's status as an American hero, see Robinson, "Uncertain Borders," 8; and Dekker, *James Fenimore Cooper: The American Scott*, 82–97. On masculinity and American identity, see Caleb Crain, *American Sympathy: Men, Friendship, and Literature in the New Nation* (New Haven: Yale University Press, 2001); Julie Ellison, *Cato's Tears and the Making of Anglo-American Emotion* (Chicago: University of Chicago Press, 1999); and Glenn Hendler, *Public Sentiments: Structures of Feeling in Nineteenth-Century American Literature* (Chapel Hill: University of North Carolina Press, 2001).

57. Nelson, "Cooper's Leatherstocking Conversations: Identity, Friendship, and Democracy in the New Nation," in *A Historical Guide to James Fenimore Cooper*, ed. Leland S. Person (New York: Oxford University Press, 2007), 141.

58. Nelson, "Cooper's Leatherstocking Conversations," 141.

59. Davie, *Heyday of Sir Walter Scott*, 109. See also Fiedler, *Love and Death in the American Novel*, 205–209; and Jane Tompkins, *Sensational Designs: The Cultural Work of American Fiction, 1790–1860* (New York: Oxford University Press, 1985), 94–121.

60. Baym, *Feminism and American Literary History*, 19.

61. Alexander Welsh, *The Hero of the Waverley Novels* (New Haven: Yale University Press, 1963), 71.

62. James Fenimore Cooper, letter to Samuel Carter Hall, May 21, 1831, in *The Letters and Journals of James Fenimore Cooper*, ed. James Franklin Beard, 6 vols. (Cambridge, MA: Belknap Press of Harvard University Press, 1960–1968), vol. 2, 83.

63. William Joseph Snelling, *Tales of the Northwest; or Sketches of Indian Life and Character* (Boston: Hilliard, 1830), vi. Subsequent references will be made parenthetically.

64. J. M. Bumsted, *The People's Clearance*, xi.

Chapter 4

1. James Horn, "British Diaspora: Emigration from Britain, 1680–1815," in *Oxford History of the British Empire*, vol. 2, *The Eighteenth Century*, ed. P. J. Marshall (Oxford: Oxford University Press, 1998), 38. For accounts of Welsh migration that might call into question Horn's claim, see A. H. Dodd, *The Character of Early Welsh Emigration to the United States* (Cardiff: University of Wales Press, 1953); and H. M. Davies, "'Very Different Springs of Uneasiness': Emigration from Wales to the United States of America during the 1790s," *Welsh History Review* 15.3 (1991), 368–398.

2. On Elizabethan versions of the Madoc myth see Gwyn A. Williams, *The Welsh in Their History* (London: Croom Helm, 1982), 16–26.

3. Gwyn A. Williams, *Madoc: The Making of a Myth* (London: Eyre Methuen, 1979), 67, 85.

4. George Burder, *The Welch Indians; or a Collection of Papers; Respecting a people whose ancestors emigrated from Wales to America, in the Year 1170, with Prince Madoc* (London: T. Chapman, 1797), 10.

5. Williams, *Madoc*, 84.

6. Richard Deacon, *Madoc and the Discovery of America: Some New Light on an Old Controversy* (London: Muller, 1967); Samuel Eliot Morison, *The European Discovery of America: The Northern Voyages, A.D. 500–1600* (New York: Oxford University Press, 1971), 84–87; Williams, *Madoc*.

7. Williams, *Madoc*, 66.

8. The origins of the ancient Britons were a matter of dispute. Geoffrey of Monmouth and his followers accorded Britain Roman origins, claiming that the Britons were descended from Brutus, grandson of Aeneas of Troy, while later historians claimed northern European Celtic or Teutonic origins for the Britons. See Colin Kidd, *British Identities before Nationalism: Ethnicities and Nationhood in the Atlantic World, 1600–1800* (Cambridge, UK: Cambridge University Press, 1999), 61–68, 186–187; and Hugh A. MacDougall, *Racial Myth in English History: Trojans, Teutons, and Anglo-Saxons* (Hanover, NH: University Press of New England, 1982), 8–10, 47–48.

9. Nicholas Canny, *Kingdom and Colony: Ireland in the Atlantic World, 1560–1800* (Baltimore: Johns Hopkins University Press, 1988); R. R. Davies, "Colonial Wales," *Past and Present* 65 (1974), 3–23; Richard Wyn Jones, "The Colonial Legacy in Welsh Politics," in *Postcolonial Wales*, ed. Jane Aaron and Chris Williams (Cardiff: University of Wales Press, 2005), 23–28.

10. Jones, "Colonial Legacy," 25–26. Jones quotes from Davies, "Colonial Wales," 3.

11. See MacDougall, *Racial Myth*, 15–16; and Peter Roberts, "Tudor Wales, National Identity, and the British Inheritance," in *British Consciousness and Identity: The Making of Britain, 1533–1707*, ed. Brendan Bradshaw and Peter Roberts (Cambridge, UK: Cambridge University Press, 1998), 8–42.

12. Roberts, "Tudor Wales," 35, 8.

13. Roberts, "Tudor Wales," 13; Philip Schwyzer, "British History and 'The British History': The Same Old Story," in *British Identities and English Renaissance Literature*, ed. David J. Baker and Willy Maley (Cambridge, UK: Cambridge University Press, 2002), 21. Philip Jenkins similarly argues that Wales' position "within the early modern British state can be discussed in terms of negatives" because between 1530 and 1790, there were no "distinctively Welsh" insurrections. See "Seventeenth-Century Wales: Definition and Identity," in *British Consciousness and Identity: The Making of Britain, 1533–1707*, ed. Brendan Bradshaw and Peter Roberts (Cambridge, UK: Cambridge University Press, 1998), 213–235.

14. See Shawna Lichtenwalner, *Claiming Cambria: Invoking the Welsh in the Romantic Era* (Newark: University of Delaware Press, 2008), 141–148; and Prys Morgan, "From a Death to a View: The Hunt for the Welsh Past in the Romantic Period," in *The Invention of Tradition*, ed. Eric Hobsbawm and Terence Ranger (Cambridge, UK: Cambridge University Press, 1983), 43–100, esp. 56–60.

15. Branwen Jarvis, "Iolo Morganwg and the Welsh Cultural Background," in *A Rattleskull Genius: The Many Faces of Iolo Morganwg*, ed. Geraint H. Jenkins (Cardiff: University of Wales Press, 2005), 29–49.

16. Quoted in Williams, *Madoc*, 135.

17. Quoted in Williams, *Madoc*, 135. On Welsh emigration to America in the late eighteenth and early nineteenth centuries see Gwyn A. Williams, *The Search for Beulah Land: The Welsh and the Atlantic Revolution* (New York: Holmes & Meier, 1980).

18. Mary-Ann Constantine, "'This Wildernessed Business of Publication': The Making of *Poems, Lyric and Pastoral* (1794)," in *A Rattleskull Genius: The Many Faces of Iolo Morganwg*, ed. Geraint H. Jenkins (Cardiff: University of Wales Press, 2005), 149. The subscription list for *Poems, Lyric and Pastoral* included names such as Hannah More, Anna Letitia Barbauld, James Boswell, Rev. John Evans, Rev. Richard Price, John Horne Took, William Wilberforce, and General George Washington.

19. Mary-Ann Constantine, "'This Wildernessed Business,'" 149, 126.

20. Edward Williams [Iolo Morganwg], *Poems, Lyric and Pastoral*, 2 vols. (London: J. Nichols, 1794), vol. 1, 41. Subsequent references to this edition will be made by volume and page number. All italics are in the original.

21. On Iolo's criticisms of the "ignorance and brutality" of life in rural Wales see Jarvis, "Iolo Morganwg," 46–47.

22. Sarah Prescott, *Eighteenth-Century Writing from Wales: Bards and Britons* (Cardiff: University of Wales Press, 2008), 153.

23. The phrase is Katie Trumpener's and describes the literary appropriation or invention of traditions to resist the Anglicization of the Celtic peripheries. See *Bardic Nationalism: The Romantic Novel and the British Empire* (Princeton: Princeton University Press, 1997), 19–34.

24. William's and Mary's names perhaps reflect Jacson's republicanism, alluding to the 1688 Glorious Revolution that placed William of Orange and his wife Mary on the throne in James II's stead. Mary's escape from her tyrannical parents, who imprison her in order

to prevent her marriage to William, implies that revolution, or disobedience, is justified when authority is exercised arbitrarily, as it was by the Stuart monarchs.

25. [Frances Jacson], *Disobedience*, 4 vols. (London: William Lane, 1797), vol. 4, 60.

26. [Jacson], *Disobedience*, vol. 4, 60.

27. [Jacson], *Disobedience*, vol. 4, 93.

28. Jane Aaron, "'Saxon, Think not All Is Won': Felicia Hemans and the Making of the Britons," *Cardiff Corvey: Reading the Romantic Text* 4.1 (May 2000), 2, online (12 June 2010): http://www.cf.ac.uk.offcampus.lib.washington.edu/corvey/articles/cc04_n01.html. Hemans lived in northern Wales for most of her adult life and, according to Aaron, "regarded herself as a naturalized Welsh woman" (2).

29. William Brewer, "Felicia Hemans, Byronic Cosmopolitanism and the Ancient Welsh Bards," in *English Romanticism in the Celtic World*, eds. Gerard Carruthers and Alan Rawes (Cambridge, UK: Cambridge University Press, 2003), 176.

30. Felicia Dorothea Browne Hemans, *Works*, 6 vols. (London: 1839), vol. 4, 235, lines 3–4.

31. Hemans, *Works*, vol. 4, 236, line 8.

32. Hemans, *Works*, vol. 4, 236, lines 13–18.

33. Hemans, *Works*, vol. 4, 230, lines 7–8. In contrast to my very literal reading, Catherine Brennan sees "The Cambrian in America" as figuratively dramatizing "the conflict between the nineteenth-century woman writer's impulse to conform to the widely propagated ideal of domesticity and her aspirations to wider worldly encounters." See her *Angers, Fantasies and Ghostly Fears: Nineteenth-Century Women from Wales and English-Language Poetry* (Cardiff: University of Wales Press, 2003), 82.

34. Nanora Sweet, "History, Imperialism, and the Aesthetics of the Beautiful: Hemans and the Post-Napoleonic Moment," in *At the Limits of Romanticism: Essays in Cultural, Feminist, and Materialist Criticism*, ed. Mary A. Favret and Nicola J. Watson (Bloomington: Indiana University Press, 1994), 173.

35. The critical examination of Wales's centrality to English Romanticism owes a great deal to *English Romanticism and the Celtic World*, ed. Gerard Carruthers and Alan Rawes (Cambridge, UK: Cambridge University Press, 2003). See also *Wales and the Romantic Imagination*, ed. Damian Walford Davies and Lynda Pratt (Cardiff: University of Wales Press, 2007); and Shawna Lichtenwalner, *Claiming Cambria*.

36. Gerard Carruthers and Alan Rawes, "Introduction: Romancing the Celt," in *English Romanticism and the Celtic World*, ed. Gerard Carruthers and Alan Rawes (Cambridge, UK: Cambridge University Press, 2003), 4.

37. On the decade-long composition of *Madoc*, see Paul Jarman, "*Madoc*, 1795: Robert Southey's Misdated Manuscript," *The Review of English Studies*, new series, 55 (2004), 355–373; and Lynda Pratt, "Revising the National Epic: Coleridge, Southey and *Madoc*," *Romanticism* 2 (1996), 149–164.

38. On Southey's correspondence with Iolo, see Caroline Franklin, "The Welsh American Dream: Iolo Morganwg, Robert Southey and the Madoc Legend," in *English Romanticism and the Celtic World*, ed. Gerard Carruthers and Alan Rawes (Cambridge, UK: Cambridge University Press, 2003), 69–84.

39. For the specifics of the projected Pantisocracy, see Nigel Leask, "Pantisocracy and the Politics of the 'Preface' to *Lyrical Ballads*," in *Reflections of Revolution: Images of Romanticism*, ed. Alison Yarrington and Kelvin Everest (London: Routledge, 1993), 39–58;

and Michael Wiley, *Romantic Migrations: Local, National, and Transnational Dispositions* (New York: Palgrave, 2008), 56–80.

40. Lynda Pratt, "Southey in Wales: Inscriptions, Monuments, and Romantic Prosperity," in *Wales and the Romantic Imagination*, ed. Damian Walford Davies and Lynda Pratt (Cardiff: University of Wales Press, 2007), 87.

41. Leask, "Pantisocracy," 44. Conversely, Tim Fulford calls Pantisocracy an "anticolonialist colony." See *Romantic Indians: Native Americans, British Literature, and Transatlantic Culture 1756–1830* (Oxford: Oxford University Press, 2006), 121.

42. On Southey's objections to and revisions of the epic as a genre, see Pratt, "Revising the National Epic."

43. On Southey's invention of the Hoamen, see Nigel Leask, "Southey's *Madoc*: Reimagining the Conquest of America," in *Robert Southey and the Contexts of English Romanticism*, ed. Lynda Pratt (Aldershot: Ashgate, 2006), 145.

44. Lynda Pratt, "Southey in Wales: Inscriptions, Monuments, and Romantic Prosperity," in *Wales and the Romantic Imagination*, ed. Damian Walford Davies and Lynda Pratt (Cardiff: University of Wales Press, 2007), 90.

45. Robert Southey, *The Poetical Works, 1793–1810*, ed. Lynda Pratt, vol. 2 (London: Pickering & Chatto, 2004), I.V.29–34. Subsequent references will be made parenthetically.

46. Elisa E. Bashero-Bondar, "British Conquistadors and Aztec Priests: The Horror of Southey's *Madoc*," *Philological Quarterly* 82 (2003), 87–113. Rebecca Cole Heinowitz makes a similar argument in *Spanish America and British Romanticism, 1777–1826: Rewriting Conquest* (Edinburgh: Edinburgh University Press, 2010), 93–131. Joselyn M. Almeida illuminates the broader implication of such British critiques of Spanish empire in *Reimagining the Transatlantic, 1780–1890* (Burlington, VT: Ashgate, 2011), 19–61.

47. For further explorations of the poem's colonial implications, see Beshero-Bondar, "British Conquistadors"; Heinowitz, *Spanish America*, 93–131; and Leask, "Southey's *Madoc*."

48. Benedict Anderson, *Imagined Communities: Reflections on the Origins and Spread of Nationalism*, 2nd ed. (London: Verso, 1991); Homi K. Bhabha, *The Locations of Culture* (London: Routledge, 1994), 148.

49. Gilbert Imlay, *The Emigrants; or the History of an Expatriated Family*, ed. W. M. Verhoeven and Amanda Gilroy (New York: Penguin, 1998), 204. Subsequent references to this edition will be made parenthetically.

50. Gilbert Imlay, *A Topographical Description of the Western Territory of North America*, 3rd ed. (London: J. Debrett, 1797), 367.

51. Imlay, *Topographical Description*, 368.

52. Imlay, *Topographical Description*, 369.

53. See W. M. Verhoeven, *Gilbert Imlay: Citizen of the World* (London: Pickering & Chatto, 2008).

54. On Enlightenment philosophers' analyses of Native Americans, see Fulford, *Romantic Indians*, 41–48.

55. On relations between settlers and Native Americans in Kentucky, see Ellen Eslinger ed. *Running Mad for Kentucky: Frontier Travel Accounts* (Lexington: University Press of Kentucky, 2004), 57–58; and Craig Thompson Friend, "Introduction," in *The Buzzel about*

Kentuck: Settling the Promised Land, ed. Craig Thompson Friend (Lexington: University Press of Kentucky, 1999), 11–13.

56. Fulford, *Romantic Indians*, 122.

57. John Filson, *The Discovery, Settlement and Present State of Kentucke* (New York: Corinth Books, 1962), 101.

58. William Godwin, *Imogen: A Pastoral Romance. In Two Volumes. From the Ancient British*, in *Collected Novels and Memoirs of William Godwin*, vol. 2, ed. Pamela Clemit (London: Pickering, 1992), 173.

59. On land ownership and political participation in Jefferson's republicanism see David N. Mayer, *The Constitutional Thought of Thomas Jefferson* (Charlottesville: University Press of Virginia, 1994), 53–118. The British origins of Jefferson's thought can be traced to James Harrington's *The Commonwealth of Oceana* (1656) and Andrew Fletcher's *A Discourse of Government With Relation to Militias* (1698).

60. Laura Doyle, *Freedom's Empire: Race and the Rise of the Novel in Atlantic Modernity, 1640–1940* (Durham, NC: Duke University Press, 2008), 4.

61. Prescott, *Eighteenth-Century Writing from Wales*, xx.

62. Fulford, *Romantic Indians*, 196.

63. Fiona Stafford, "*Lodore*: A Tale of the Present Time?" in *Mary Shelley's Fictions from Frankenstein to Falkner*, ed. Michael Eberle-Sinatra (London: Macmillan, 2000), 182. On *Lodore* as a silver-fork novel, see also Richard Cronin, "Mary Shelley and Edward Bulwer: *Lodore* as Hybrid Fiction," in *Mary Shelley's Fictions*, ed. Eberle-Sinatra, 39–54.

64. Mary Shelley, *Lodore*, ed. Fiona Stafford, in *The Novels and Selected Works of Mary Shelley*, ed. Nora Crook and Pamela Clemit, vol. 6 (London: Pickering, 1996), 41. Subsequent references to this edition will be made parenthetically.

65. Lisa Vargo, "Introduction," in *Lodore*, by Mary Shelley (Peterborough, ON: Broadview, 1997), 27–28. On the New Harmony community with which Birkbeck was affiliated, see Donald E. Pitzer, "The New Moral World of Robert Owen and New Harmony," in *America's Communal Utopias*, ed. Donald E. Pitzer (Chapel Hill: University of North Carolina Press, 1997), 88–134.

Chapter 5

1. William Carleton, *Traits and Stories of the Irish Peasantry*, foreword by Barbara Hayley, 2 vols. (Gerrards Cross, Buckinghamshire: Colin Smythe, 1990), vol. 1, v. This reprint is based on an 1842 edition that brought together the first series of *Traits and Stories*, published in 1830, and the second, published in 1832.

2. Carleton, *Traits and Stories*, vol. 1, vii.

3. Carleton, *Traits and Stories*, vol. 1, v.

4. Carleton, *Traits and Stories*, vol. 1, vi.

5. Carleton, *Traits and Stories*, vol. 1, vi.

6. It is worth noting that, in addition to the many Scottish, Irish, and American collections of tales and sketches, a few Welsh and Cornish collections appeared in the 1820s and '30s, including *Tales of Welsh Society and Scenery* (1827), *Tales of Welshland and Welsherie* (1831), and John Carne's *Tales of the West* (1828). Keith D. M. Snell surmises that Wales did

not produce much English-language fiction in the nineteenth century because of the relative vitality of Welsh-language fiction. See *The Bibliography of Regional Fiction in Britain
and Ireland, 1800–2000* (Aldershot: Ashgate, 2002), 8.

7. I borrow the term "metrocentric" from Bernard Bailyn's introduction to *Strangers
within the Realm: Cultural Margins of the First British Empire*, ed. Bernard Bailyn and
Philip D. Morgan (Chapel Hill: University of North Carolina Press, 1991), 9.

8. On the generic conventions of the sketch and the history of the genre's development in
Britain and the United States respectively, see Amanpal Garcha, *From Sketch to Novel: The
Development of Victorian Fiction* (Cambridge, UK: Cambridge University Press 2009); and
Kristie Hamilton, *America's Sketchbook: The Cultural Life of a Nineteenth-Century Literary
Genre* (Athens, OH: Ohio University Press, 1998).

9. Katie Trumpener, *Bardic Nationalism: The Romantic Novel and the British Empire*
(Princeton: Princeton University Press, 1997).

10. Josephine Donovan, *New England Local Color Literature: A Women's Tradition* (New
York: Frederick Ungar, 1983), 7. See also Roberto M. Dainotto, *Place in Literature: Regions,
Cultures, Communities* (Ithaca: Cornell University Press, 2000); W. J. Keith, *Regions of
the Imagination: The Development of British Rural Fiction* (Toronto: University of Toronto
Press, 1988); Judith Fetterley and Marjorie Pryse, *Writing Out of Place: Regionalism,
Women, and American Literary Culture* (Urbana: University of Illinois Press, 2003). For an
argument in favor of locating the origins of regionalism earlier than the nineteenth cen-
tury, see Evan Gottlieb and Juliet Shields, "Introduction," in *Representing Place in British
Literature and Culture, 1660–1830: From Local to Global* (Aldershot: Ashgate, 2013), 1–12.

11. Donovan, *New England*, 2.

12. Franco Moretti, "Graphs, Maps, Trees: Abstract Models for Literary History—2,"
New Left Review 26 (2004), 84.

13. Ian Duncan, "The Provincial or Regional Novel," in *A Companion to the Victorian
Novel*, ed. Patrick Brantlinger and William Thesing (Malden: Blackwell, 2002), 322.

14. Duncan, "The Provincial or Regional Novel," 322.

15. Dainotto, *Place in Literature*, 23. See also Lawrence Buell, *New England Literary
Culture: From Revolution through Renaissance* (Cambridge, UK: Cambridge University
Press, 1986), 300–306; and Francesco Loriggio, "Regionalism and Theory," in *Regionalism
Reconsidered: New Approaches to the Field*, ed. David Jordan (New York: Garland,
1994), 17–21.

16. Duncan, "The Provincial or Regional Novel," 323.

17. Richard Sha, *The Visual and Verbal Sketch in British Romanticism* (Philadelphia:
University of Pennsylvania Press, 1998).

18. Sha, *Visual and Verbal Sketch*, 63.

19. Ina Ferris discusses this convention in *The Romantic National Tale and the Question
of Ireland* (Cambridge, UK: Cambridge University Press, 2002), 47–56.

20. Frank Davey, "Toward the Ends of Regionalism," in *A Sense of Place: Re-evaluating
Regionalism in Canadian and American Writing*, ed. Christian Riegel and Herb Wylie
(Edmonton: University of Alberta Press, 1998), 4. See also Fetterley and Pryse, *Writing
Out of Place*, 6–7.

21. Sidney Owenson, *Patriotic Sketches of Ireland, Written in Connaught* (Baltimore:
Dobbin & Murphy, 1809), ix.

22. Owenson, *Patriotic Sketches*, 17.

23. William St. Clair suggests that British copyright law was respected by Americans rather than enforced by the British prior to the Revolution. See *The Reading Nation in the Romantic Period* (Cambridge, UK: Cambridge University Press, 2004), 379. On the reprinting of British works in the early republic, see Robert A. Gross, "Introduction: An Extensive Republic," in *An Extensive Republic: Print, Culture, and Society in the New Nation, 1790–1840*, vol. 2 of *A History of the Book in America*, ed. Robert A. Gross and Mary Kelley (Chapel Hill: University of North Carolina Press, 2010), 24–29, and Eve Tavor Bannet, *Transatlantic Stories and the History of Reading, 1720–1810: Migrant Fictions* (Cambridge, UK: Cambridge University Press, 2011), 6–11.

24. Owenson, *Patriotic Sketches*, n.pag.

25. A. G. L'Estrange, *The Life of Mary Russell Mitford: Related in a Selection from her Letters to her Friends*, 3 vols. (London: Bentley, 1870), vol. 2, 172.

26. Jeffrey Rubin-Dorsky, "Washington Irving and the Genesis of the Fictional Sketch," *Early American Literature* 21.3 (1986–1987), 229.

27. Washington Irving, *The Works of Washington Irving*, 21 vols. (New York: Putnam, 1860–1863), vol. 2, 13.

28. Irving, *Works*, vol. 2, 278.

29. Edward Watts, *Writing and Postcolonialism in the Early Republic* (Charlottesville: University Press of Virginia, 1998), 173.

30. James Lawson, *Tales and Sketches, by a Cosmopolite* (New York: Elam Bliss, 1830), 9.

31. Irving, *Works*, vol. 2, 6. On the English publication of *The Sketch Book* and Irving's ensuing literary celebrity in Britain, see Ben Harris McClary, *Washington Irving and the House of Murray* (Knoxville: The University of Tennessee Press, 1969).

32. Gary Kelly, *English Fiction of the Romantic Period, 1780–1830* (London: Longman, 1989), 64–65.

33. Buell, *New England*, 294.

34. Fetterley and Pryse, *Writing Out of Place*, 67–68.

35. Elizabeth Helsinger, *Rural Scenes and National Representations, Britain 1815–1850* (Princeton: Princeton University Press, 1997), 121.

36. Mary Russell Mitford, *Our Village: Sketches of Rural Character and Scenery*, 4 vols. (London: Whittaker, 1824), vol. 1, 11, and vol. 4, 258.

37. Helsinger, *Rural Scenes*, 121.

38. Tim Killick, *British Short Fiction in the Early Nineteenth Century: The Rise of the Tale* (Aldershot: Ashgate, 2008), 120.

39. Jackie Turton, "Making It National; or, the Art of the Tale: Correspondence between William Carleton and His Publisher," *Irish Studies Review* 13 (2005), 176.

40. Mitford, *Our Village*, vol. 1, 100.

41. Helsinger, *Rural Scenes*, 128. See also Fetterley and Pryse, who conclude that Mitford "lacks any sense" that the regional sketch "could be used to create a space of critique." *Writing Out of Place*, 68.

42. Mitford, *Our Village*, vol. 2, 204–205.

43. Andrew Picken, *Tales and Sketches of the West of Scotland* (Glasgow: Robertson and Atkinson; Edinburgh: Oliver & Boyd; London: G. & W. B. Whittaker, 1824), 122. Picken published the collection under the pseudonym Christopher Keelivine, using Keelivine, a Scots word for pencil, to explore the aesthetics of the literary sketch.

44. Picken, *Tales and Sketches*, 202.

45. Benjamin Drake, *Tales and Sketches from the Queen City* (Cincinnati: Morgan, 1838), 7.

46. Drake, *Tales and Sketches*, 8.

47. Sarah Hale, *Sketches of American Character*, 4th ed. (Boston: Freeman Hunt, 1831), 8.

48. Hale, *Sketches*, 208.

49. Hale, *Sketches*, 270.

50. Hale, *Sketches*, 287.

51. Owenson, *Patriotic Sketches*, 48–49.

52. Owenson, *Patriotic Sketches*, 49–50.

53. Trumpener, *Bardic Nationalism*, 19–34.

54. Gross, "Introduction," 5. For more on the decentralization of publishing in the early nineteenth-century United States, see Ronald J. Zboray, "Antebellum Reading and the Ironies of Technological Innovation," *American Quarterly* 40 (1998), 65–82. Hamilton argues that the early nineteenth-century American "proliferation of prose sketches" was also influenced by "the explosion of magazine and newspaper publication and the growth of public education." See Hamilton, *America's Sketchbook*, 14. On London's dominance of the transatlantic literary market, see Joseph Rezek, *London and the Making of Provincial Literature: Aesthetics and the Transatlantic Book Trade, 1800–1850* (Philadelphia: University of Pennsylvania Press, 2015).

55. See Meredith McGill, *American Literature and the Culture of Reprinting, 1834–1853* (Philadelphia: University of Pennsylvania Press, 2003).

56. Gross, "Introduction," 11.

57. Hsuan L. Hsu, *Geography and the Production of Space in Nineteenth-Century American Literature* (New York: Cambridge University Press, 2010), 165.

58. Hale, *Sketches*, 190.

59. Hale, *Sketches*, 190.

60. Sandra A. Zagarell, "'America' as Community in Three Antebellum Village Sketches," in *The (Other) American Traditions: Nineteenth-Century Women Writers*, ed. Joyce W. Warren (New Brunswick, NJ: Rutgers University Press, 1993), 156.

61. Lydia Sigourney, *A Sketch of Connecticut, forty years since* (Hartford: Oliver D. Cooke, 1824), 32. Subsequent references will be made parenthetically.

62. Catharine Maria Sedgwick, *Tale and Sketches*, Second Series (New York: Harper, 1844), n. pag. Subsequent references will be made parenthetically.

63. Catharine Maria Sedgwick, *The Power of her Sympathy: The Autobiography and Journal of Catharine Maria Sedgwick*, ed. Mary Kelley (Boston: Northeastern University Press, 1993), 50–53. These statistics are from Kerby A. Miller, *Emigrants and Exiles* (New York: Oxford University Press, 1985), 193–194.

64. Kevin Kenny, *The American Irish, A History* (Harlow, UK: Longman, 2000), 45.

65. David H. Bennett, *Party of Fear: From Nativist Movements to the New Right in American History* (Chapel Hill: University of North Carolina Press, 1988), 27–60.

66. In her autobiography, Sedgwick favorably compares Irish servants' "half-savage ways—their blunders—their imaginativeness—indefiniteness—and *curve-lines* every way" to "shiftless, lazy, unfaithful" black servants (*The Power of her Sympathy*, 51). On Sedgwick's attitudes towards the Irish, see also Juliet Shields, "Pedagogy in the Post-Colony: Documentary Didacticism and the 'Irish Problem,'" *Eighteenth-Century Novel* 6 (2009), 465–493.

67. William Carleton, *Tales and Sketches, Illustrating the Character, Usages, Traditions, Sports and Pastimes of the Irish Peasantry* (Dublin: James Duffy, 1845), viii.

68. Alexander Bethune, *Tales and Sketches of the Scottish Peasantry* (Edinburgh: Fraser; and London: W. S. Orr, 1838), 131. Subsequent references will be made parenthetically.

69. Franco Moretti, *Atlas of the European Novel 1800–1900* (London: Verso, 1998), 165; italics in original.

Epilogue

1. Hallvard Dahlie's *Varieties of Exile: The Canadian Experience* (Vancouver: University of British Columbia Press, 1986) discusses writing by Canadian immigrants from the mid-eighteenth to the mid-twentieth century. Much Canadian writing published before the Canadian Confederation of 1867 could be considered literature of migration, as W. H. New suggests in *A History of Canadian Literature*, 2nd ed. (Montreal: McGill-Queen's University Press, 2003), 25–78.

2. See the Introduction, note 24, for a list of this scholarship.

3. There are some exceptions to this Anglocentrism. Scottish writing about the West Indies receives a fair amount of attention in Elizabeth Bohls, *Slavery and the Politics of Place: Representing the Colonial Caribbean, 1770–1833* (Cambridge, UK: Cambridge University Press, 2014); and Keith Albert Sandiford, *The Cultural Politics of Sugar: Caribbean Slavery and Narratives of Colonialism* (Cambridge, UK: Cambridge University Press, 2000). Elizabeth Waterston examines Canadian literary connections to Scotland in *Rapt in Plaid: Canadian Literature and Scottish Tradition* (Toronto: University of Toronto Press, 2003).

4. Katie Trumpener, *Bardic Nationalism: The Romantic Novel and the British Empire* (Princeton: Princeton University Press, 1997), 291. The question of whether Canadian literature is postcolonial—or is amenable to analysis through a postcolonial lens—is open to debate. For a range of perspectives on this question, see the essays collected in Laura Moss, ed., *Is Canada Postcolonial? Unsettling Canadian Literature* (Waterloo, ON: Wilfred Laurier University Press, 2003).

5. Francis Russell Hart, *The Scottish Novel* (Cambridge, MA: Harvard University Press, 1978), 31.

6. Regina Hewitt posits that Galt used the term "theoretical histories" because his fiction "applied the methods from large-scale studies of multiple peoples from prehistory to modernity on a small scale"—for instance, to a single parish or town. But of course these "histories" are also theoretical in the sense that they are fictional, describing the possible or hypothetical rather than the factual. See Hewitt, "Introduction: Observations and Conjectures on John Galt's Place in Scottish Enlightenment and Romantic-Era Studies," in *John Galt: Observations and Conjectures on Literature, History, and Society*, ed. Regina Hewitt (Lewisburg, PA: Bucknell University Press, 2012), 2; and Keith M. Costain, "Theoretical History and the Novel: The Scottish Fictions of John Galt," *ELH* 43 (1976), 342–63.

7. The Canada Company was a chartered British land development company formed ostensibly to promote the colonization of Upper Canada. Its investors purchased Crown

Lands in Ontario which they sold back to British emigrants at a profit in what Galt described in his *Autobiography* as "land-jobbing huxtry." On Galt's role in the company see *The Autobiography of John Galt*, 2 vols. (London: Cochrane and McCrone, 1833), vol. 2, 158; and Robert C. Lee, *The Canada Company and the Huron Tract, 1826–1853: Personalities, Profits, and Politics* (Toronto: Natural Heritage Books, 2004).

8. The abridged version of *Bogle Corbet* inspired a collection of essays: Elizabeth Waterston, ed., *John Galt: Reappraisals* (Guelph, ON: University of Guelph Press, 1985). In addition to Trumpener's *Bardic Nationalism*, Ian Duncan's *Scott's Shadow: The Romantic Novel in Edinburgh* (Princeton: Princeton University Press, 2007) also has contributed significantly to the renewed critical interest in Galt's Scottish novels, inspiring new work such as the essays in *John Galt: Observations and Conjectures on Literature, History, and Society*, ed. Regina Hewitt (Lewisburg, PA: Bucknell University Press, 2013).

9. P. H. Scott, *John Galt* (Edinburgh: Scottish Academic Press, 1985), 99. On *Lawrie Todd* see Charles E. Shain's "John Galt's America," *American Quarterly* 8 (1956), 254–263; and Scott, *John Galt*, 92–104.

10. Elizabeth Waterston, "Introduction," in *Bogle Corbet*, by John Galt, ed. Elizabeth Waterston (Toronto: Stewart and Mclelland, 1977), 2.

11. *The Counsel for Emigrants* (Aberdeen: John Mathison, 1834), 19–20. Like many guidebooks for emigrants, this one is made up of excerpts from periodical essays and correspondence.

12. *Counsel for Emigrants*, ix.

13. *Counsel for Emigrants*, ix.

14. Kenneth McNeil, "Time, Emigration, and the Circum-Atlantic World: John Galt's *Bogle Corbet*," in *John Galt: Observations and Conjectures on Literature, History, and Society*, ed. Regina Hewitt (Lewisburg, PA: Bucknell University Press, 2013), 302, 310.

15. Trumpener, *Bardic Nationalism*, 281, 288.

16. Trumpener, *Bardic Nationalism*, 284.

17. Trumpener, *Bardic Nationalism*, 274.

18. The abridged version of the novel issued by McClelland and Stewart in 1977 includes only the Canadian section of Corbet's story (part of the second and all of the third volume), ironically cutting him off from the colonial past that he seems destined to repeat.

19. Scott, *John Galt*, 94.

{ WORKS CITED }

Aaron, Jane. "'Saxon, Think not All Is Won': Felicia Hemans and the Making of the Britons." *Cardiff Corvey: Reading the Romantic Text* 4 (2000). http://www.cf.ac. uk.offcampus.lib.washington.edu/corvey/articles/cc04_no1.html.

Almeida, Joselyn M. *Reimagining the Transatlantic, 1780–1890*. Burlington, VT: Ashgate, 2011.

Anderson, Benedict. *Imagined Communities: Reflections on the Origins and Spread of Nationalism*. 2nd ed. London: Verso, 1991.

Anderson, James. *The Interest of Great Britain, with Regard to her American Colonies, Considered*. London: Cadell, 1782.

Annals of Congress. 1st Congress. 2nd session. February, 1790.

Armitage, David. *The Ideological Origins of the British Empire*. Cambridge, UK: Cambridge University Press, 2000.

Armitage, David, and Michael J. Braddick, eds. *The British Atlantic World, 1500–1800*. New York: Palgrave, 2002.

Armstrong, Nancy, and Leonard Tennenhouse. "The American Origins of the English Novel." *ALH* 4 (1992): 386–410.

Ayscough, Samuel. *Remarks on the Letters from an American Farmer; or a detection of the errors of Mr. J. Hector St. John; Pointing out the pernicious Tendency of these Letters to Great Britain*. London: John Fielding, 1783.

Bailyn, Bernard. *The Ideological Origins of the American Revolution*. Cambridge, MA: The Belknap Press, 1967.

Bailyn, Bernard. *Voyagers to the West: A Passage in the Peopling of America on the Eve of Revolution*. New York: Vintage, 1988.

Bailyn, Bernard, and Philip D. Morgan, eds. *Strangers within the Realm: Cultural Margins of the First British Empire*. Chapel Hill: University of North Carolina Press, 1991.

Bannet, Eve Tavor. *An Empire of Letters: Letter Manuals and Transatlantic Correspondence, 1688–1820*. Cambridge, UK: Cambridge University Press, 2005.

Bannet, Eve Tavor. *The Transatlantic History of Reading, 1720–1810: Migrant Fictions*. Cambridge, UK: Cambridge University Press, 2011.

Bannet, Eve Tavor. "Charles Brockden Brown and England: Of Genres, the Minerva Press, and the Early Republican Reprint Trade." In *Transatlantic Literary Exchanges 1790–1870: Gender, Race, and Nation*. Ed. Kevin Hutchings and Julia M. Wright. Farnham, Surrey: Ashgate, 2011. 133–152.

Bannet, Eve Tavor, and Susan Manning, eds. *Transatlantic Literary Studies, 1660–1830*. Cambridge, UK: Cambridge University Press, 2012.

Banton, Michael. *The Idea of Race*. London: Tavistock, 1977.

Barfoot, C. C. "Deserting the Village." In *The Clash of Ireland: Literary Contrasts and Connections*. Amsterdam: Rodopi, 1989. 52–97.

Basker, James G. "Johnson and Slavery." *Harvard Library Bulletin* 20 (2009): 29–50.

Baucom, Ian. "Found Drowned: The Irish Atlantic." *Nineteenth-Century Contexts* 22 (2000): 103–138.

Bauer, Ralph. *The Cultural Geography of Colonial American Literatures*. Cambridge, UK: Cambridge University Press, 2003.

Baym, Nina. *Feminism and American Literary History: Essays*. New Brunswick, NJ: Rutgers University Press, 1992.

Belich, James. *Replenishing the Earth: The Settler Revolution and the Rise of the Anglo-World, 1783–1939*. Oxford: Oxford University Press, 2009.

Bennett, David H. *Party of Fear: From Nativist Movements to the New Right in American History*. Chapel Hill: University of North Carolina Press, 1988.

Berkhofer, Jr., Robert F. *The White Man's Indian: Images of the American Indian from Columbus to the Present*. New York: Alfred A. Knopf, 1978.

Berry, Christopher J. *Social Theory of the Scottish Enlightenment*. Edinburgh: Edinburgh University Press, 1997.

Beshero-Bondar, Elisa E. "British Conquistadors and Aztec Priests: The Horror of Southey's Madoc." *Philological Quarterly* 82 (2003): 87–113.

Bethune, Alexander. *Tales and Sketches of the Scottish Peasantry*. Edinburgh: Fraser; and London: W. S. Orr, 1838.

Bhabha, Homi K. *The Locations of Culture*. London: Routledge, 1994.

Bilder, Mary Sarah. *The Transatlantic Constitution: Colonial Legal Culture and the Empire*. Cambridge, MA: Harvard University Press, 2008.

Bland, Richard. "The Colonel Dismounted: Or, the Rector Vindicated." In *Pamphlets of the American Revolution, 1750–1776*. Ed. Bernard Bailyn and Jane N. Garrett. Cambridge, MA: The Belknap Press, 1965. 292–354.

Bohls, Elizabeth. *Slavery and the Politics of Place: Representing the Colonial Caribbean, 1770–1833*. Cambridge, UK: Cambridge University Press, 2014.

Borden, Morton, ed. *The Antifederalist Papers*. Lansing: Michigan State University Press, 1965.

Brackenridge, Hugh Henry. *Modern Chivalry*. Ed. Claude M. Newlin. New York: American Book Company, 1937.

Brennan, Catherine. *Angers, Fantasies and Ghostly Fears: Nineteenth-Century Women from Wales and English-Language Poetry*. Cardiff: University of Wales Press, 2003.

Brewer, William. "Felicia Hemans, Byronic Cosmopolitanism and the Ancient Welsh Bards." In *English Romanticism in the Celtic World*. Eds. Gerard Carruthers and Alan Rawes. Cambridge, UK: Cambridge University Press, 2003. 167–181.

Brown, Charles Brockden. "A Sketch of American Literature, for 1806-7." *The American Register; or, General Repository of History, Politics, and Science*. Vol. 1 (1807): 173–187.

Brown, Charles Brockden. *Edgar Huntly, or Memoirs of a Sleepwalker*. Ed. Norman S. Grabo. New York: Penguin, 1988.

Brown, Charles Brockden. *Wieland; or, the Transformation: an American Tale* and *Memoirs of Carwin the Biloquist*. Ed. Jay Fliegelman. New York: Penguin, 1991.

Bucci, Richard. "John Jay and 'The Federalist No. V': A Bibliographic Discussion." *The Papers of the Bibliographical Society of America* 105 (2011): 377–406.

Buell, Lawrence. *New England Literary Culture: From Revolution through Renaissance*. Cambridge, UK: Cambridge University Press, 1986.

Buell, Lawrence. "American Literary Emergence as a Postcolonial Phenomenon." *ALH* 4.3 (1992): 411–442.

Bumsted, J. M. *The People's Clearance: Highland Emigration to North America 1770–1815.* Edinburgh: Edinburgh University Press, 1982.

Burder, George. *The Welch Indians; or a Collection of Papers; Respecting a people whose ancestors emigrated from Wales to America, in the Year 1170, with Prince Madoc.* London: T. Chapman, 1797.

Burke, Edmund. *Reflections on the Revolution in France.* Ed. L. G. Mitchell. Oxford: Oxford University Press, 1993.

Burke, Edmund. "Speech on American Taxation, 19 April 1774." In *The Writings and Speeches of Edmund Burke.* Vol. 2. Ed. Paul Langford. Oxford: Oxford University Press, 1981. 406–463.

Burke, Edmund. "Speech on Conciliation with America, 22 March 1775." In *Writings and Speeches of Edmund Burke.* Vol. 3. Ed. Warren M. Elofson. Oxford: Oxford University Press, 1996. 103–169.

Burnard, Trevor. "European Migration to Jamaica, 1655–1780." *William and Mary Quarterly* 53 (1996): 769–794.

Cagidemetrio, Alide. "A Plea for Fictional Histories and Old-Time Jewesses." In *The Invention of Ethnicity.* Ed. Werner Sollors. New York: Oxford University Press, 1989. 14–43.

Campbell, Mildred. "'Of People Either too Few or too Many': The Conflict of Opinion on Population and Its Relation to Emigration." In *Conflict in Stuart England: Essays in Honour of Wallace Notestein.* Ed. William Appleton Aiken and Basil Duke Henning. London: Jonathan Cape, 1960. 169–202.

A Candid Enquiry into the Causes of the Late and the Intended Migrations from Scotland, in a letter to J--- R--- Esq; Lanark-shire. Glasgow: P. Tait, 1771.

Canny, Nicholas. *Kingdom and Colony: Ireland in the Atlantic World, 1560–1800.* Baltimore: Johns Hopkins University Press, 1988.

Canny, Nicholas. "Introduction." In *The Oxford History of the British Empire.* Vol. 1. *The Origins of Empire.* Ed. Nicholas Canny. Oxford: Oxford University Press, 1998. 1–33.

Carleton, William. *Tales and Sketches, Illustrating the Character, Usages, Traditions, Sports and Pastimes of the Irish Peasantry.* Dublin: James Duffy, 1845.

Carleton, William. *Traits and Stories of the Irish Peasantry.* 2 vols. Gerrards Cross, Buckinghamshire: Colin Smythe, 1990.

Carretta, Vincent. *George III and the Satirists from Hogarth to Byron.* Athens: University of Georgia Press, 1990.

Carruthers, Gerard, and Alan Rawes. "Introduction: Romancing the Celt." In *English Romanticism and the Celtic World.* Ed. Gerard Carruthers and Alan Rawes. Cambridge, UK: Cambridge University Press, 2003. 1–19.

Carter II, Edward C. "A 'Wild Irishman' Under Every Federalist's Bed: Naturalization in Philadelphia, 1789–1806." *Proceedings of the American Philosophical Society* 133.2 (1989): 178–189.

Cassuto, Leonard. "'[Un]consciousness Itself is the Malady': *Edgar Huntly* and the Discourse of the Other." *Modern Language Studies* 23.4 (1993): 118–130.

Christophersen, Bill. *The Apparition in the Glass: Charles Brockden Brown's American Gothic.* Athens: University of Georgia Press, 1993.

Clark, J. C. D. *The Language of Liberty, 1660–1832: Political Discourse and Social Dynamics in the Anglo-American World*. New York: Cambridge University Press, 1994.

Claybaugh, Amanda. *The Novel of Purpose: Literature and Social Reform in the Anglo-American World*. Ithaca: Cornell University Press, 2006.

Clemit, Pamela. *The Godwinian Novel: The Rational Fictions of Godwin, Brockden Brown, and Mary Shelley*. Oxford: Clarendon, 1993.

Cobbett, William. "Detection of a Conspiracy, Formed by the United Irishmen, with the Evident Intention of Aiding the Tyrants of France in Subverting the Government of the United States of America." In *Peter Porcupine in America: Pamphlets on Republicanism and Revolution*. Ed. David A. Wilson. Ithaca: Cornell University Press, 1994. 241–257.

Colley, Linda. *Britons: Forging a Nation 1707–1832*. New Haven: Yale University Press, 1992.

Cone, Carl B. *Burke and the Nature of Politics: The Age of the American Revolution*. Louisville: University of Kentucky Press, 1957.

Connolly, Clare. *A Cultural History of the Irish Novel, 1790–1829*. Cambridge, UK: Cambridge University Press, 2012.

Connolly, S. J. "Eighteenth-Century Ireland: Colony or *ancien régime*?" In *The Making of Modern Irish History: Revisionism and the Revisionist Controversy*. Ed. D. George Boyce and Alan O'Day. London: Routledge, 1996. 15–33.

Constantine, Mary-Ann. "'This Wildernessed Business of Publication': The Making of *Poems, Lyric and Pastoral* (1794)." In *A Rattleskull Genius: The Many Faces of Iolo Morganwg*. Ed. Geraint H. Jenkins. Cardiff: University of Wales Press, 2005. 123–146.

Conway, Stephen. *The British Isles and the War of American Independence*. Oxford: Oxford University Press, 2000.

Conway, Stephen. "From Fellow-Nationals to Foreigners: British Perceptions of the Americans, circa 1739–1793." *William and Mary Quarterly*. 3rd ser. LIX (2002): 65–99.

Cook, Elizabeth Heckendorn. *Epistolary Bodies: Gender and Genre in the Eighteenth-Century Republic of Letters*. Stanford: Stanford University Press, 1997.

Cooper, James Fenimore. *The Letters and Journals of James Fenimore Cooper*. Ed. James Franklin Beard. 6 vols. Cambridge, MA: Belknap Press of Harvard University Press, 1960–1968.

Cooper, James Fenimore. *The Last of the Mohicans; a Narrative of 1757*. Ed. James A. Sappenfield and E. N. Feltskog. Albany: State University of New York Press, 1983.

Cooper, James Fenimore. *The Deerslayer; or, the First War-Path*. Ed. James Franklin Beard, et al. Albany: State University of New York Press, 1987.

Costain, Keith M. "Theoretical History and the Novel: The Scottish Fictions of John Galt." *ELH* 43 (1976): 342–63.

The Counsel for Emigrants. Aberdeen: John Mathison, 1834.

Crain, Caleb. *American Sympathy: Men, Friendship, and Literature in the New Nation*. New Haven: Yale University Press, 2001.

Cressy, David. *Coming Over: Migration and Communication between England and New England in the Seventeenth Century*. Cambridge, UK: Cambridge University Press, 1987.

de Crèvecoeur, J. Hector St. John. *Letters from an American Farmer and Sketches of Eighteenth-Century America*. Ed. Albert Stone. New York: Penguin, 1981.

Cronin, Richard. "Mary Shelley and Edward Bulwer: *Lodore* as Hybrid Fiction." In *Mary Shelley's Fictions from* Frankenstein *to* Falkner. Ed. Michael Eberle-Sinatra. London: Macmillan, 2000. 39–54.

Curley, Thomas M. "Johnson and Burke: Constitutional Evolution versus Political Revolution." *Studies on Voltaire and the Eighteenth Century* 263 (1989): 265–268.

Dahlie, Hallvard. *Varieties of Exile: The Canadian Experience.* Vancouver: University of British Columbia Press, 1986.

Dainotto, Roberto M. *Place in Literature: Regions, Cultures, Communities.* Ithaca: Cornell University Press, 2000.

Davey, Frank. "Toward the Ends of Regionalism." In *A Sense of Place: Re-evaluating Regionalism in Canadian and American Writing.* Ed. Christian Riegel and Herb Wylie. Edmonton: University of Alberta Press, 1998. 1–18.

Davidson, Cathy N. *Revolution and the Word: The Rise of the Novel in America.* Expanded ed. Oxford: Oxford University Press, 2004.

Davie, Donald. *The Heyday of Sir Walter Scott.* London: Routledge and Kegan Paul, 1961.

Davies, Gwendolyn. "Publishing Abroad." In *History of the Book in Canada.* Vol. 2. Ed. Patricia Lockhart Fleming, Yvan Lamonde, and Fiona Black. Toronto: University of Toronto Press, 2005. 139–146.

Davies, H. M. "'Very Different Springs of Uneasiness': Emigration from Wales to the United States of America during the 1790s." *Welsh History Review* 15 (1991): 368–398.

Davies, R. R. "Colonial Wales." *Past and Present* 65 (1974): 3–23.

Deacon, Richard. *Madoc and the Discovery of America: Some New Light on an Old Controversy.* London: Muller, 1967.

The Declaration by the Representatives of the United Colonies of North America, now met in General Congress at Philadelphia. London, 1775.

Defoe, Daniel. *A Tour Through the Whole Island of Great Britain.* 7th ed. 4 vols. London: J. and F. Rivington, 1769.

Dekker, George. *James Fenimore Cooper: The American Scott.* New York: Barnes and Noble, 1967.

Dekker, George. *The American Historical Romance.* Cambridge, UK: Cambridge University Press, 1987.

Dennis, Ian. "The Worthlessness of Duncan Heyward: A Waverley Hero in America." *Studies in the Novel* 29 (1997): 1–16.

DeWolfe, Barbara. "Introduction." In *Discoveries of America: Personal Accounts of British Emigrants to North America during the Revolutionary Era.* Ed. Barbara DeWolfe. Cambridge, UK: Cambridge University Press, 1997. 1–37.

Dobson, David. *Scottish Emigration to Colonial America, 1607–1785.* Athens: University of Georgia Press, 1994.

Dodd, A. H. *The Character of Early Welsh Emigration to the United States.* Cardiff: University of Wales Press, 1953.

Donovan, Josephine. *New England Local Color Literature: A Women's Tradition.* New York: Frederick Ungar, 1983.

Doyle, Laura. *Freedom's Empire: Race and the Rise of the Novel in Atlantic Modernity, 1640–1940.* Durham, NC: Duke University Press, 2008.

Drake, Benjamin. *Tales and Sketches from the Queen City.* Cincinnati: Morgan, 1838.

Dulany, Daniel. *Considerations on the Propriety of Imposing Taxes in the British Colonies.* London: J. Almon, 1776.

Duncan, Christopher M. *The Anti-Federalists and Early American Political Thought.* DeKalb: Northern Illinois University Press, 1995.

Duncan, Ian. "The Provincial or Regional Novel." In *A Companion to the Victorian Novel.* Ed. Patrick Brantlinger and William Thesing. Malden: Blackwell, 2002. 318–335.

Duncan, Ian. *Scott's Shadow: The Romantic Novel in Edinburgh.* Princeton: Princeton University Press, 2007.

Durey, Michael. *Transatlantic Radicals and the Early American Republic.* Lawrence: University of Kansas Press, 1997.

Dwan, David, and Christopher J. Insole. *The Cambridge Companion to Edmund Burke.* Cambridge, UK: Cambridge University Press, 2012.

Dyer, Gary. "Irresolute Ravishers and the Sexual Economy of Chivalry in the Romantic Novel." *Nineteenth-Century Literature* 55 (2000): 340–368.

Earle, Edward Mead, ed. *The Federalist: A Commentary on the Constitution of the United States, Being a Collection of Essays written in Support of the Constitution agreed upon September 17, 1787 by the Federal Convention.* New York: The Modern Library, 1937.

Edmunds, R. David. *American Indian Leaders: Studies in Diversity.* Lincoln: University of Nebraska Press, 1980.

Elliott, Emory. *Revolutionary Writers: Literature and Authority in the New Republic.* New York: Oxford University Press, 1986.

Elliott, J. H. "A Europe of Composite Monarchies." *Past and Present* 137 (1992): 48–71.

Ellison, Julie. *Cato's Tears and the Making of Anglo-American Emotion.* Chicago: University of Chicago Press, 1999.

Eslinger, Ellen ed. *Running Mad for Kentucky: Frontier Travel Accounts.* Lexington: University Press of Kentucky, 2004.

Estes, Todd. "The Voices of Publius and the Strategies of Persuasion in *The Federalist.*" *Journal of the Early Republic* 28 (2008): 523–558.

The Exile of Erin! Dublin: Wholesale and Retail Book Warehouse, n.d.

Fender, Stephen. *Sea Changes: British Emigration and American Literature.* Cambridge, UK: Cambridge University Press, 1992.

Ferguson, Robert A. "The Forgotten Publius: John Jay and the Aesthetics of Ratification." *Early American Literature* 34 (1999): 223–240.

Ferris, Ina. *The Romantic National Tale and the Question of Ireland.* Cambridge, UK: Cambridge University Press, 2002.

Fetterley, Judith, and Marjorie Pryse. *Writing out of Place: Regionalism, Women, and American Literary Culture.* Urbana: University of Illinois Press, 2003.

Fiedler, Leslie. *Love and Death in the American Novel.* 3rd ed. New York: Stein and Day, 1982.

Filson, John. *The Discovery, Settlement and Present State of Kentucke.* New York: Corinth Books, 1962.

Fischer, David Hackett. *Albion's Seed: Four British Folkways in America.* New York: Oxford University Press, 1989.

Flynn, Christopher. *Americans in British Literature, 1770–1832: A Breed Apart.* Aldershot: Ashgate, 2008.

Fogleman, Aaron Spencer. *Hopeful Journeys: German Immigration, Settlement, and Political Culture in Colonial America, 1717–1775.* Philadelphia: University of Pennsylvania Press, 1996.

Folkenflik, Robert. "Johnson's Politics." In *The Cambridge Companion to Johnson.* Ed. Greg Clingham. Cambridge, UK: Cambridge University Press, 1997. 102–113.

Frank, Armin Paul. "Writing Literary Independence: The Case of Cooper—the 'American Scott' and the Un-Scottish American." *Comparative Literature Studies* 34 (1997): 41–70.

Franklin, Benjamin. *Writings*. Ed. J. A. Leo Lemay. New York: Library of America, 1987.

Franklin, Caroline. "The Welsh American Dream: Iolo Morganwg, Robert Southey and the Madoc Legend." In *English Romanticism and the Celtic World*. Ed. Gerard Carruthers and Alan Rawes. Cambridge, UK: Cambridge University Press, 2003. 69–84.

Freud, Sigmund. "The Uncanny." In *The Standard Edition of the Complete Works of Sigmund Freud*. Trans. and ed. James Strachey, et al. Vol. 17. London: The Hogarth Press, 1964. 219–256.

Friend, Craig Thompson. "Introduction." In *The Buzzel about Kentuck: Settling the Promised Land*. Ed. Craig Thompson Friend. Lexington, Kentucky: University Press of Kentucky, 1999. 1–22.

Fulford, Tim. *Romantic Indians: Native Americans, British Literature, and Transatlantic Culture, 1756–1830*. Oxford: Oxford University Press, 2006.

Galt, John. *Lawrie Todd; or, The Settlers in the Woods*. 3 vols. London: Henry Colburn, 1830.

Galt, John. *Bogle Corbet; or, The Emigrants*. 3 vols. London: Henry Colburn, 1831.

Galt, John. *Autobiography*. 2 vols. London: Cochrane and M'Crone, 1833.

Garcha, Amanpal. *From Sketch to Novel: The Development of Victorian Fiction*. Cambridge, UK: Cambridge University Press 2009.

[Gardiner, W. H.]. Rev. of *The Spy, A Tale of Neutral Ground*. By James Fenimore Cooper. *North American Review* 15 (1822): 258.

Gardner, Jared. *Master Plots: Race and the Founding of an American Literature, 1787–1845*. Baltimore: The Johns Hopkins University Press, 1998.

Gerber, David A. "Epistolary Ethics: Personal Correspondence and the Culture of Emigration in the Nineteenth Century." *Journal of American Ethnic History* 19 (2000): 3–23.

Gerson, Carole. "Writers without Borders: The Global Framework of Canada's Early Literary History." *Canadian Literature* 201 (2009): 15–33.

Gibbons, Luke. *Edmund Burke and Ireland: Aesthetics, Politics, and the Colonial Sublime*. Cambridge, UK: Cambridge University Press, 2003.

Gibbons, Luke. "Ireland, America, and Gothic Memory: Transatlantic Terror in the Early Republic." *boundary 2* 31.1 (2004): 25–47.

Giles, Paul. *Transatlantic Insurrections: British Culture and the Formation of American Literature, 1730–1860*. Philadelphia: University of Pennsylvania Press, 2001.

Giles, Paul. *The Global Remapping of American Literature*. Princeton: Princeton University Press, 2011.

Gilman, Chandler Robbins. *Life on the Lakes: Being Tales and Sketches collected during A Trip to the Pictured Rocks of Lake Superior*. 2 vols. New York: George Dearborn, 1836.

Godwin, William. *An Enquiry Concerning Political Justice*. Ed. Isaac Kramnick. Harmondsworth: Penguin, 1976.

Godwin, William. "Imogen: A Pastoral Romance. In Two Volumes. From the Ancient British." In *Collected Novels and Memoirs of William Godwin*. Vol. 2. Ed. Pamela Clemit. London: Pickering & Chatto, 1992.

Goldsmith, Oliver. *The Poetical Works of Oliver Goldsmith*. Ed. Austin Dobson. Oxford: Oxford University Press, 1949.

Gottlieb, Evan, and Juliet Shields. "Introduction." In *Representing Place in British Literature and Culture, 1660–1830: From Local to Global*. Aldershot: Ashgate, 2013. 1–12.

Gould, Eliga H. *The Persistence of Empire: British Political Culture in the Age of the American Revolution*. Chapel Hill: University of North Carolina Press, 2000.

Grabo, Norman S. "Crèvecoeur's American: Beginning the World Anew." *William and Mary Quarterly*. 3rd series. 48 (1991): 159–172.

Grant, Alexander, and Keith J. Stringer, eds. *Uniting the Kingdom? The Making of British History*. London: Routledge, 1995.

Gravil, Richard. *Romantic Dialogues: Anglo-American Continuities, 1776–1862*. New York: St. Martin's Press, 2000.

Greene, Donald. *The Politics of Samuel Johnson*. 2nd ed. Athens: University of Georgia Press, 1990.

Greene, Jack P. *Peripheries and Center: Constitutional Development in the Extended Polities of the British Empire, and the United States, 1607–1788*. Athens: University of Georgia Press, 1986.

Greene, Jack P. *Creating the British Atlantic: Essays on Transplantation, Adaptation, and Continuity*. Charlottesville: University of Virginia Press, 2013.

Griffin, Michael. "Delicate Allegories, Deceitful Mazes: Goldsmith's Landscapes." *Eighteenth-Century Ireland/Iris an dá chultúr* 16 (2001): 104–117.

Gross, Robert A. "Introduction: An Extensive Republic." In *A History of the Book in America*. Vol. 2. *An Extensive Republic: Print, Culture, and Society in the New Nation, 1790–1840*. Ed. Robert A. Gross and Mary Kelley. Chapel Hill: University of North Carolina Press, 2010. 1–50.

Haims, Lynn. "Of Indians and Irishmen: A Note on Brackenridge's Use of Sources for Satire in 'Modern Chivalry'." *Early American Literature* 10 (1975): 88–92.

Hale, Sarah. *Sketches of American Character*. 4th ed. Boston: Freeman Hunt, 1831.

Hamilton, Kristie. *America's Sketchbook: The Cultural Life of a Nineteenth-Century Literary Genre*. Athens: Ohio University Press, 1998.

Hancock, David. "Scots in the Slave Trade." In *Nation and Province in the First British Empire: Scotland and the Americas, 1600–1800*. Ed. Ned C. Landsman. Lewisburg, PA: Bucknell University Press, 2001. 60–93.

Hanlon, Christopher. *America's England: Antebellum Literature and Atlantic Sectionalism*. Oxford: Oxford University Press, 2013.

Hart, Francis Russell. *The Scottish Novel*. Cambridge, MA: Harvard University Press, 1978.

Hechter, Michael. *Internal Colonialism: The Celtic Fringe in British National Development*. 2nd ed. New Brunswick, NJ: Transaction Publishers, 1999.

Heinowitz, Rebecca Cole. *Spanish America and British Romanticism, 1777–1826: Rewriting Conquest*. Edinburgh: Edinburgh University Press, 2010.

Helsinger, Elizabeth. *Rural Scenes and National Representations, Britain 1815–1850*. Princeton: Princeton University Press, 1997.

Hemans, Felicia Dorothea Browne. *Works*. 6 vols. London: Cadell, 1839.

Hendler, Glenn. *Public Sentiments: Structures of Feeling in Nineteenth-Century American Literature*. Chapel Hill: University of North Carolina Press, 2001.

Hewitt, Regina, ed. *John Galt: Observations and Conjectures on Literature, History, and Society*. Lewisburg, PA: Bucknell University Press, 2013.

Horn, James. "British Diaspora: Emigration from Britain, 1680–1815." In *The Oxford History of the British Empire*. Vol. 2. *The Eighteenth Century*. Ed. P. J. Marshall. Oxford: Oxford University Press, 1998. 28–52.

Horsman, Reginald. *Race and Manifest Destiny: The Origins of American Racial Anglo-Saxonism*. Cambridge, MA: Harvard University Press, 1981.

Hsu, Hsuan L. *Geography and the Production of Space in Nineteenth-Century American Literature*. New York: Cambridge University Press, 2010.

Hudson, Nicholas. "From 'Nation' to 'Race': The Origins of Racial Classification in Eighteenth-Century Thought." *Eighteenth-Century Studies* 29 (1996): 247–264.

Hudson, Nicholas. *Samuel Johnson and the Making of Modern England*. Cambridge, UK: Cambridge University Press, 2003.

Ignatiev, Noel. *How the Irish Became White*. New York: Routledge, 1995.

Imlay, Gilbert. *A Topographical Description of the Western Territory of North America*. 3rd ed. London: J. Debrett, 1797.

Imlay, Gilbert. *The Emigrants; or the History of an Expatriated Family*. Ed. W. M. Verhoeven and Amanda Gilroy. New York: Penguin, 1998.

Irving, Washington. *The Works of Washington Irving*. 21 vols. New York: Putnam, 1860–1863.

[Jacson, Frances]. *Disobedience*. 4 vols. London: William Lane, 1797.

Jarman, Paul. "*Madoc*, 1795: Robert Southey's Misdated Manuscript." *The Review of English Studies*, new series, 55 (2004): 355–373.

Jarvis, Branwen. "Iolo Morganwg and the Welsh Cultural Background." In *A Rattleskull Genius: The Many Faces of Iolo Morganwg*. Ed. Geraint H. Jenkins. Cardiff: University of Wales Press, 2005. 29–49.

[Jefferson, Thomas]. *A Summary View of the Rights of British America*. London: G. Kearsley, 1774.

Jefferson, Thomas. *Notes on the State of Virginia*. Philadelphia: Prichard and Hall, 1788.

Jenkins, Philip. "Seventeenth-Century Wales: Definition and Identity." In *British Consciousness and Identity: The Making of Britain, 1533–1707*. Ed. Brendan Bradshaw and Peter Roberts. Cambridge, UK: Cambridge University Press, 1998. 213–235.

Johnson, Samuel. *The Political Writings*. Ed. Donald J. Greene. New Haven: Yale University Press, 1977.

Johnson, Samuel. "A Journey to the Western Islands of Scotland." In *A Journey to the Western Islands of Scotland and The Journal of a Tour to the Hebrides*. Ed. Peter Levi. London: Penguin, 1984.

Jones, Maldwyn A. "The Scotch-Irish in British America." In *Strangers within the Realm: Cultural Margins of the First British Empire*. Ed. Bernard Bailyn and Philip D. Morgan. Chapel Hill: University of North Carolina Press, 1991. 284–313.

Jones, Richard Wyn. "The Colonial Legacy in Welsh Politics." In *Postcolonial Wales*. Ed. Jane Aaron and Chris Williams. Cardiff: University of Wales Press, 2005. 23–38.

Jones, Robert W. *Literature, Gender, and Politics in Britain, 1770–1785*. Cambridge, UK: Cambridge University Press, 2011.

Kafer, Peter. *Charles Brockden Brown's Revolution and the Birth of the American Gothic*. Philadelphia: University of Pennsylvania Press, 2004.

Keith, W. J. *Regions of the Imagination: The Development of British Rural Fiction*. Toronto: University of Toronto Press, 1988.

Kelly, Gary. *English Fiction of the Romantic Period, 1789–1830*. London: Longman, 1989.

Kenny, Kevin. *The American Irish: A History*. Harlow, UK: Longman, 2000.

Kenyon, Cecilia M. *The Antifederalists*. Indianapolis: Bobbs-Merrill, 1966.

Kerrigan, John. *Archipelagic English: Literature, History, and Politics 1603–1707*. Oxford: Oxford University Press, 2008.

Kettner, James H. *The Development of American Citizenship, 1608–1870*. Chapel Hill: University of North Carolina Press, 1978.

Kidd, Colin. *British Identities before Nationalism: Ethnicities and Nationhood in the Atlantic World, 1600–1800*. Cambridge, UK: Cambridge University Press, 1999.

Killen, Jarlath. *Gothic Ireland: Horror and the Irish Anglican Imagination in the Long Eighteenth Century*. Dublin: Four Courts, 2005.

Killick, Tim. *British Short Fiction in the Early Nineteenth Century: The Rise of the Tale*. Aldershot: Ashgate, 2008.

Klinck, Carl F. "Biographical Introduction." In *The Journal of Major John Norton, 1816*. Ed. Carl F. Klinck and James J. Talman. Toronto: The Champlain Society, 1970. xiii–xcvii.

Klooster, Wim. *The Dutch in the Americas*. Providence, RI: The John Carter Brown Library, 1997.

Kramnick, Isaac. *The Rage of Edmund Burke: Portrait of an Ambivalent Conservative*. New York: Basic, 1977.

Kramnick, Isaac. "The 'Great National Discussion': The Discourse of Politics in 1787." *William and Mary Quarterly*. 3rd ser. 45 (1988): 3–32.

Kumar, Krishan. *The Making of English National Identity*. Cambridge, UK: Cambridge University Press, 2003.

Lamont, Claire. "Jane Austen and the Nation." In *A Companion to Jane Austen*. Ed. Claudia L. Johnson and Clara Tuite. Oxford: Wiley-Blackwell, 2009. 304–313.

Langford, Paul. *Englishness Identified: Manners and Character, 1650–1850*. New York: Oxford University Press, 2000.

Lawson, James. *Tales and Sketches, by a Cosmopolite*. New York: Elam Bliss, 1830.

Leask, Nigel. "Pantisocracy and the Politics of the 'Preface' to *Lyrical Ballads*." In *Reflections of Revolution: Images of Romanticism*. Ed. Alison Yarrington and Kelvin Everest. London: Routledge, 1993. 39–58.

Leask, Nigel. "Irish Republicans and Gothic Eleutherarchs: Pacific Utopias in the Writing of Theobald Wolfe Tone and Charles Brockden Brown." *Huntington Library Quarterly* 63 (2000): 347–367.

Leask, Nigel. "Southey's Madoc: Reimagining the Conquest of America." In *Robert Southey and the Contexts of English Romanticism*. Ed. Lynda Pratt. Aldershot: Ashgate, 2006. 133–150.

Lee, Robert C. *The Canada Company and the Huron Tract, 1826–1853: Personalities, Profits and Politics*. Toronto: Natural Heritage Books, 2004.

Lennox, Charlotte. *Euphemia*. Ed. Susan Kubica Howard. Peterborough, ON: Broadview, 2013.

L'Estrange, A. G. *The Life of Mary Russell Mitford: Related in a Selection from Her Letters to Her Friends*. 3 vols. London: Bentley, 1870.

Levine, Robert S. "Race and Nation in Brown's Louisiana Writings of 1803." In *Revising Charles Brockden Brown*. Ed. Philip Barnard, Mark Kamrath, and Stephen Shapiro. Knoxville: University of Tennessee Press, 2004. 332–353.

Lichtenwalner, Shawna. *Claiming Cambria: Invoking the Welsh in the Romantic Era.* Newark: University of Delaware Press, 2008.

Looby, Christopher. *Voicing America: Language, Literary Form, and the Origins of the United States.* Chicago: University of Chicago Press, 1996.

Loriggio, Francesco. "Regionalism and Theory." In *Regionalism Reconsidered: New Approaches to the Field.* Ed. David Jordan. New York: Garland, 1994. 3–25.

MacDougall, Hugh A. *Racial Myth in English History: Trojans, Teutons, and Anglo-Saxons.* Hanover, NH: University Press of New England, 1982.

Mackillop, Andrew. *"'More Fruitful than the Soil': Army, Empire, and the Scottish Highlands, 1715–1815.* East Linton, Scotland: Tuckwell Press, 2000.

Macpherson, James. *Rights of Great Britain Asserted against the Claims of America.* London: Cadell, 1776.

Marshall, Humphry. *The Aliens: A Patriotic Poem.* Philadelphia, 1798.

Marshall, Peter J. "British North America, 1760–1815." In *The Oxford History of the British Empire.* Vol. 2. *The Eighteenth Century.* Ed. Peter J. Marshall. Oxford: Oxford University Press, 1998. 372–393.

Marshall, Peter J. *Remaking the British Atlantic: The United States and the British Empire after American Independence.* Oxford: Oxford University Press, 2012.

Martin, Susan F. *A Nation of Immigrants.* Cambridge, UK: Cambridge University Press, 2011.

Mayer, David N. *The Constitutional Thought of Thomas Jefferson.* Charlottesville: University Press of Virginia, 1994.

Mazzeo, Tilar J. "The Impossibility of Being Anglo-American: The Rhetoric of Emigration and Transatlanticism in British Culture, 1791–1830." *European Romantic Review* 16 (2005): 59–78.

McClary, Ben Harris. *Washington Irving and the House of Murray.* Knoxville: The University of Tennessee Press, 1969.

McDowell, R. B. *Ireland in the Age of Imperialism and Revolution, 1760–1801.* Oxford: Clarendon, 1979.

McGill, Meredith. *American Literature and the Culture of Reprinting, 1834–1853.* Philadelphia: University of Pennsylvania Press, 2003.

McNeil, Kenneth. "Time, Emigration, and the Circum-Atlantic World: John Galt's *Bogle Corbet.*" In *John Galt: Observations and Conjectures on Literature, History, and Society.* Ed. Regina Hewitt. Lewisburg, PA: Bucknell University Press, 2013. 299–321.

A Memorial of the Case of the German Emigrants Settled in the British Colonies of Pensilvania, and the back Parts of Maryland, Virginia, etc. London, 1754.

Millar, John. *The Origin of the Distinction of Ranks.* 3rd ed. London: J. Murray, 1779.

Miller, Kerby A. *Emigrants and Exiles.* New York: Oxford University Press, 1985.

Mitford, Mary Russell. *Our Village: Sketches of Rural Character and Scenery.* 4 vols. London: Whittaker, 1824.

Moretti, Franco. *Atlas of the European Novel 1800–1900.* London: Verso, 1998.

Moretti, Franco. "Graphs, Maps, Trees: Abstract Models for Literary History—2." *New Left Review* 26 (2004): 79–103.

Morgan, Prys. "From a Death to a View: The Hunt for the Welsh Past in the Romantic Period." In *The Invention of Tradition.* Ed. Eric Hobsbawm and Terence Ranger. Cambridge, UK: Cambridge University Press, 1983. 43–100.

Morison, Samuel Eliot. *The European Discovery of America: The Northern Voyages, A.D. 500–1600.* New York: Oxford University Press, 1971.

Morley, Vincent. *Irish Opinion and the American Revolution, 1760–1783.* Cambridge, UK: Cambridge University Press, 2002.

Moss, Laura, ed. *Is Canada Postcolonial? Unsettling Canadian Literature.* Waterloo, ON: Wilfred Laurier University Press, 2003.

Mount, Nicholas. *When Canadian Literature Moved to New York.* Toronto: University of Toronto Press, 2005.

Nelson, Dana D. "Cooper's Leatherstocking Conversations: Identity, Friendship, and Democracy in the New Nation." In *A Historical Guide to James Fenimore Cooper.* Ed. Leland S. Person. Oxford: Oxford University Press, 2007. 123–154.

New, W. H. *A History of Canadian Literature.* 2nd ed. Montreal: McGill-Queen's University Press, 2003.

Newman, Gerald. *The Rise of English Nationalism: A Cultural History, 1720–1830.* New York: St. Martin's Press, 1987.

O'Brien, Conor Cruise. *The Great Melody: The Thematic Biography and Commented Anthology of Edmund Burke.* London: Sinclair-Stevenson, 1992.

O'Brien, Karen. "Johnson's View of the Scottish Enlightenment in *A Journey to the Western Islands of Scotland*." *The Age of Johnson* 4 (1991): 59–82.

Owenson, Sidney. *Patriotic Sketches of Ireland, Written in Connaught.* Baltimore: Dobbin & Murphy, 1809.

Paine, Thomas. *Rights of Man, Common Sense, and Other Political Writings.* Ed. Mark Philp. Oxford: Oxford University Press, 1998.

Parker, George. *The Beginnings of the Book Trade in Canada.* Toronto: University of Toronto Press, 1985.

Perkins, Pam. "Imagining Eighteenth-Century Quebec: British Literature and Colonial Rhetoric." In *Is Canada Postcolonial? Unsettling Canadian Literature.* Ed. Laura Moss. Waterloo, ON: Wilfred Laurier University Press, 2003. 151–161.

Picken, Andrew [Christopher Keelivine]. *Tales and Sketches of the West of Scotland.* Glasgow: Robertson and Atkinson; Edinburgh: Oliver & Boyd; London: G. & W. B. Whittaker, 1824.

Pitzer, Donald E. "The New Moral World of Robert Owen and New Harmony." In *America's Communal Utopia.* Ed. Donald E. Pitzer. Chapel Hill: University of North Carolina Press, 1997. 88–134.

Pocock, J. G. A. "The Limits and Divisions of British History: In Search of the Unknown Subject." *The American Historical Review* 87 (1982): 311–36.

Pratt, Lynda. "Revising the National Epic: Coleridge, Southey and *Madoc*." *Romanticism* 2 (1996): 149–164.

Pratt, Lynda. "Southey in Wales: Inscriptions, Monuments, and Romantic Prosperity." In *Wales and the Romantic Imagination.* Ed. Damian Walford Davies and Lynda Pratt. Cardiff: University of Wales Press, 2007. 86–103.

Prescott, Sarah. *Eighteenth-Century Writing from Wales: Bards and Britons.* Cardiff: University of Wales Press, 2008.

Public Advertiser. February 27, 1783.

Radner, John. "The Significance of Johnson's Changing Views of the Hebrides." In *The Unknown Samuel Johnson.* Ed. John Burke Jr. and Donald Kay. Madison: University of Wisconsin Press, 1983. 131–147.

Rhees, Morgan J. *The Good Samaritan. An Oration delivered . . . in behalf of the Philadelphia Society for the Information and Assistance of persons Emigrating from Foreign Countries.* Philadelphia: Lang & Ustick, 1796.

Rice, Grantland S. *The Transformation of Authorship in America.* Chicago: University of Chicago Press, 1997.

Richards, Eric. "Scotland and the Uses of the Atlantic Empire." In *Strangers within the Realm: Cultural Margins of the First British Empire.* Ed. Bernard Bailyn and Philip D. Morgan. Chapel Hill: University of North Carolina Press, 1991. 67–114.

Richards, Eric. *The Highland Clearances: People, Landlords and Rural Turmoil.* Edinburgh: Birlinn, 2000.

Richards, Eric. *Britannia's Children: Emigration from England, Scotland, Wales and Ireland since 1600.* London: Hambledon, 2004.

Robbins, Caroline. *The Eighteenth-Century Commonwealthman: Studies in the Transmission, Development, and Circumstance of English Liberal Thought from the Restoration of Charles II until the War with the Thirteen Colonies.* Cambridge, MA: Harvard University Press, 1961.

Roberts, Peter. "Tudor Wales, National Identity, and the British Inheritance." In *British Consciousness and Identity: The Making of Britain, 1533–1707.* Ed. Brendan Bradshaw and Peter Roberts. Cambridge, UK: Cambridge University Press, 1998. 8–42.

Robertson, John. "An Elusive Sovereignty: The Course of the Union Debate in Scotland 1698–1707." In *A Union for Empire: Political Thought and the British Union of 1707.* Ed. John Robertson. Cambridge, UK: Cambridge University Press, 1995. 198–227.

Robinson, Forrest G. "Uncertain Borders: Race, Sex, and Civilization in *The Last of the Mohicans.*" *Arizona Quarterly* 47 (1991): 1–28.

Roche, Regina Maria. *The Munster Cottage Boy: A Tale.* 4 vols. London: A. K. Newman, 1820.

Rogers, Pat. *Journey to the Western Islands* in *Johnson and Boswell: The Transit of Caledonia.* Oxford: Oxford University Press, 1996.

Rubin-Dorsky, Jeffrey. "Washington Irving and the Genesis of the Fictional Sketch." *Early American Literature* 21.3 (1986–1987): 226–247.

Samuels, Shirley. "Wieland: Alien and Infidel." *Early American Literature* 25.1 (1990): 46–66.

Sandiford, Keith Albert. *The Cultural Politics of Sugar: Caribbean Slavery and Narratives of Colonialism.* Cambridge, UK: Cambridge University Press, 2000.

Schmitt, Cannon. *Alien Nation: Nineteenth-Century Gothic Fictions and English Nationality.* Philadelphia: University of Pennsylvania Press, 1997.

Schroeder, Natalia. "Maria Regina Roche and the Early Nineteenth-Century Irish Novel." *Eire-Ireland* 19.2 (1984): 116–130.

Schwyzer, Philip. "British History and 'The British History': The Same Old Story?" In *British Identities and English Renaissance Literature.* Ed. David J. Baker and Willy Maley. Cambridge, UK: Cambridge University Press, 2002. 11–23.

Scott, P. H. *John Galt.* Edinburgh: Scottish Academic Press, 1985.

Sebastiani, Silvia. *The Scottish Enlightenment: Race, Gender, and the Limits of Progress.* Trans. Jeremy Carden. New York: Palgrave Macmillan, 2013.

Sedgwick, Catharine Maria. *Tale and Sketches. Second Series.* New York: Harper, 1844.

Sedgwick, Catharine Maria. *The Power of Her Sympathy: The Autobiography and Journal of Catharine Maria Sedgwick.* Ed. Mary Kelley. Boston: Northeastern University Press, 1993.

Sedgwick, Eve Kosofsky. *The Coherence of Gothic Conventions*. New York: Arno Press, 1980.

Sha, Richard. *The Visual and Verbal Sketch in British Romanticism*. Philadelphia: University of Pennsylvania Press, 1998.

Shain, Charles E. "John Galt's America." *American Quarterly* 8 (1956): 254–263.

Shelley, Mary. *Lodore*. Ed. Fiona Stafford. *The Novels and Selected Works of Mary Shelley*. Vol. 6. Ed. Nora Crook and Pamela Clemit. London: Pickering & Chatto, 1996.

Sher, Richard B. "Transatlantic Books and Literary Culture." In *Transatlantic Literary Studies, 1660–1830*. Ed. Eve Tavor Bannet and Susan Manning. Cambridge, UK: Cambridge University Press, 2012. 10–27.

Shields, David S. *Oracles of Empire: Poetry, Politics, and Commerce in British America, 1690–1750*. Chicago: University of Chicago Press, 1990.

Shields, Juliet. "Pedagogy in the Post-Colony: Documentary Didacticism and the 'Irish Problem.'" *Eighteenth-Century Novel* 6 (2009): 465–493.

Shields, Juliet. *Sentimental Literature and Anglo-Scottish Identity, 1745–1820*. Cambridge, UK: Cambridge University Press, 2010.

Sigourney, Lydia. *A Sketch of Connecticut, forty years since*. Hartford: Oliver D. Cooke, 1824.

Smith, Adam. *The Theory of Moral Sentiments*. Ed. D. D. Raphael and A. L. Macfie. Oxford: Clarendon Press, 1976.

Smith, Herb. "Hugh Henry Brackenridge's Debt to the Stage Irish Convention." *Ball State University Forum* 30 (1989): 14–19.

Snell, K. D. M. *The Bibliography of Regional Fiction in Britain and Ireland, 1800–2000*. Aldershot: Ashgate, 2002.

Snelling, William Joseph. *Tales of the Northwest; or Sketches of Indian Life and Character*. Boston: Hilliard, 1830.

Spender, Stephen. *Love-Hate Relations: English and American Sensibilities*. New York: Random House, 1974.

Stafford, Fiona. "*Lodore*: A Tale of the Present Time?" In *Mary Shelley's Fictions from Frankenstein to Falkner*. Ed. Michael Eberle-Sinatra. London: Macmillan, 2000. 181–196.

St. Clair, William. *The Reading Nation in the Romantic Period*. Cambridge, UK: Cambridge University Press, 2004.

Stepan, Nancy. *The Idea of Race in Science: Great Britain 1800–1960*. London: Macmillan, 1982.

Stone, Albert E. "Introduction." In *Letters from an American Farmer and Sketches of Eighteenth-Century America*. New York: Penguin, 1981. 7–32.

Stoyle, Mark. *West Britons: Cornish Identities and the Early Modern British State*. Exeter: University of Exeter Press, 2002.

The Strong-Box Opened; or, a Fund found at Home for the Immediate Employment of our People and for Preventing Emigration. Dublin: T. T. Faulkner, 1780.

Sussman, Charlotte. "The Colonial Afterlife of Political Arithmetic: Swift, Demography, and Mobile Populations." *Cultural Critique* 56 (2004): 96–126.

Sweet, Nanora. "History, Imperialism, and the Aesthetics of the Beautiful: Hemans and the Post-Napoleonic Moment." In *At the Limits of Romanticism: Essays in Cultural, Feminist, and Materialist Criticism*. Ed. Mary A. Favret and Nicola J. Watson. Bloomington: Indiana University Press, 1994. 170–184.

Tamarkin, Elisa. *Anglophilia: Deference, Devotion, and Antebellum America*. Chicago: University of Chicago Press, 2008.

Tennenhouse, Leonard. *The Importance of Feeling English: American Literature and the British Diaspora, 1750–1850.* Princeton: Princeton University Press, 2007.

Todd, Emily B. "Walter Scott and the Nineteenth-Century American Literary Marketplace." *Papers of the Bibliographical Society of America* 93 (1999): 495–517.

Todd, William B. and Anne Bowden, eds. *Walter Scott: A Bibliographic History, 1796–1832.* Newcastle, DE: Oak Knoll Press, 1998.

Tompkins, Jane. *Sensational Designs: The Cultural Work of American Fiction, 1790–1860.* New York: Oxford University Press, 1985.

Tone, Theobald Wolfe. *Life of Theobald Wolfe Tone: Memoirs, Journals and Political Writings, Compiled and Arranged by William T.W. Tone, 1826.* Ed. Thomas Bartlett. Dublin: The Lilliput Press, 1998.

Totten, Robbie. "National Security and U.S. Immigration Policy, 1776–1790." *Journal of Interdisciplinary History* 39 (2008): 37–64.

Trumpener, Katie. *Bardic Nationalism: The Romantic Novel and the British Empire.* Princeton: Princeton University Press, 1997.

Turton, Jackie. "Making It National; or, the Art of the Tale: Correspondence between William Carleton and His Publisher." *Irish Studies Review* 13.2 (2005): 175–86.

United States Statutes at Large. Vol. 1. Public Acts of the Fifth Congress. Second Session. Chapter LVIII.

Vargo, Lisa. "Introduction." In *Lodore.* By Mary Shelley. Peterborough, ON: Broadview, 1997. 9–40.

Verhoeven, W. M. *Revolutionary Histories: Transatlantic Cultural Nationalism, 1775–1815.* London: Palgrave, 2002.

Verhoeven, W. M. "'This blissful period of intellectual liberty': Transatlantic Radicalism and Enlightened Conservatism in Brown's Early Writings." In *Revising Charles Brockden Brown: Culture, Politics, and Sexuality in the Early Republic.* Ed. Philip Barnard, Mark L. Kamrath, and Stephen Shapiro. Knoxville: University of Tennessee Press, 2004. 7–40.

Verhoeven, W. M. *Gilbert Imlay: Citizen of the World.* London: Pickering & Chatto, 2008.

A View of the Present State of Ireland. Dublin: L. Fay, 1780.

A Vindication of the Rights of the Americans. London, 1765.

Waterman, Bryan. "The Bavarian Illuminati, the Early American Novel, and Histories of the Public Sphere." *William and Mary Quarterly* 3rd ser. 62.1 (2005): 9–30.

Waterston, Elizabeth. "Introduction." *Bogle Corbet.* By John Galt. Ed. Elizabeth Waterston. Toronto: Stewart and Mclelland, 1977. 1–7.

Waterston, Elizabeth ed., *John Galt: Reappraisals.* Guelph, ON: University of Guelph Press, 1985.

Waterston, Elizabeth. *Rapt in Plaid: Canadian Literature and Scottish Tradition.* Toronto: University of Toronto Press, 2003.

Watts, Edward. *Writing and Postcolonialism in the Early Republic.* Charlottesville: University Press of Virginia, 1998.

Watts, Steven. *The Romance of Real Life: Charles Brockden Brown and the Origins of American Culture.* Baltimore: The Johns Hopkins University Press, 1994.

Weisbuch, Robert. *Atlantic Double-Cross: American Literature and British Influence in the Age of Emerson.* Chicago: University of Chicago Press, 1986.

Welsh, Alexander. *The Hero of the Waverley Novels.* New Haven: Yale University Press, 1963.

Wheeler, Roxann. *The Complexion of Race: Categories of Difference in Eighteenth-Century British Culture*. Philadelphia: University of Pennsylvania Press, 2000.

White, Ed. "Carwin the Peasant Rebel." In *Revising Charles Brockden Brown: Culture, Politics, and Sexuality in the Early Republic*. Knoxville: University of Tennessee Press, 2004. 41–59.

Wiley, Michael. *Romantic Migrations: Local, National, and Transnational Dispositions*. New York: Palgrave, 2008.

Williams Edward [Iolo Morganwg]. *Poems, Lyric and Pastoral*. 2 vols. London: J. Nichols, 1794.

Williams, Gwyn A. *Madoc: The Making of a Myth*. London: Eyre Methuen, 1979.

Williams, Gwyn A. *The Search for Beulah Land: The Welsh and the Atlantic Revolution*. New York: Holmes & Meier, 1980.

Williams, Gwyn A. *The Welsh in Their History*. London: Croom Helm, 1982.

Wills, Garry. *Explaining America: The Federalist*. Garden City, NJ: Doubleday, 1981.

Wilson, David A. *United Irishmen, United States: Immigrant Radicals in the Early American Republic*. Ithaca: Cornell University Press, 1998.

Wokeck, Marianne S. "German and Irish Immigration to Colonial Philadelphia." *Proceedings of the American Philosophical Society* 133.2 (1989): 128–143.

Wolfe, Eric A. "Ventriloquizing Nation: Voice, Identity, and Radical Democracy in Charles Brockden Brown's Wieland." *American Literature* 78 (2006): 431–457.

Womack, Peter. *Improvement and Romance: Constructing the Myth of the Highlands*. London: Macmillan, 1989.

Wood, Gordon S. *The Creation of the American Republic, 1776–1787*. Chapel Hill: University of North Carolina Press, 1969.

Yokota, Kariann Akemi. *Unbecoming British: How Revolutionary America Became a Postcolonial Nation*. Oxford: Oxford University Press, 2011.

Young, Robert J. C. *Colonial Desire: Hybridity in Theory, Culture and Race*. London: Routledge, 1995.

Zagarell, Sandra A. "'America' as Community in Three Antebellum Village Sketches." In *The (Other) American Traditions: Nineteenth-Century Women Writers*. Ed. Joyce W. Warren. New Brunswick, NJ: Rutgers University Press, 1993. 143–163.

Zboray, Ronald J. "Antebellum Reading and the Ironies of Technological Innovation." *American Quarterly* 40 (1998): 65–82.

Ziff, Larzer. *Writing in the New Nation: Prose, Print, and Politics in the Early United States*. New Haven: Yale University Press, 1991.

Zolberg, Aristide R. *A Nation by Design: Immigration Policy in the Fashioning of America*. Cambridge, MA: Harvard University Press, 2006.

{ INDEX }